CREATIVE WRITING

For People Who Can't Not Write

OTHER BOOKS BY KATHRYN LINDSKOOG

The C.S. Lewis Hoax
How To Grow a Young Reader
C.S. Lewis: Mere Christian
Around the Year with C.S. Lewis and His Friends
A Child's Garden of Christian Verses
The Gift of Dreams
Loving Touches
Up from Eden
The Lion of Judah in Never-Never Land

Newsletter by Kathryn Lindskoog

The Lewis Legacy

Kathryn Lindskoog

Academie
Books Grand Rapids, Michigan
Zondervan Publishing House

CREATIVE WRITING
Copyright © 1989 by Kathryn Lindskoog

ACADEMIE BOOKS is an imprint of Zondervan Publishing House,
1415 Lake Drive, S.E., Grand Rapids, Michigan 49506.

Library of Congress Cataloging in Publication Data

Lindskoog, Kathryn Ann
    Creative writing : for people who can't not write / Kathryn
  Lindskoog
      p.   cm.
  Bibliography: p.
  Includes index.
  ISBN 0-310-25321-7
  1. English language–Rhetoric. 2. Creative writing.
  3. Authorship.   I. Title.
  PE1408.L56   1989
  808'.042–dc20   89-32182
                                                          CIP

"A Black November Turkey" from *Things of This World*, Copyright © 1956 and renewed 1984 by
Richard Wilbur, reprinted by permission of Harcourt Brace Jovanovich, Inc.

Edited by Tom Raabe and Leonard G. Goss
Designed by Leonard G. Goss
Cover Art by The Aslan Group, Ltd.
Internal Illustrations by Patrick Wynne

Printed in the United States of America

90 91 92 93 94 / DH / 10 9 8 7 6 5 4 3 2

To Walter Zadrozny and Ranelda Hunsicker
First My Students, Then My Friends and Teachers

Contents

Written to That End

First came delicious crayon scribbles on the walls of my mind,
Then unpleasant pencil practice on lines of conformity.
We yearned to write our names right. I still do.

I walked through paper snow to a country school
Where we all blotched accidental Rorschachs from bent nibs
Often plunged an inch down into the clotted glory
Of each desk's deep, deep well of inkiness.
I almost fell in, and maybe I did.
How dirty and sinister the ink smelled.
It was full of soot, they said, because of the war,
But it could have been coffee grounds.
We did as we were told then, because of the war.
We are all part of the war effort; I can see it now.
How awkward our scratchings for beauty, and how wise.

The portentous first fountain pen, bulky to hold,
Bulky of line, hard to fill, short-lived.
I kept it forty years, large and dark and dry. A better gift of hope
Never stopped flowing, the fountain inside me.

Then came an old metal mystery too heavy for a mind to lift —
The mechanical universe —
Each letter (to someone) struck by a slow forefinger of thought,
Each key eager for openings.
Ancient Underwood, dim Gutenberg dream.
I did not know yet that people ever got new ribbons,
But I discovered carbon paper, and could believe in loaves
     and fishes.

O the magical roll and flow of newly ballpoint youth,
All novelty-loving, with giddy lines of inquiry.
Just in case (and out of case) I needed it, I got a Royal portable

To type the world. (Of course I did.)
I wonder at how fast our platens hardened.
How regular the clicks and zings have been, how frequent the
    returns,
How tragic the footnotes.
(I try to drop all tragedy to the bottom of the page.)
I have banged and battered my way this way
Through half the chapters of my life,
A fairly good machine with fairly good machines.
I keep adding power and extra features as I age —
With trashbins of typos.

Then suddenly I am computing with whirs and blips and ease,
Peering at a crystal screen that shows what I know I know.
So it has come to this, whatever this is, flicker and all.
I believe my font will change when the trumpet sounds,
And final revision must mean letter-perfect freedom.
There is surely a default we did not set ourselves.
I almost know how to write my name, as God knows it —
That mysterious scribble in His mind that lets me read Him.
I'm starting now to read His love aloud;
All my life I've written to that end.

Introduction

C. S. Lewis wrote to me in 1957, "If you understand me so well, you will understand other authors too."

I hope he was right.

The purpose of this book is to enable authors — people who want to write or have to write — to do it better and to enjoy it more. I designed the book for creative writing classes and for creative writers far from the classroom. But I frankly hope the book will be used also as a supplementary textbook for college composition classes and for homiletics classes in seminaries. I am always thinking of the people who want to express themselves better for personal or professional reasons.

Today's wonderful new technology enables people to cover more pages faster with turgid writing that no one will ever really read. What the writer experienced as mindless drudgery is worse than mindless drudgery for readers. Both writers and readers need all the help they can get.

Writing carelessly is easy enough for most people, but writing one's very best is hard, hard work; so we might as well be clear about what we are doing and why. All the things we write are in essence various kinds of letters to ourselves or to other people. Further, they are letters that we *have to write*, or that we *should write*, or that we *want to write*.

Everyone understands the *need* to write reports, applications, and business letters. And everyone understands the *duty* to write greetings, personal records, and family letters. But not everyone understands the *desire* to write. Some of us desire to write in order to be creative, to develop an inborn talent, to find out what we think and feel, to share our ideas and feelings, to intensify life by writing about it, or to experiment on paper because we have a love affair with words.

Needless to say, in a given case we may change our minds about whether we have to write something, whether we should write something, or whether we want to write something. But those are the three valid reasons behind the struggle to put words on paper well. In every chapter of this book the emphasis is upon making conscious, informed choices.

I wrote the book with serious purpose but with the intentionally warm and lively style reflected in the title. Throughout, I was modeling some of the techniques that I am teaching. Because the book is far-ranging, it touches only lightly on most topics and often refers students to good sources for further reading. Many of the footnotes contain valuable material that would have cluttered the text; I hope that readers refer to them. At the end of every chapter I suggest activities meant to illustrate and apply part of what was in the chapter.

Topics in this book include discoveries about creativity, the cost of clarity and brevity, common pitfalls, evocative prose, peculiar properties of the English language, word wealth, rewards of writing, facts about publication, the nature of poetry, how to hit the heart, pathways to print, writers' temperament types, writing tools, and writers as readers. The next-to-last chapter contains an outpouring of reflections and advice from an array of contemporary writers who were kind enough to contribute; and the final chapter brings together for the first time a collection of writing advice from one of our century's foremost writers and teachers, C. S. Lewis.

Acknowledgments

Thanks to the teachers, editors, and fellow writers who have added joy to my own writing career.

Thanks to Cornelius Plantinga and Robert Siegel for their generous contributions to chapter 6.

Thanks to John Alexander, Lloyd Alexander, Isabel Anders, Dennis Baker, K. L. Billingsley, Marian Bray, Marjorie Chandler, Russell Chandler, Arthur C. Clarke, Gracia Fay Ellwood, Eli Haugen, Virginia Hearn, Walter Hearn, Melvin Maddocks, Bruce McAllister, Paul McCusker, Carole Gift Page, Richard V. Pierard, Rosalind Rinker, Jack Rowe, Luci Shaw, Robert Siegel, Kevin Springer, Hugh Steven, Sheldon Vanauken, Carolyn Vash, Walter Wangerin, Ron Wilson, Karen Wojahn, and Charles Wrong, who contributed their personal insights to chapter 9.

Thanks to Ranelda Hunsicker and Virginia Hearn for their astute manuscript suggestions.

Thanks to editor Len Goss for his gentle shepherding.

And thanks to all the students who have enriched me through the years with their delightful minds and eagerness to write.

Chapter 1

The Wonder of Creativity

The world will never starve for want of wonders, but only for want of wonder.

— G. K. Chesterton

In a modest house in Dublin there lives a young man who has never said a word. He has never been able to print the letters of the alphabet. He can't go to college.

Christopher Nolan lives strapped in a wheelchair because he has been severely spastic since birth. His face contorts, and his head lolls and jerks. All that he can control well is his eye movement, and so he communicates

with his mother, father, and sister with his brightly blinking eyes. His mother has developed an uncanny ability to read his eyes. How else could anyone read him?

When he was eleven years old Nolan learned to type one letter at a time with a stick strapped to his forehead. (To do this he has to have his mother hold his head steady for him, and it can still take him up to fifteen minutes to type one word.) After all his years of being mute, Nolan described his slow typing as a "dam-burst of dreams"; and he soon started typing out the prose and poetry that he had been secretly composing in his head since he was three years old.

Nolan's mother was amazed at her silent son's vocabulary and literary talent. His collection *Dam-burst of Dreams* was published when he was only fourteen years old, and it won him much literary acclaim. Then at the age of twenty-two Nolan won Britain's coveted $35,400 Whitbread Book of the Year prize for his second book, a 1987 autobiography titled *Under the Eye of the Clock*. This book also won the prestigious Whitbread Biography Award.[1]

The chairman of the literary panel that selected Nolan's book for the Whitbread Biography Award insists that sympathy played no part in the decision. "He won because of the merits of his book, period." British literary critic John Carey says that completely aside from his handicap, Nolan is "a brilliantly gifted young writer."

In response to a contact from a Hollywood film producer, Nolan said, "I want to highlight the creativity within the brain of a cripple and while not attempting to hide his crippledom I want instead to filter all sob-storied sentiment from his portrait and dwell upon his life, his laughter, his vision." He is determined not to allow Hollywood to tell his story wrong.

Thousands of people have written letters to Christopher Nolan. His mother says, "He has shown them that life is worth living, and it doesn't matter whether you're in a wheelchair or a bed; it's what's going on in your mind and your soul that is important."

Nolan believes that his creativity and gift for language were planted in him. This is how he describes it: "My mind is just like a spin dryer at full speed. My thoughts fly around my skull, while millions of beautiful words cascade down into my lap. Images gunfire across my consciousness and, while trying to discipline them, I jump in awe of the soul-filled beauty of the mind's expanse."

Inspired Creativity

Tradition says that truly creative writing is that which comes in mysterious bursts of inspiration. (Teachers are usually down to earth and emphasize that writing requires ten percent inspiration and ninety percent perspiration.) For most of us the bursts are so tiny and mild that we are not apt to notice them. We modestly miss the mystery of our own creativity. We tend to focus on other people's dramatic dam-bursts of genius that seem far more exciting than our own accomplishments. And that is a mistake.

Abraham Maslow pointed out correctly that a first-rate soup is more creative than a second-rate painting; and ordinary activities like home-making and parenthood, done with insight and resourcefulness, are actually more creative than writing run-of-the-mill poetry. Sublime poetry is sublime; but some poetry is like canned soup, and we might as well admit it — the world likes lots of canned soup. Feeling arty is no sign of great artistic talent, and feeling sentimental about sentimentality is no sign of refined perception. Spattering human emotion onto reams of paper may feel good, but it is not necessarily very creative.

We are too easily awed by stereotypes. For example, the phrase "poetry and prose" certainly sounds more creative than ordinary writing. Actress Kim Novak once told a reporter that she loves to read, and that she reads mainly poetry and prose. I wondered what else she thought she read.

When I ask classrooms of adult students if they can speak or write prose, most are too modest to answer yes. I say, "Congratulations! If you are not writing poetry, you are writing prose. You have been speaking prose since you were two years old and writing prose since you first printed 'See Spot run' in first grade." Many students seem rather awed by the news. It's as if they've been doing calculus all these years and didn't know it.

Nonfiction prose is what most of us write most often, and it can be marvelously creative — which means insightful and resourceful. But in many schools "Creative Writing" includes only poetry, fiction, and drama. I think that definition of creative writing is too narrow. There is nothing very creative about copycat dramas by hack writers, but even an ordinary thank-you or sympathy letter can be inspired. What kinds of writing are creative? It all depends upon the writer.

Joyce Carol Oates is a one-woman fountain of fiction who has published at least two books a year for over twenty years. She says, "People are curious about the creative process. And I try to explain, particularly to my students with whom I work, that the creative process is inherent in all human beings and that people who don't think they are creative, in fact, often are." Like many authors, Oates finds creative inspiration a mystery (she says that long walks help), but she finds the conscious part of her writing extremely hard work. She claims that she sometimes types and throws away the same page of a book seventeen times in one hour. (Most of us can't even type that fast.)

Although she says she enjoys teaching college even more than writing, year after year she turns out an amazing stream of novels, short stories, poetry, and nonfiction. It looks as if she may be addicted to creative writing. (Perhaps creativity causes the brain to release endorphins, our natural chemistry of pleasure.) Inspired creativity in any field is one of life's most unfailing delights. And it does not matter whether the creative act is sublime, practical, or ridiculous.

Inspired Humor

One of my favorite inspired-creativity stories is about nonfiction author and editor Leo Rosten and his most embarrassing moment. In 1939 he was a little-known writer working on a serious sociological study of the movie colony in Hollywood. He was surprised and thrilled when he received a telegram inviting him to a banquet in honor of W. C. Fields at the Masquers' Club. (W. C. Fields was the popular red-nosed comedian who acted outrageously rough and gruff.)

When Rosten arrived at the dinner, he was being paged urgently over the loudspeakers. Then he found out that he should have arrived early because he was going to be seated at the head table with the celebrity guests of honor. He had to make a grand entry with the likes of W. C. Fields, Groucho Marx, Bob Hope, Jack Benny, Red Skelton, Jimmy Durante, George Burns, Edgar Bergen, and Milton Berle. The star-filled audience clapped madly for the others and then looked at him, the last one, with puzzled disappointment. He was nobody and he knew it.

After the delicious dinner, a famous wit named William Collier, Sr., got up and began what is now called a roast. He delivered a brilliant series of affectionate insults to W. C. Fields. Then without warning he looked at his notes and said that the next speaker was Leo Boston. He looked again and said, "No — *Rosten.*" The room was almost silent.

Rosten was paralyzed. It was either Red Skelton or George Burns who jabbed him and forced him to his feet. Then he stood there silently praying that he would somehow disappear. Seconds dragged by. He was a total blank. He heard a hoarse, disgusted-sounding voice nearby mutter, "Say *some*thin!" He gulped helplessly.

Next he heard some words come out of his own throat. They were "The only thing I can say about W. C. Fields . . . is this: any man who hates dogs and babies can't be all bad." That one sentence brought down the house, and Rosten sank back into his seat bathed in glory.

Newspapers around the world repeated the quip the next day, and both CBS and BBC featured it on the radio. Both *Time* and *Newsweek* ran it. Overnight, Rosten was an international wit.

Ironically, in a few weeks the quip was accidentally attributed to W. C. Fields himself, and it has been repeated that way ever since. It has proved useless for Leo Rosten to try to remind the world that he was the joke's real creator. But he admits that he didn't consciously invent it; it just came out of his mouth as a gift.[2]

According to Arthur Koestler, who wrote a 700-page book called *The Act of Creation*,[3] humor is the first of three main branches of creativity. The other two are science[4] and the arts. As if to illustrate Koestler's point, cartoonist Jules Feiffer once remarked that when he spent three-and-one-half years writing a serious novel, it was almost like being a scientist or mathematician working over a very precise problem that takes forever and shows no sign of being solved until right at the end " — and then the thrill of discovering that you're right — your intuition plus some reasoning and some precision has panned out."[5] That's the thrill of long-term creative discovery. In contrast, Feiffer particularly likes cartooning because it is almost instantaneous. "It is a great kick to have an idea, write it, execute it, and two or three or four hours later, there it is finished and shining up at me, in glistening black ink." That sounds like a creative high.

When Koestler wrote his chapters about humor, he probably didn't know Leo Rosten's story, but he named the kind of humor Rosten came up with — the pseudo-proverb. Koestler defines it as two logically incompatible statements that have been combined into a line whose rhythm and style make it sound like a virtuous moral adage or golden rule of right living. Koestler gives three examples.

> One should never work between meals.
> One should not carry moderation to extremes.
> The only way to get rid of a temptation is to yield to it.

In all humor, Koestler says, there has to be a collision of material that causes a mental jolt. Except for gag writers who follow formulas in a mechanical way, people create humor by getting help from their fringe-conscious or unconscious process that puts the material together in a new and surprising way. It interlocks in a new combination. The new combination seems to come almost as a gift.

How Creativity Works

Koestler explains that although God created something out of nothing, human beings create by making new combinations of what is already here. We uncover, select, reshuffle, combine, and synthesize the words, facts, ideas, and skills we already have. And the more familiar the things are that we are using, the more exciting our new products seem to be. So it was that when Newton took some common data like man's age-old knowledge of tides and changes of the moon and ripe apples falling to the earth, and gave us his theory of gravity, he radically changed our view of the world.

My own father knew an easy but wonderful trick when he was a little boy back near the turn of the century, and Arthur Koestler has used that very trick to demonstrate how creativity works. It is great fun. All you need is a dollar bill and two regular metal paper clips. (I like to use large ones, but that is not necessary.)

First, fold the dollar bill into thirds, Z-style. Then carefully slide the two paper clips over the top edge of the folded bill. With the clips, fasten one outer fold to the center fold, and then fasten the other outer fold to the center fold. The two paper clips do not touch. Grasping the two ends of the dollar bill firmly, suddenly pull them apart, snapping the dollar bill out straight. This makes the paper clips pop off the top. When you pick up the paper clips, you will find them magically interlocked!

That's how creativity works, Koestler says. Routine thinking takes place on one level. But the creative act always takes place on more than one level, whether it is in humor, science, or art. Koestler gives Gutenberg's invention of the printing press as one example. Gutenberg knew all about how to print designs from carved woodblocks. But he wanted to print entire pages of the Bible, and he couldn't carve all 1,300 pages of the Bible out of blocks of wood. He thought quite a bit about how coins were cast in molds and how seals were used to print designs in sealing wax. Then he took part in the local wine harvest and noticed the power of the winepress that squeezed the juice out of the grapes. There was his answer! He invented the letterpress by combining the separate skills of stamping with a seal and pressing wine. No one had connected these two methods before.

Gutenberg's story included the three steps that are common to many creative discoveries.

1. The inventor has seriously studied his subject and has thought hard about it. He is seeking something.
2. The inventor's mind relaxes and gets receptive as he does something else.
3. The inventor notices something that other people haven't considered, and it turns out to be the major key he needed.

How can ordinary people get the time to pursue a subject carefully, put it aside while relaxing, and then discover the desired solution? These optimum conditions aren't always available.

About twenty years ago a distinguished British medical professor named Sir George Pickering was sick in bed for a long time and wanted to do something creative in spite of his illness. So he decided to use his time in bed to write a book about how people can be creative while they are sick in bed.[6] He chose to write about how physical illness helped the creative lives of six famous people: Charles Darwin, Florence Nightingale, Mary Baker Eddy, Sigmund Freud, Marcel Proust, and Elizabeth Barrett Browning. He titled his book *Creative Malady*, and obviously he was writing also about himself. He decided in the end that just one of the six would have been as creative healthy as sick, and that was poet Elizabeth Barrett Browning — who happened to write best lying down.

There are three things you need in order to be creatively ill, according to Pickering:

1. You must be intelligent.
2. You must be protected and cared for by other people.
3. You must stay sick enough to be excused from life's demands, but well enough to pursue your creative interests.

Pickering didn't mention it, but there are places where a few physically healthy writers are treated that way: at writers' colonies. Writer Doris Grumbach, reflecting upon the pros and cons of writers' colonies, observed that the daily luxury of eight hours of complete solitude and silence without any interruptions caused some writers to go to pieces. Although many thrive as expected in such a perfect environment, many others write better with some distractions caused by the ordinary duties of life. For them, interruptions are necessary tension breakers.[7]

It seems that all creative people like to encounter a little chaos in their environment. Frank Barron, a psychologist at the University of California at Santa Cruz, once tested a group of artists and scientists who had made distinguished contributions in their fields. He showed them cards with orderly, symmetrical designs and other cards with unbalanced, disorderly designs to see which they preferred. Most people like the orderly cards best, but highly creative people prefer disorderly cards. It is not that highly creative people like confusion for its own sake; quite the contrary. They enjoy challenge. They like to discover hidden order where it was not evident, and they like to produce order where it did not seem easy to do so. Chaos or disorder is the raw material that they use all the time, and they find it interesting.

John W. Gardner claims that highly creative people are not outlaws, but lawmakers. They are nonconformists in a special sense of the word. They allow their hunches and wild ideas to come to the surface, and they are willing to take risks; but in everyday life they usually conform to what is standard and look and act quite normal. Their independence shows up mainly in their ideas. There they are flexible, playful, and open. They like to discover relatedness and connect things that did not seem to be connected. "Every great creative performance since the initial one has been in some measure a bringing order out of chaos."[8]

According to psychologist Rollo May in his book *The Courage To Create*,[9] the search for a pattern in apparent chaos is a way of trying to find meaning in life. Whenever we try to make life meaningful, we are being creative, and being creative is the only way to make life meaningful. May says that our only hope for immortality is in artistic creations we leave behind when we die. Rollo May's philosophy is *aestheticism*, a kind of atheistic existentialism in which an artist imposes some kind of order and meaning upon a universe that otherwise has none. The artist's meaning is imaginary, but supposedly it is better than none at all. Rollo May's basic belief system is unacceptable to many of us, but some of his insights about creativity are interesting.

The key to creativity is receptivity. A really creative person is not just lazily and passively waiting for inspiration to strike. Receptivity is a kind of alertness and readiness, nimbleness, fine-honed sensitivity. It is being open and alive, with a high degree of attention. It is like a diver poised on the end of the board, balanced, waiting for the right moment. Sometimes everything clicks together just right, and then the result is creative success.

Playwright Harold Pinter doesn't know where his plays come from. "I've never been able to sit down and say, 'Now I'm going to write a play.' I just have no alternative but to wait for the thing to be released in me. . . . Something is taking place and my task is just to allow that thing to take place and follow it."[10]

Rollo May points out how common it is for people to say things like "it suddenly hit me," "this thought popped up," "it came out of the blue," and "the idea dawned on me." We often refer to insights that we didn't achieve by consciously working them out. They came as gifts from our unconscious mental processes that we can't control. They came as the trout come to a trout fisherman. Trout and creative ideas can't be landed by willpower or good intentions alone. They require patience and readiness.

May can't explain creativity, but he does give advice about cooperating with it instead of quenching it. He recommends "the constructive use of solitude." *Be still.* In our hectic civilization, with the constant racket of TV and radio, with constant rush and conversation and activity, it is difficult for insights from the unconscious depths to break through. For many people, being alone is a sign of social failure, and they won't be alone if they can help it. Many others are basically afraid of any part of reality they can't control rationally, and so they have to keep busy to block out hidden mental processes such as sudden intuitions and dreams.

Rollo May likes to repeat Kierkegaard's illustration about noise. Just as early American settlers used to bang on pots and pans at night to keep the wolves away, so many people today keep lots of busy "noise" (activity and projects and distraction) going on to keep fears at bay. The noise creates a sense of security and fights our anxiety about life and death and losses. But the noise also diminishes our receptivity and makes us less creative.

On July 18, 1874, Lewis Carroll, the author of *Alice in Wonderland*, was quietly walking alone on a hillside on a bright summer day when suddenly the line "The Snark *was* a Boojum, you see" popped into his head. Then the rest of the stanza gradually came to him:

> In the midst of the word he was trying to say,
>   In the midst of his laughter and glee,
> He had softly and suddenly vanished away —
>   For the Snark *was* Boojum, you see.

Over the next year or two, 140 more stanzas occurred to Carroll, and the poem pieced itself together. As soon as it was complete, he published it as a book. He never was quite sure what the nonsense meant. (Lewis Carroll was really the Reverend Charles Dodgson, a devout Oxford mathematics professor.)

A few years later, A. E. Housman had a similar experience of walking creativity. He was a Latin scholar who eventually taught at Cambridge, but now he is best remembered for his slim volumes of poetry, not his scholarship.

> As I went along, thinking of nothing in particular, only looking at things around me and following the progress of the seasons, there would flow into my mind, with sudden and unaccountable emotion, sometimes a line or two of verse, sometimes a whole stanza at once, accompanied, not preceded, by a vague notion of the poem which they were destined to form part of.[11]
>
> Then there would usually be a lull of an hour or so, then perhaps the spring would bubble up again. I say bubble up, because, so far as I could make out, the source of the suggestions thus proffered to the brain was . . . the stomach.
>
> When I got home I wrote them down, leaving gaps, and hoping that further inspiration might be forthcoming another day. Sometimes

it was, if I took my walks in a receptive and expectant frame of mind; but sometimes the poem had to be taken in hand and completed by the brain, which was apt to be a matter of trouble and anxiety, involving trial and disappointment, and sometimes ending in failure.

I happen to remember distinctly the genesis of the piece which stands last in my first volume. Two of the stanzas, I do not say which, came into my head, just as they are printed, while I was crossing the corner of Hampstead Heath between the Spaniard's Inn and the footpath to Temple Fortune. A third stanza came with a little coaxing after tea. One more was needed, but it did not come; I had to turn to and compose it myself, and that was a laborious business. I wrote it thirteen times, and it was more than a twelvemonth before I got it right.[12]

Delightful as Housman's poems are, they were minor productions. In contrast, Wolfgang Amadeus Mozart was a true creative giant. And, like Housman, he got some of his best inspiration while taking walks.

When I am, as it were, completely myself, completely alone, and of good cheer — say, travelling in a carriage, or walking after a good meal, or during the night when I cannot sleep; it is on such occasions that my ideas flow best and most abundantly. WHENCE and HOW they come, I know not; nor can I force them. Those pleasures that please me I retain in memory, and am accustomed, as I have been told, to hum them to myself. If I continue in this way, it soon occurs to me how I may turn this or that morsel to account, so as to make a good dish of it, that is to say, agreeably to the rules of counterpoint, to the peculiarities of the various instruments, etc.

All this fires my soul, and provided I am not disturbed, my subject enlarges itself, becomes methodised and defined, and the whole, though it be long, stands almost complete and finished in my mind, so that I can survey it, like a fine picture or a beautiful statue, at a glance. Nor do I hear in my imagination the parts SUCCESSIVELY, but I hear them, as it were, all at once. What a delight this is I cannot tell! All this inventing, this producing, takes place in a pleasing lively dream. Still the actual hearing of the whole thing is after all the best. What has been thus produced I do not easily forget, and this is perhaps the best gift I have my Divine Maker to thank for.[13]

Mozart knew his brand-new compositions so well that he could write them down automatically at his convenience later as if taking dictation. Distractions didn't bother him at all then, and he could even talk with someone while writing down the music for the first time.

He had no idea where he got his style; he had made no attempt to be original. He figured that the distinct style of his music came to him just like the distinct shape of his large nose. It was inborn. But his knowledge of music was not entirely inborn; he had studied and was well trained from early childhood.

Dreams and Diaries

Mozart's story of dreamy musical creativity is a bit like that of Robert Penn Warren, America's recent first Poet Laureate. "I get many ideas while on long swims. I sort of half-dream. It's a numbing, bemusing experience. And a thousand ideas drift into the head. There's rhythm and blankness, and you feel detached from yourself. It opens the head to suggestion."

This sounds a bit like the great German organic chemist Friedrich Kekulé. One day in a dreamy state he came up with the right theory of molecular structure. He liked to tell about it.

> I turned my chair to the fire and dozed. Again the atoms were gambolling before my eyes. This time the smaller groups kept modestly in the background. My mental eye, rendered more acute by repeated visions of this kind, could now distinguish larger structures, of manifold conformation; long rows, sometimes more closely fitted together; all twining and twisting in snakelike motion. But look! What was that? One of the snakes had seized hold of its own tail, and the form whirled mockingly before my eyes. As if by a flash of lightning I awoke.

He realized that the image of a snake biting its tail was an image of molecules in closed chains or rings. This insight into molecular structure was a major breakthrough in chemistry. Kekulé said to his fellow scientists, "Let us learn to dream, gentlemen."

Another favorite story of dream creativity is Samuel Taylor Coleridge's account about how he wrote his haunting poem "Kubla Khan." He took a strong drugstore medicine for dysentery, then dozed off while reading dull prose about a palace built by Kubla Khan. While he slept, he saw images as real as life and composed at least two hundred or three hundred lines of poetry about what he saw.

> In Xanadu did Kubla Khan
> A stately pleasure-dome decree;
>   Where Alph, the sacred river ran
> Through caverns measureless to man
>   Down to a sunless sea. . . .

Then he woke up, remembered the entire poem perfectly, and started to write it down. But when he had recorded only fifty-four lines, a visitor from the village of Porlock arrived to talk business and stayed for over an hour. When the man left, Coleridge returned to his poem and realized to his horror that he had total amnesia for the rest of it. For him the poem itself was lost, and the fifty-four lines were only a fragment. But that fragment became one of the all-time favorite poems in English literature.

One of the oldest and most beautiful accounts of dream creativity was recorded by the British historian named Bede in about A.D. 700. He told about a simple Christian family man named Caedmon who was getting along in years and had never learned any poems or songs, so was never able to take part after dinner in the monastery when people took turns singing. One night Caedmon was asleep in the stable guarding the cattle, and a man came to him in a dream and told him to sing about the beginning of the world. When Caedmon tried to obey, he found himself singing a beautiful new song. He remembered the entire song after he woke up, and sang it to the monks the next day.

They all recognized that this was great poetry inspired by God. Furthermore, they discovered that Caedmon could compose more biblical hymns when he was awake. For the rest of his life, they read Bible passages to him and he transformed them into hymns which they wrote down. So it was that Caedmon, who never learned to read and write, was our first English poet. His poems led many people away from sin and into godly lives.

This story is more than just a pretty little Christian myth; it was seriously recorded by the first great scholar in England, whose life overlapped that of Caedmon. It is as if a reputable historian in England today told what he believed true about C. S. Lewis's life, and people read his account over one thousand years later. Alas, of all of Caedmon's many poems in Old English, only a few lines have survived to this day; but he is still rightly remembered as a creative genius, the father of English poetry.

Although Sigmund Freud wrongly insisted at the turn of the century that no one can really write anything in a sleeping dream, and some people still believe him, many writers are doing it to this day. When they can remember what they wrote after they wake up, however, it isn't always as good as they thought it was in their dreams. The following verse has been attributed to more than one author, but it is commonly said that Dorothy Parker wrote it in a dream. She thought it was the answer to the problems of the world, woke up enough to write it down, and then read it with dismay the next morning.

> Hoggimous, higgimous,
> Men are polygamous.

> Higgimous, Hoggimous,
> Women monogamous.

In contrast to Dorothy Parker, when I made up a short verse in a dream once, I didn't take it seriously at all. I thought it was hilarious. I laughed so hard I was gasping, and I literally woke myself up; then I wrote the funny verse down. Here is what I read the next morning:

> Some people use tobacco-stuff;
> I don't, 'cause I'm not up to snuff.

Needless to say, this is a pun, and mildly clever rather than hilarious. Puns are very common in our sleeping dreams; but most people don't notice them, and so they usually slip by. In his book about creativity, Arthur Koestler says that puns are a basic form of creativity related to rhyming. In puns two strings of thought are tied together by the knot of a similar sound, such as "have lots of pun," or "the write answer."

A bizarre biological discovery about punning was made by a German surgeon named Forster in 1929. Dr. Forster was operating on a patient's brain to remove a tumor. Whenever the surgeon manipulated the spot where the tumor was located, the patient would start with whatever words the doctor had just uttered and make a series of puns about his own brain surgery. He didn't mean to do it; he couldn't help it. The surgeon had discovered the spot in this patient's brain that made him pun. Since then the rare disorder of compulsive punning has been called Forster's Syndrome. It is a physical affliction a bit like epilepsy.

Whether we catch the creative puns in our sleeping dreams or not, we are bursting with creativity at night. Many writers have claimed that they woke up with the basis for a new novel that came in a dream. Some writers specifically think about what they need to come up with for their books when they are going to bed, expecting their minds somehow to work things out while they are asleep. They say that after a week or so of calmly filing the mental request at bedtime, they often find that whatever they needed comes to mind with no effort at all.

Many people feel that simply writing down some of our sleeping creativity can make us more creative in our waking hours. Taking a little vitamin B6 for a period of time, consciously intending at night to remember some dreams later, and having a dream diary in easy reach are three tricks that often work against dream amnesia and increase dream recall.

Morton Kelsey, an Episcopal priest and author, has told people about his handy combination dream diary and journal. He uses an ordinary spiral notebook. At the back he starts jotting down his dreams and his ideas about them, working forward. At the front he writes down his waking thoughts and feelings and ideas. When he meets himself somewhere in the middle of the notebook, he starts a new one. That way the journal and dream diary for a certain period are permanently together, and it keeps life simpler to have only one notebook going at a time.

Personal journal writing itself is supposed to be a stimulus to creativity. When we write things out, we are sometimes surprised by insight and understanding that we didn't know we had. The journal is also a healthy way to let off emotional steam and relieve tension, much like confiding in a friend. The journal often shows us the causes and meanings behind the events and patterns of life. The journal can include drawings, clippings, and diagrams, but it is usually made up mainly of writing. It might include favorite quotations, high points of life, strong feelings, early memories, letters to God, inner arguments, goals, life review, irritations and fears, aids to growth, and bright ideas. Just having the heading "bright ideas" can encourage them to come.

Ira Progoff, a teacher of depth psychology, became interested in journals while working with artists who were suffering from creative blocks. He came to agree with an early psychoanalyst, Otto Rank, that the reason people become frustrated and neurotic is that they are failing to be creative enough. A personal journal is an ideal way to let creativity flow, and it helps a person to see the immense drama of life. Every person's life is in reality as interesting as any fiction or biography. The journal becomes a treasure chest of dreams, thoughts, memories, and experiences.

There are two groups of people who get the most good out of keeping a journal: the very creative and those who take their inner lives seriously. But one doesn't have to be a good writer or even a fair writer to succeed with a personal journal. One who knows English imperfectly because it is a second language can write a marvelously helpful journal in broken English. Ira Progoff says that the journal enables people to discover within themselves resources they didn't know they possessed. It seems to free and accelerate creativity.

Using Biology

Keeping a journal may work well to increase creativity, but another common prescription, relaxation, doesn't seem to work at all. In his book *The Courage to Create*, Rollo May said that he meditated twenty minutes a day, but only after he did his creative writing. If he meditated first, he felt relaxed and had nothing to say. Most people's brains produce alpha waves (8 to 30 cycles per second) when they are relaxing, and beta waves (30 to 60 cycles per second) when they are working on a problem. It seems that the faster waves are needed for alertness and focused attention. But nothing about brains is that simple. For one thing, the alpha and beta waves are combined.

It seems that creative and uncreative students use different brain wave patterns.[14] Uncreative students produce the same amount of alpha waves whether they are asked to make up ordinary stories or highly original stories. But creative students produce more alpha waves when they are asked to be original than when they are asked to produce ordinary stories. It is as if naturally creative students have an alpha switch they turn on when they need to do creative work. And, to complicate things more, the highly creative students produce less alpha than the other people do when relaxing. (This could explain why ordinary distractions of everyday life sometimes torment them unduly.) It seems that they are somehow more alert mentally while relaxing and more relaxed mentally when thinking.

It would be natural to assume that biofeedback training could teach creative people to produce even more alpha waves while doing imaginative work and thereby improve creativity. But experimenters have found that creative students are inferior at biofeedback training. Creative people control their brain waves unconsciously and aren't good at doing it consciously. It seems that the people who excel at biofeedback are not very creative in the first place. They tend to concentrate better and are less sensitive. They tend to be comfortable people.

Creative people tend to amplify sights, sounds, and textures. They are oversensitive because they overreact physiologically due to their brain wave pattern. Another peculiarity of creative people is that they have the same amount of alpha activity on both sides of the brain. Normal people have more alpha on the right side than on the left, which means that the rational left side is more active for most people. In the highly creative, the intuitive right side of the brain is a bit more active, we've been told.

There is a little test that you can try on people that will supposedly show if they are more intuitive and creative or more rational. Have the person look at you while you ask a thought question such as "What is the meaning of the proverb 'Better a bad peace than a good war'?' or "How do you think we should handle the AIDS problem?" The person will unconsciously glance to one side or the other while beginning to think about the answer. Most people will be fairly consistent about the direction of their first glance, and so people can be called "right-movers" and "left-movers." This shows which side of the brain is slightly quicker and more active.[15]

"Right-movers" have a slightly quicker left side of the brain; they are harder to hypnotize, they are probably better with numbers than with words, and they tend to be more matter-of-fact. "Left-movers," in contrast, are more easily hypnotized, more apt to major in the arts and humanities in college, more apt to have rich inner experiences, more apt to follow inner impulses, and more deeply imaginative. If all of this is true (don't swallow intriguing theories too quickly), it seems obvious that most creative writers will unconsciously glance to the left when they start to ponder a question.

If creativity is partly a matter of having the right brain waves going in the right part of the brain, and if biofeedback is no help, what can a person do physically to enhance creativity? Many writers and thinkers have come up with ideas of their own. Bossuet wrapped his head in furs, Schiller wrote with his feet in ice water and smelled rotten apples, Proust lined his room with cork and kept the windows shut tight, Turgenev kept his feet in a bucket of hot water, Swinburne isolated himself, Oswald Sitwell wrote best in hotel bedrooms, Thackeray wrote best inside the busy Athenaeum Club in London, Voltaire dictated while sitting in bed, Descartes and Rossini created flat in bed, Victor Hugo composed on top of a bus, Samuel Johnson thought best in a moving carriage, Trollope wrote in a train, Thackeray and Southey could get ideas only when holding a pen, Balzac drank poisonous quantities of black coffee, Tennyson got his best ideas in spring and summer, and Einstein got his best ideas while shaving. Woody Allen prefers to write on a bed, with no noise or music to distract him. Agatha Christie said that the best time for planning a book is when you're doing the dishes.

There used to be an elderly writer in Philadelphia who for fifteen years went to bed sixty-five to eighty-five minutes later every night, therefore getting up that much later the next morning. He lived a more-than-twenty-five hour day. He said that his body was built for that schedule, and that he never felt good in his life until he finally started to obey his own body-time. He planned his calendar in advance so that he knew which third of each day he would spend in bed; that way he could schedule appointments with people for times when he would be awake. Sometimes he ate breakfast with people who were eating dinner. He was happy and productive that way.

The Natures of Creativity

Why do creative people often have a reputation for being eccentric? First, they are not overly afraid of being different or wrong, or they couldn't be creative. They are uninhibited in their thinking, although they often prefer to conform in most areas. They are playful. They are enthusiastic. They feel free to entertain wild ideas. They feel like discoverers. They are curious. They notice odd things along the way. They like surprises and challenges. They get ideas when their minds are drifting. They don't like pat answers. They don't always think what they are told to think. They are spontaneous rather than guarded. They tend to be joyful and may be mystical. They tend to get carried away with what they are thinking. They retain much of the freshness and enthusiasm and openness of childhood.

One of the most successful creative writers of our century was J. R. R. Tolkien. He was a devout Roman Catholic, and in his opinion his creativity was a gift from God. Sometimes he prayed for a new story, and God gave him a new story. Tolkien said that psychologists sometimes explain spiritual things as a result of the functions of the glands, forgetting that God also made the glands. But like most writers, Tolkien had to work and slave over his writing in addition to receiving gifts of inspiration. It took him seventeen years to complete *The Lord of the Rings*.

It is amazing how much creative people need to be creative, although it isn't always practical to be creative. Sometimes it is costly. Many teachers favor students who have high intelligence but who are not high in creativity, students who are careful and don't come up with surprises and odd answers. (It is common knowledge that Albert Einstein, Thomas Edison, and Winston Churchill were a pain to their teachers, who considered them dim-witted.) Creative workers are sometimes penalized instead of rewarded for having good ideas. Yet people will usually be creative if they can be, even if they have to hide what they created. Creativity is a built-in drive. It is necessary play. It often gives joy; and when joy is impossible, it gives relief from boredom and solace for pain.

Henry Wadsworth Longfellow was always creative, but when his beloved wife burned to death in a household accident, he threw himself into his creative writing in a new way. He translated the entire *Divine Comedy* by Dante into English as a refuge in his sorrow, and he wrote the sonnets that were his finest poetry.

Those who know the story of author Corrie ten Boom remember the trick she used to keep herself mentally healthy when she was locked up in a Nazi prison because she had been caught hiding Jews in her house in Holland. She had a little bit of colored thread, and she secretly embroidered flower designs over and over on her old pajamas. Her bit of colored thread was in a sense the thread that led her through that period of suffering.

Creativity is a wonderful part of life under God, but as an idol it is as foolish or wicked as the rest. And, like most things on earth, creativity can be used for good or evil. It can go demonic. While Corrie ten Boom was embroidering flowers on old cloth to keep sane in a Nazi prison, a Nazi woman reportedly took an innovative look at Jews. She combined the idea of Jewish skin with the idea of novelty lamps. That is why after a while some Nazi homes had new lampshades made of human skin. That bit of hellishness was evil creativity. Destructive creativity is often valued by leaders because it can be used to hurt other groups in the competition of business, politics, or war. Destructive creativity can be a useful tool for expressing hatred or beating other people into submission.

But creativity is not always heavenly or demonic; sometimes it is just good animal fun. My favorite example of the joy of creativity is found in a 1918 book called *The Mentality of Apes*. The author Wolfgang Kohler told about teaching chimpanzees to use sticks to pull in objects that were outside their cages. Kohler had a star chimpanzee named Sultan who was a chimpanzee genius. He quickly got the idea of how to pull fruit into his cage with a stick.

Once Kohler left a banana outside the cage and put a small tree in the cage. Sultan sized up the situation, went to the tree, broke off a limb, and used it as a stick to get the banana. Then finally one day Kohler put two short hollow sticks into the cage, neither one long enough to reach the banana. Sultan tried in vain for a long time. At last he fit the two sticks together to make one long stick and managed to reach the banana and pull it in. He was elated. His discovery pleased him so immensely that he kept repeating the creative new trick and forgot to eat the banana.

Not many people have heard of the creative genius named Sultan, but most people have heard of the creative genius named Milton. John Milton was the greatest scholar of all English poets. He said he could write his best only between October and March. Milton wore out his eyes with overwork; and when he was only forty-seven, he went blind. For three years he did not write. Then he dictated a sonnet expressing his grief over the fact that he could no longer serve God with his creative writing. He based his poem on the parable of the servant who displeased his master by burying his talent instead of using it. Milton complained to God that it was unfair that he couldn't create anything to give to God anymore.

The poem's message said, "When I think of how my vision is gone at the midpoint of my life, and how my writing talent is useless now, and how much I want to serve God with that talent, and how I may displease God by being unproductive — I find myself asking, 'Does God demand daylight labor from me when I have no daylight?' But Patience answered me: 'God doesn't need anyone's work or talent. People who accept their fate with their faith intact are the ones who serve God best. He is the ruler of the universe; he has all his angels to do his bidding. He is also served by those who are just quietly attentive.'"

The poem reads,

> When I consider how my light is spent
> Ere half my days, in this dark world and wide,
> And that one talent which is death to hide
> Lodged with me useless, though my soul more bent
> To serve therewith my Maker, and present
> My true account, lest he returning chide;
> "Doth God exact day-labor, light denied?"
> I fondly ask. But Patience, to prevent
> That murmur, soon replied, "God doth not need
> Either man's work or his own gifts. Who best
> Bear his mild yoke, they serve him best. His state
> Is Kingly; thousands at his bidding speed,
> And post o'er land and ocean without rest;
> They also serve who only stand and wait.

Then Milton realized that God needed Milton's heart, not Milton's creative writing. Milton teaches us that faith in God's kindness and receptivity to God's will are more important than any creativity. After this discovery, Milton went on and somehow, almost miraculously, created the masterpieces that he is most famous for today. He said that much of this poetry came to him through his dreams.

John Milton was a rather heroic man, of giant intellect and remarkable character, and he lived three hundred years ago. But just like the rest of us, he had to depend upon something other than his conscious mind to help him with his work. (I like to call it the hyperconscious instead of the unconscious.) Times change and talents vary, but there are some basic rules that seem to help people to become as receptive as possible to gifts of creative insight and resourcefulness:

1. Learn all that you can (furnish your mind).
2. Think hard about interesting things (exercise your mind).
3. Turn off the television (quiet your mind).
4. Take walks (refresh your mind).
5. Save time for contemplation (free your mind).
6. Associate with creative people (stimulate your mind).
7. Notice your dreams (respect your mind).
8. Keep a personal journal (tune in to your mind).
9. Be quick to question authority (alert your mind).
10. Trust God (surrender your mind).

Creative writing is much like gardening. It takes hard work, but hard work alone can never produce the flowers and fruit. There is a mysterious kind of germination that takes place. A writer named G. C. Lichtenberg summed it up this way in 1799: "There is something in our minds like sunshine and the weather, which is not under our control. When I write, the best things come to me from I know not where." All we can do is to prepare, cooperate, and then enjoy the fruits and flowers when they come.

SUGGESTED ACTIVITIES

1. Try three weeks of daily journaling that is completely different from regular diary entries. Here are some possible examples:
   a. Record your sleeping dreams every time you can remember them.
   b. When you can't recall any sleeping dreams, write down your first thoughts every time you wake up, no matter how absurd they are.
   c. Choose an ordinary event from your day and make a page of "what-ifs" that would completely alter the course of your life.
   d. Choose one kind of sense stimulation, such as color, odor, soft touches, or background noise, and concentrate on it for several days. Make descriptive notes about some of your new or increased impressions. Then go on to a different kind of sense stimulation for several days.
2. Make imaginary journal entries for someone very different from yourself. Put yourself into that person's position and mindset, and experience the part. Can you stretch enough to feel along with that person and to make the journal entries seem convincing to yourself? This person might become part of a short story or novel for you someday.
3. Alone or with one or two acquaintances, write down a dozen abstract qualities (ideas or concepts) like youth, old age, hope, fear, and loyalty on scraps of paper and put them upside down in a pile. Write down a dozen concrete items (physical things) like scissors, keys, wildflowers, stars, a city, or a river, and place these upside down in a second pile. Next, draw two words — one from each pile — and think of ways in which the two items are alike. You might have to tell how loyalty is like lemons or how cruelty is like the moon. Either pool all your group's ideas and discuss them, or else write out one page on each pair you tackle. The more mismatched your two words seem to be, the more innovative your comparison becomes.
4. If you use the words *like* or *as* when you make an analogy, we call the figure of speech a simile. If you do not, we call it a metaphor. Examples: "She squawked and flapped like a chicken." "The old man

slumped there, a piece of twisted driftwood left by the tide." If you switch from one figure of speech to another too abruptly you get what is called a mixed metaphor. Examples: "She squawked and flapped around the room like a chicken that was just about to cut anchor and set sail." "The old man slumped there like a piece of twisted driftwood in which the fire had gone out." Try writing a lengthy figure of speech about each of these subjects: (1) a slender, proud, and almost arrogant woman, (2) an extremely handsome and virile middle-aged hero, and (3) a shy teenager suffering at a high school dance.

NOTES

[1] Linda Joffee, "A Voice From the Mute World Sings," *Christian Science Monitor* (January 27, 1988), 1, 6.

[2] Leo Rosten, "My Most Embarrassing Moment," *Saturday Review* (June 12, 1976), 12.

[3] Arthur Koestler, *The Act of Creation* (New York: Macmillan, 1964).

[4] For a scientist's thoughts about creativity, read *Creativity and Intuition: A Physicist Looks at East and West* (New York: Harper & Row, 1973) by Hideki Yukawa, a colleague of Albert Einstein.

[5] Jo Ann Levine, "Cartoon, Novel, or Play? Just Wait," *Christian Science Monitor* (Oct. 12, 1977), 28.

[6] Sir George Pickering, *Creative Malady* (Cambridge, England: Oxford University Press 1974), 273–74.

[7] Doris Grumbach, "Fine Print," *Saturday Review* (Oct. 15, 1977), 33.

[8] John W. Gardner, "Stand Out of My Light," *Christian Science Monitor* (January 11, 1977), 25, taken from *Self-Renewal* (New York: Harper & Row, 1963).

[9] Rollo May, *The Courage to Create* (New York: Norton, 1975), 89.

[10] Jack Kroll, "The Puzzle Of Pinter," *Newsweek* (Nov. 29, 1976), 77.

[11] One of the most popular of Housman's poems is "When I Was One-and-Twenty."

> When I was one-and-twenty
>   I heard a wise man say,
> "Give crown and pounds and guineas,
>   But not your heart away;
> Give pearls away and rubies
>   But keep your fancy free."
> But I was one-and-twenty,
>   No use to talk to me.
>
> When I was one-and-twenty
>   I heard him say again,
> "The heart out of the bosom

Was never given in vain;
'Tis paid with sighs a plenty
And sold for endless rue."
And I am two-and-twenty,
And oh, 'tis true, 'tis true.

[12] Sir George Pickering, *Creative Malady* (Cambridge, England: Oxford University Press 1974), 273–74.

[13] Rollo May, *The Courage to Create* (New York: Norton, 1975), 89.

[14] Colin Martindale, "What Makes Creative People Different," *Psychology Today* (July, 1975), 44–50.

[15] James H. Austin, "Eyes Left! Eyes Right!" *Saturday Review* (August 9, 1975), 32.

Chapter 2

To Communicate or Obfuscate

To write simply is as difficult as to be good.
— W. Somerset Maugham

Our society demands clear drinking water, but accepts murky writing. (If our water supply were as muddy as much of our pretentious prose, all flavors of Jell-O would look brown.) The first virtue of good writing is clarity. For this a writer needs a correct — not necessarily large — vocabulary, untangled thinking, and the mental energy to keep sentences from going awry. Then, be-

cause sentences often go awry anyway, a writer needs the patience to repair them.

Clear thinking and clear writing go together. Say what you mean to say. That's clarity. And it's easier when your writing is simple and direct.[1]

With effort, most young children do a good job of writing clear prose like "The cat sat on the mat." That is like learning to bounce one ball. But when we get to sentences like "The salesman that the doctor met departed," it is not enough to have the scenario straight and put the words together grammatically. This particular sentence makes readers' eyes jump about because it is hard to process mentally.[2] A good writer senses that it is an unpleasant sentence and tries to shift the parts around to improve it. That is like bouncing several balls at once.

As ideas get more complex, it is hard to keep all the phrases and idioms under control. One successful article writer published a 1987 book full of writing advice, stressing that writers should cut out all unnecessary words — and he let this sentence slip through: "Writing classes should be taught by working writers, but few seldom are." (Either *few* or *seldom* needs to be cut out.) It could happen to any of us.

If our language were orderly and dependable, like a set of Tinker Toys or Legos, life would be easier. To many Europeans, English seems to be an illogical and chaotic language, unsuited for clear thinking and clear writing. The other European languages are far better organized and easier to use. In contrast, our language can seem like Silly Putty. To write well in English is difficult, and to write perfectly in it is impossible. Experts can find bits of confused wording in even the best English books.[3]

Juggling Words and Ideas

If writing a baby sentence is like bouncing a ball, more ambitious writing is like juggling several pieces of china while pedaling a unicycle. Doing this with difficult ideas and subtlety or artistry is like juggling a set of china while pedaling a unicycle on a highwire above Niagara Falls. It takes natural ability, years of practice,[4] and immense concentration.

Good writers of English are like chess players and concert pianists combined. But they make the writing look easy.[5] Raymond Chandler explained how he did it this way:

> Me, I wait for inspiration, although I don't necessarily call it by that name. I believe that all writing that has any life in it is done with the solar plexus. It is hard work in the sense that it may leave you tired, even exhausted. In the sense of conscious effort it is not work at all. The important thing is that there should be a space of time, say four hours a day at least, when a professional writer doesn't do anything else but write. He doesn't have to write, and if he doesn't feel like it he shouldn't try. He can look out of the window or stand on his head or writhe on the floor, but he is not to do any other positive

thing, not read, write letters, glance at magazines, or write checks. Either write or nothing. . . . Two very simple rules: A. You don't have to write, B. You can't do anything else. The rest comes of itself.[6]

Chandler had an excellent British education and an extraordinary facility with English. He didn't run into sentence snarls as often as most writers do. The very richness and irregularity and ambiguity of the English language often trick ordinary American writers into confusion and muddles and misstatements. When these are silly enough, we call them bloopers. A recent collection of student bloopers making the rounds included the following composite:

> Abraham Lincoln became America's greatest Precedent. Lincoln's mother died in infancy, and he was born in a log cabin which he built with his own hands. When Lincoln was President, he wore only a tall silk hat. Abraham Lincoln wrote the Gettysburg Address while traveling from Washington to Gettysburg on the back of an envelope. He also freed the slaves by signing the Emasculation Proclamation, and the Fourteenth Amendment gave the ex-Negroes citizenship. But the Clue Clux Clan would torcher and lynch the ex-Negroes and other innocent victims. It claimed it represented law and odor. On the night of April 14, 1865, Lincoln went to the theater and got shot in his seat by one of the actors in a moving picture show. The believed assinator was John Wilkes Booth, a supposingly insane actor. This ruined Booth's career.[7]

I cannot prove that these were genuine student bloopers, but as one well acquainted with the writing of public school pupils, I don't doubt it for a minute. Many teachers start collections like this. For all its flaws and gaffes, this piece of writing has a couple of excellent qualities. First, it is brief. Second, it is (unintentionally) amusing. That can't be said for enough writing in the United States today.

I have my own folders full of student bloopers that I dip into every few years. "The alarm went off at 6:00 A.M. and slowly crawled out of bed." The author wrote that on her nineteenth birthday. I notice now for the first time that although this paper was written on 12/6/84, the author accidentally dated it 12/6/65. I don't blame her; I make slips also.

If the first virtue of good writing is clarity, the second virtue is brevity. When asked how tall a man should be, Abraham Lincoln answered tall enough to reach from the top of his head to the soles of his feet. Just as tall as necessary, and not taller. Similarly, a piece of writing should be no longer and wordier than necessary. I suggest to students that they pretend they have to pay me one dollar for each word they use, to see how many dollars they can save if they try. It is easier to write loose, fat prose than to write lean and muscular prose. The battle of the bulge never ends for most writers; they belong to an unofficial "Word Watchers" league, forever trimming off unnecessary words that pad their phrases, bloat their paragraphs, and add flab to their ideas.

This anonymous verse says it best:

> The written word
> Should be clean as bone,
> Clear as light,
> Firm as stone.
> Two words are not
> As good as one.

Just as there are two primary virtues for writers, there are two prime sins. The first sin is to bore the reader. Many readers claim to be bored, but no writers claim to be boring. W. Somerset Maugham said, "I never met an author who admitted that people did not buy his book because it was dull." Most writers admit almost anything before they admit they are boring.

The second sin for a writer is to insult the reader accidentally, which is like bumping into him and sloshing his coffee onto his shirt without even noticing. I feel insulted when a writer informs me that nine comes just before ten (a truism) or that all women love Frank Sinatra (an exaggeration). I want to say, "Who do you think you're talking to?"

Both boring and insulting the reader show lack of sensitivity to the person whose mental room you have entered. A good writer is a graceful guest in the reader's brain. Intentionally shocking or disturbing the reader or arguing with the reader can be fine, but clumsily irritating the reader is a sign of incompetence. Readers need all the consideration they can get.

E. B. White claimed that a reader is in serious trouble most of the time, like a man floundering in a swamp. He said it is the duty of anyone attempting to write English to drain this swamp quickly and get his man up on dry ground, or at least throw him a rope.

"You may say that the serious writer doesn't have to bother about the tired reader," Flannery O'Connor said, "but he does, because they are all tired." Of course the writers are tired, too, whether they know it or not.

Most of us use English so naturally that we are hardly aware of it, just as we drive our cars automatically on crowded freeways. But our brains are doing complicated work for us every minute. One of the best ways to become aware of the chaos and confusion our brains have to sort through all the time with English is to observe how immigrants struggle with our language.[8] As a young man from Vietnam wrote about his friends, "Although they spent a lot of time, they do not catch up with the ideas in the books if they do not try themselves to conquer the laziness. Sometimes, they fall in sleep early." (I can hardly catch up with the ideas in the books myself, most of the time.)

Another Vietnamese student wrote, "The number of unemployees will increase." I congratulate her for her logic.[9]

I also liked the logic of an enthusiastic student from Mexico who said, "I personally prefer to watch the news on television rather than to read them on newspapers." (News looks plural, and *on* newspapers makes as much sense as *on* television. The print is *on* the paper, but the picture is *in* the screen, isn't it?)

I had a student from the Philippines that year who wrote, "Sometimes, most of us overemphasize the fact of God's one attribute over another that our perception of Him is not anymore balanced as it should be." I wonder if he has a job now working on instruction manuals for my brand of computer. I seem to recognize the thinking style.

In 1977 an extraordinary immigrant named Lev Landa arrived in the United States from the Soviet Union, where he was a leading professor of learning theory and an expert in practical logic.[10] He was glad to escape Soviet bureaucracy, and he expected to enjoy American efficiency; so he was flummoxed by the confusion and waste he soon encountered here. He has named his teaching methods "Landamatics" and started a consulting firm. He worked on the Dutch tax form, reduced it from 3,199 to 1,182 words, and helped cut the error rate from about fifty percent to less than ten percent. He would like to help our Internal Revenue Service cut down on incoherence also.

Mr. Landa dreams of enlisting Ralph Nader to start a movement to make American business talk plan English. He says we waste billions on badly written forms. He knows of one telephone equipment company that wastes more than $2 million a year on service calls because its instruction books are incomprehensible. Chase Manhatten, the bank that provided him with his first credit card, wastes more than $20 million a year trying to explain badly written forms to its customers. For some strange reason, companies like to hire and train employees to give oral explanations instead of hiring professional writers to make the printed materials clear. Application forms, assembly instructions, tax guidelines, insurance policies, claim forms, instruction booklets — all of these are full of unnecessary complexities and obfuscation. They take up years of our lives and cost our nation billions. Landa says that Americans are legally free people, but in practical terms their freedom of choice is severely limited by printed obfuscation — important writing that is ridiculously unclear.

Many people take the official confusion for granted and also pay little attention to their own words in everyday life. Consider this sentence: "The quiet moments are spent walking slowly down a deserted, endless path that is filled with pinecones and large, overstuffed trees." I asked the bright, pleasant American college student who wrote this how the path could be endless unless it was one big circle, and how she could walk on it if it was filled with pinecones. She didn't know. Then I told her that I loved the idea of big, soft overstuffed trees, like giant cushions. She said she thought overstuffed meant bushy. She was amazed that I paid so much attention to her words; she never had.

Easy Writing

Our church newsletter once included this sentence from an engineer: "At the church we meet, greet, meander around and have more fellowship with the cat at home than we do with our brother-in-Christ on the weekend." I tucked it away for safekeeping. I have read that in England one can find lower-class people who mangle their sentences, but no professional people who do so. In the United States this is common among professional people.

Here is a more recent sample:

> Along with the traditional fillings which accompany our church's life during the Easter season, I have been faced with many personal fillings as well. For me those personal fillings have centered around my own "futuring" and how this relates to the future of the church. This process of "futuring" has surfaced many thoughts and feelings of thanks for the acceptance, support and love which I feel from you. The strengthening of our relationship together over the last seven months has made our prospects of movement from this church family more and more difficult to imagine. I am sincerely grateful for your encouragement of this difficulty. . . .

Here are the bones of the sentences:

1. I have been faced with fillings.
2. Fillings have been centered around futuring.
3. Process has surfaced thoughts.
4. Strengthening has made process difficult.
5. I am grateful (for encouragement of difficulty).

That is from an intelligent and sensitive youth minister who has always spoken English. But like many native speakers today, he sometimes writes a strange kind of English indeed. Although his message is meant to be warm and personal, it lacks clarity, brevity, and simplicity. It needs work.

Ernest Hemingway said, "The first and most important thing of all, at least for writers today, is to strip language clean, to lay it bare down to the bone." He also said, "Easy writing makes hard reading."

The peculiar kind of itchy, scabby, oozy writing that I see spreading like a fungus infection in our country seems to thrive in the warm, damp atmosphere of schools. (Most people who try to teach English know very little about it, and they have far too many students and too many other duties anyway.) Here is a sample bulletin from our local high school principal who had received complaints from parents that school materials were unclear and poorly written:

> All material sent directly home or sent home with a student should be proofread by two or more staff members. Everything sent out from our office is read by a member of the English Department before the final copy is typed. Please diminish the chances of sending something to parents or being given to students that is sub-standard. This procedure applies to items that go into the school paper. Curriculum papers or other handouts given to students and parents require proofreading as well. Criticism in this area cannot be defended.

Since this serious-sounding announcement was too vague and confused to make real sense, no one paid attention, and things went on as usual. I suspect that the principal felt that his bulletin should pacify the parents. My guess is that the concerned parents saw what they were up against and gave up the fight.

An English professor named Richard Mitchell went on the warpath about gobbledygook a few years ago and published two books about the subject: *Less Than Words Can Say* (Little, Brown and Company, 1979) and *The Leaning Tower of Babel* (Little, Brown and Company, 1984). He claims that our schools foster overblown, inane writing, and that manglers of language and thought — administrators and bureaucrats who cannot adequately read or write or think — are running and ruining our language, our schools, our institutions, and our society.

Mitchell says the Department of Transportation issued this directive once: "If a guest becomes intoxicated . . . take his or her car keys and send them home in a taxi." If that were a student blooper, it would be funny. But it makes Mitchell angry.

Intimidation

Mitchell sees the misuse of English especially common in education, government, psychology, and the social sciences, but he sees it everywhere else also. He points out unintelligible public documents, imperial-sounding administrative memoranda, threatening "legalese," and bizarre obscurity of all kinds.

He is a witty, feisty grumbler, and he claims that ordinary American people are still intimidated by rank and power — and by language that suggests financial wealth or power, including academic, governmental, and bureaucratic power. (Think of your reaction if you get an obscure, unfriendly letter from a government agency.) Most people are unconsciously intimidated by language that they cannot themselves use easily. This psychological fact is a great advantage to those who want to control others, so they tend to write in an impersonal power-jargon. Like fast-talking hucksters, they bluff and bamboozle by obfuscating. Then this lingo becomes standard in institutions.

The sign "Eschew Obfuscation" says it all.

When the Normans ruled England, Mitchell says, it was obvious which language people spoke — plain words (English) or control words (French). The government might possibly *pardon* you in French for a crime, but only your friend could *forgive* you in English for a sin. Both words are English now, but there is still a shade of difference in their meanings. Likewise, we say that our hearts are broken in English, not fractured in French. Winston Churchill knew this when he advised writers to use native English words whenever possible. They communicate common humanity best. But communicating common humanity is exactly what some people want least.

Because spokesmen for science and technology have the most authority in our society today, language that sounds scientific or technical easily intimidates or impresses ordinary people. Science has the sanction today that the Church had in the Middle Ages. Therefore a technical or pseudo-scientific style is the prized style in many classrooms, even those far removed from science and technology.[11] It is also the style sometimes desired by editors and publishers. It can lead to lazy and superficial writing. (This is no indictment of real science or of scientists who are real writers. Three of my all-time favorite authors are Loren Eiseley, Lewis Thomas, and Oliver Sacks — all twentieth-century American science writers.)[12]

As D. Bruce Lockerbie (author of *The Cosmic Center* and *So You're Going to College*, and editor of *The Christian, the Arts, and Truth*) has complained, writers used to observe human phenomena and rely on their common sense in uttering wisdom. But today we are often expected to use graphs, statistics, and the jargon of social science to justify our common-sense conclusions. An education article he read announced the old truism that parental unemployment and divorce are the main causes for the poverty of children. This was suddenly "news" because it was the result of a current scientific study conducted by a university economics professor on a ten-year grant from a foundation. (Word lovers are apt to shake their heads over a boondoggle.)

Lockerbie wryly observed that if Thomas Paine were to publish his revolutionary 1776 pamphlet *Common Sense* today, he would probably have to rename it *Statistics Show. . .* or *A Study Reveals. . . .* This is especially true when people are writing about human behavior such as politics, religion, or education.[13]

Marjorie Holmes, one of our country's most popular inspirational writers, noted several years ago that editors suddenly started asking her to refer to authorities (anyone in print) when she made a point about family life or similar common-sense topics. So she got the habit of saying what she had to say, then scouting to find something in print that more or less agreed with her, so she could cite it as a source. (Needless to say, it is possible to plant your own sources in print sometimes, either intentionally or by happy accident, and refer to them later.)[14]

The trick here is to make ideas look as if they have been approved by some kind of state-certified authorities with technical expertise. If you have any fresh ideas and original insights, this is like giving them the bleach treatment — for the recycled look fashionable in new jeans. And indeed the pseudo-scientific style is an intellectual fashion. If a graph or a few sets of numbers can be worked in anywhere to add a dash of "quantification," so much the better. The slightest suggestion of laboratory methods or statistical research helps, no matter how illogical the connection is.[15] And if it seems that a large sum of money or a powerful computer touched some aspect of the subject in any way at all, that adds clout.

This pseudo-scientific style creates an aura of credibility even if the material says little that is definite or nothing that is new. It's the art of illusion. People writing in this style at its worst choose long words instead of short ones and confusing sentences instead of clear ones. Further, they use too many passive verbs instead of active verbs ("The method is based on" instead of "We based the method on"), and as many abstractions as possible (method, subvariables, system, priorities, data, status — all names of things you can't touch or see or easily define).

This stultifying sociological style can spread into every subject area. Here is a classroom report about finding good campsites:

> The method is based on evaluating two basic groupings the authors
> feel are vital in considering where campgrounds might be best located.
> These groupings, physical and socio-economic, are broken down into

sub-headings which in turn are expanded into lists of sub-variables. The idea was to have trained observers visit pre-determined potential campsites and rate them according to a set numerical rating system, supposedly reflecting degree of campground excellence. Priorities in campsite development were the product of socio-economic data. When the two ratings were combined a list of prioritized camp-grounds and their existing physical status would result, and hopefully provide the planner with a feeling of confidence as the next step was taken.[16]

From an entirely different source, here (in redundant legalese) is National Park Service policy statement 36 CFR 50.10 warning people not to damage vegetation:

> No person shall prune, cut, carry away, pull up, dig, fell, bore, chop, saw, chip, pick, move, sever, climb, molest, take, break, deface, destroy, set fire to, burn, scorch, carve, paint, mark, or in any manner interfere with, tamper, mutilate, misuse, disturb or damage, any tree, shrub, plant, grass, flower, or part thereof, nor shall any person permit any chemical, whether solid, fluid, or gaseous, to seep, drip, drain or be emptied, sprayed, dusted or injected upon, about or into any tree, shrub, plant, grass, flower or part thereof, except when specifically authorized by competent authority; nor shall any person build fires, or station, or use any tar kettle, heater, road roller or other engine within an area covered by this part in such a manner that the vapor, fumes or heat therefrom may injure any tree or other vegetation.

Minimal Coherency

Obviously, there is no National Language Service policy statement 36 CFR 50.10 warning the public not to injure English that way. It is often said that art critics are some of the worst offenders when it comes to doing damage with gaseous jargon. One of them, best left unnamed, claims in an expensive book that when an artist paints a picture of any tree, shrub, plant, grass, flower, or part thereof, he illegally carries away its essence and diminishes it:

> Now, if technical practice transforms its object — that is, its "subject" matter — the "original" is in some sense lost. But perhaps technique merely transfers the original, carrying its essence, so to speak, from one location to another, as if it could pass unchanged from nature to culture. Even so, originality is diminished; it is weakened in that the original is repeated. Existing in two places, or in two formal states, it becomes not only reiterative, but static. Repetition of this "essence" multiplies and fixes that which must

appear transient in its singularity. In sum, to the extent that one conceives of the original as singular, the representation of originality becomes paradoxical by either of the two estimations of pictorial metaphor: the act of painting either transfers or transforms its model (or has both effects at once); in either event, painting's "original" suffers.

Yet the very possibility of a representation and reiteration of originality forms part of the mythology of modern art (and of the modern sense of the "classic"). The paradox of representation can be resolved by the modern artist's act, regarded as original in itself. As if linked to a unique and immediate experience, artistic originality emerges within a painting that seems to have no definite model, despite its references to art and nature. Painting becomes self-referential and self-expressive, pointing to itself and to the self that generates it. The artist becomes a vehicle of discovery, one who finds what cannot be made, locating what representational technique cannot touch. Yet the modern "master" finds his "original" with such frequency that he appears able to create (make) it at will. Hence a second paradox arises, one on the level of artistic practice, as opposed to the level of a general theory of representation: a found "original" can be made. . . . the impressionists were born into a culture that defined artistic production in terms of creating the original. This myth of artistic originality and creativity, this productive play of finding and making, had already assumed a high degree of reality within their world. Despite the paradox, . . . the impressionists accepted this reality and their record of achievement could only confirm it. I believe these modern artists acted self-consciously; nevertheless, historical "accident" plays a part in the critical response [an artist's] technique provoked. He may achieve exercised control over his painting, but not over his historical fortune. To be sure, some of his admirers entertained notions of originality at variance with his own, and interpreted him accordingly, adding transformative nuances of meaning to his works. [His] painting was not only brought forth from a historical moment, but cast into one; it was polysemous at its origin.

Plato said, "Beauty of style and harmony and grace and good rhythm depend upon simplicity." But simplicity would sometimes reveal that an emperor has no clothes[17] and that a prestigious critic is saying lots of nothing. A century ago English art critic John Ruskin wrote simply and clearly about J. M. W. Turner's drawings of swans. Ruskin was mentally unstable, and his delightful writing about Turner's swans was incorrect. When clear and simple writing is out of style, it's harder to tell if an author is hallucinating.

Speaking of his own field, economics, John Kenneth Galbraith explains what has happened in many other fields as well:

> Further, it must be said, much past writing on the history of economic ideas has been aggressively dull. There are a significant number of learned men and women who hold that any successful effort to make ideas lively, intelligible and interesting is a manifestation of deficient scholarship. This is the fortress behind which the minimally coherent regularly find refuge.[18]

Jargon

Medical doctors are noted for habitually using scholarly sounding jargon. I went to my dermatologist once because I had a patch of sore skin. He looked it over and declared briskly that it was "Epidermal Schlerodoma of Idiopathic Origin" and should clear up all right without treatment. I asked to have the Latin translated. "Sore Skin, Cause Unknown," he winked. His nurse told me that they have their own office definition for *idiopathic:* The doctor is an *idiot* and the patient is *pathetic.* I left feeling that I had got a little something for my money.

At the University of Southern California School of Medicine a famous experiment once took place. Dr. John Ware and some colleagues introduced a Dr. Myron R. Fox, who gave a lecture on "Mathematical Game Theory as Applied to Physical Education" to a group of medical educators — psychologists, sociologists, physicians, and social workers. Dr. Fox was really an actor, and his lecture was a meaningless concoction of contradictions, *non sequiturs*, circular discussion, invented words, irrelevant details, and entertaining jokes that had nothing to do with the subject. He was well received, and not one member of the professional audience realized that the whole speech had said nothing at all. They reported on anonymous questionnaires that they found the lecture clear and stimulating.[19]

Later J. Scott Armstrong, associate professor of marketing at the University of Pennsylvania, followed up with a series of tests and found that some unintelligible writing from a supposedly legitimate source in a reader's area of expertise will usually win high marks from the reader. This is called the "Dr. Fox Hypothesis" after the original experiment. That is bad news for real writers, but it accounts for the frequent success of gobbledygook.

Jargon is initially the badge of the exclusive or the refuge of the verbally incompetent. Jacques Barzun says people slip into jargon when they combine the desire to appear learned with pure laziness. Covering up confused ideas with technical-sounding phrases is a quick way out.[20]

This is a problem for creative writers, because until they become alert to what is going on all around them, they may become infected with jargon.

Jargon is dull, pompous, inflated, careless, ugly, and vague. It is a way of striking a pose instead of thinking. It is a way of hiding behind a wall of empty words. But many naive people find it impressive because they don't understand the difference between clear thinking and muddy thinking.

I remember the book-length manuscript recently submitted to a publisher. It was meant to challenge and inspire ordinary people, but it had fog like this in it:

> Membership in various mediating structures — such as church, family, or any number of other significant organizations — can also exert an influence on how someone thinks of health and illness. All this diversity does not mean, however, that meaningful discussion about our culture's definition of health is impossible. While remaining sensitive to the diversity it is possible to sketch out in broad strokes the dominant ingredients that make up the parameters of health within America — and, indeed most of western — culture. The unified themes that filter through in the midst of the variations are unmistakable.

I understand that this writer was a university and seminary graduate, and I imagine that he got A's for writing that way in school. Instead of saying "a godly life" in plain English, he says "a lifestyle of godliness." (I advise people never to use "lifestyle" where "life" would do.) "It is not uncommon to find individuals wrestling as adults through the pain in facing the fact that their parents are declining." (It is painful for people to watch their parents decline?) "God makes it clear that obedience is not contrary to who Jeremiah was as a person." (Jeremiah was obedient?) "There can be no doubt that Jeremiah described himself with great accuracy in Lamentations." (Jeremiah told the truth about himself?) "Hebrews 11 comes near the end of an epistle." (Hebrews has thirteen chapters?) "Depth is replaced by the breadth of notoriety." (Fame is a shallow pleasure?) "The mass media is virtually monolithic in confirming the correlation between health and longevity." (People assume that good health means long life?) "Immediate results appear upon the horizon." *Stop!*

How can immediate results be off on the distant horizon?

I will keep this disappointed author's name secret to protect the guilty, and I hope that he rewrites his book and gets it published eventually. The suggestion I sent to him was that he must cut every chapter in half because they are so full of fat, and that he must cut out all the jargon and educationese. Every sentence should make good sense in plain English. This writer lacked both of the initial virtues all writers need, clarity and brevity. He committed both of the initial sins all writers must avoid, accidentally boring and insulting his readers. If he had taped up a picture of a typical reader near his typewriter and written with that person constantly in mind, he might have spared himself months of work. I suspect that he was accidentally, out of habit, writing to the teachers in his past. In fact, those teachers had dutifully read his papers because they were paid to wade through them and had to do it.

It is a fact that this kind of turgid writing is the only way to get an A in some classes. I explain that to my students and invite them to go ahead and write what their instructors expect, in order to get good grades. And I readily admit that some of this turgid writing gets published in respectable places. I found such an article in a prestigious religious magazine recently. It began by stating that people who get sick and die today all think that they have caused their illnesses (I was irritated by the exaggeration), and it moved on to the claim that people thus need a theology of culture that undergirds our health-policy ethics. (To me that is unclear.) Most of the article was composed of unrelated references to many books and articles (authority-citing gone to seed), and I wondered where it could possibly be leading. Here is the baffling conclusion:

> Now more than ever before, we have more opportunity for such acts as leave-taking, and for directing to some extent the mode and timing of our deaths. Yet, paradoxically, numerous factors prevent us from fully taking on this "last responsibility." Time is ripe to begin to reclaim some of the resources that might lead us to a more nuanced formulation of the relationship between moral responsibility, illness and death.

As the editor of another magazine remarked to me once, "So many writers feel obligated to end their articles with a little pirouette." Most teachers are pleased to see a bit of rhetorical flourish at the end of a floundering essay, even if it doesn't say anything, although most magazine editors are more particular. This article was featured in a magazine that is found in libraries across the country. So I must admit that this kind of writing pays off in prestige sometimes, even if readers get nothing out of it. Dullness and obscurity are sometimes rewarded by teachers and editors who haven't overcome their own dullness and obscurity.

School gives some people their deplorable writing habits. It gives them the idea that writing is easy for people who are bright. The fact is that fairly poor writing is easy for people who are bright, and that's the best that many professors look for nowadays. I have seen papers by successful graduate students that would have received a C or a D from me when I was teaching high school.

Clear, concise writing that does not bore or insult the reader costs. As Gene Fowler said, "Writing is easy; all you do is sit staring at a blank sheet of paper until the drops of blood form on your forehead." Sean Casey said, "When I stepped from hard manual work to writing, I just stepped from one kind of hard work to another." Red Barber said, "There's nothing to writing. All you do is sit down at a typewriter and open a vein." Isaac Bashevis Singer said, "The wastebasket is a writer's best friend." F. Scott Fitzgerald said, "All good writing is *swimming under water* and holding your breath." Robert Louis Stevenson said, "I hate to write, but I love to have written." Peter De Vries said, "I love being a writer. What I can't stand is the paperwork." Bernard Malamud said, "The idea is to get the pencil moving quickly." Ring Lardner said, "How can you write if you can't cry?" Vladimir Nabokov said, "I have rewritten — often several times — every word I have ever published." Morley Callaghan said, "There is only one trait that marks the writer. He is always watching." W. Somerset Maugham said, "I write twenty-four hours per day. I only *type* from 9 A.M. until noon."

And E. B. White said "Be obscure clearly."

Over fifty years ago, in his essay "Politics and the English Language," George Orwell gave us a half-dozen rules that are standing the test of time:

1. Never use a metaphor, simile, or other figure of speech which you are used to seeing in print.
2. Never use a long word where a short one will do.
3. If it is possible to cut a word out, cut it out.
4. Never use the passive where you can use the active.
5. Never use a foreign phrase, a scientific word, or a jargon word if you can think of an everyday English equivalent.
6. Break any of these rules sooner than say anything outright barbarous.

SUGGESTED ACTIVITIES

1. Locate a page of jargon (business jargon, legal jargon, technical jargon, political jargon, academic jargon, fashion jargon, sports jargon, or any other kind) and convert it into clear, natural prose. The ability to do this could land you a great job someday. On the other hand, it could get you fired.

2. Collect a bucket of "buzzwords" that are for the time being emotionally loaded or trendy and overused. (Seek examples such as *upscale, humanistic, viable,* or *networking.*) Don't be afraid to guess and to ask people's opinions about words you suspect of being "buzzwords." Why does so much of our communication hinge upon such words?

3. If you dare, try purging your next essay test or business letter of inflated language. Present all your points in practical working-class clothes rather than preppy attire or three-piece suits, but be sure to have perfect spelling and a neat appearance. How do you feel without the protection of "power language"? What responses do you get?

4. When you write your next letter to a friend or relative, try rewriting it in highly inflated language and pompous jargon. Translate sentences like "After lunch, I took a nap," into sentences like "In the period subsequent to my usual midday dietary endeavor, I thought it advisable to extend myself longitudinally in order to maximize my potential for establishing the parameters of moderate physical recuperation." Include both versions, and see what kind of response you get.

NOTES

[1] My favorite book on this topic is *Simple and Direct: A Rhetoric for Writers* by Jacques Barzun (New York: Harper & Row, 1975).

[2] Researchers at Carnegie Mellon University tracked readers' eye movements when studying the role of short-term memory in language comprehension, according to a note on page 6 of *Brain/Mind Bulletin* of April 1988. No one has yet investigated the role of short-term memory and other specialized brain functions in creative writing.

[3] Robert Graves and Alan Hodge, *The Reader Over Your Shoulder* (New York: Random House, 1979). After discussing the peculiar qualities of English, present confusion in English prose, good English, legalese, and the elements of clarity, this book analyzes muddled spots in the writing of over a dozen excellent writers including T. S. Eliot, J. B. Priestley, I. A. Richards, Bertrand Russell, George Bernard Shaw, H. G. Wells, and Alfred North Whitehead.

[4] Katherine Mansfield said, "Looking back, I imagine I was always writing. Twaddle it was too. But better far write twaddle or anything, anything, than nothing at all."

[5] The following letter from reader Joe Romeo of Uniontown, Ohio, appeared in the April 1988 issue of *NEA Today.*

Doctors earn big bucks because nobody can do what they do or read what they write; lawyers, because few can do what they do and no one can understand what they write. But public school teachers are a different matter. Most of us have experienced the classroom through 12 years of schooling. We can all do what teachers do, and everyone not only can read what teachers write, but we can understand what they write. Good teachers make their jobs look so easy, we all think we can do them. It's a case of the law of supply and demand — real or imagined.

[6] *Raymond Chandler Speaking*, edited by Dorothy Gardiner and Kathrine Sorley Walker (New York: Houghton Mifflin, 1962), 79–80.

[7] Some of these bloopers appear along with many others in *Anguished English: An Anthology of Accidental Assaults upon Our Language*, (Charleston, SC: Wyrick and Co., 1987), compiled by Richard Lederer. After 26 years as a teacher at St. Paul's School in Concord, New Hampshire, Lederer writes a weekly column — "Looking at Language" — and serves as a vice president of SPELL (Society for the Preservation of English Language and Literature).

[8] In one English class that I taught in the spring of 1984 at Santa Ana College, I had thirty students from the following nineteen countries: Afghanistan, Bahrain, Cambodia, Chile, Czechoslovakia, Dominica, France, Germany, Iran, Japan, Jordan, Korea, Kuwait, Laos, Mexico, Nigeria, Palestine, Syria, Vietnam.

[9] I did not feel inclined to congratulate the incompetent native-English-speaking feature writer on our local newspaper staff who once published the following neologism (newly invented term): "In the last several years, the number of non-support payments by one parent has risen by more than a thousand a year." What is a non-support payment, I wondered. Perhaps it's the kind of payment made by an unemployee.

[10] Jonathan Rowe, "One Soviet's Offensive," *Christian Science Monitor* (March 10, 1988), 1, 32.

[11] "Stitches" columnist John Tierney claimed in "The Heartbeat of America," (*Hippocrates*, January/February 1989, pp. 34–36) that there is a major flaw in *Huckleberry Finn*. Huck recorded, "We said there warn't no home like a raft, after all. Other places do seem so cramped up and smothery, but a raft don't. You feel mighty free and easy and comfortable on a raft." What Huck really meant to say was "Jim, although each individual reacts differently to stress according to his or her physiological and psychological makeup, the role of environmental stress should not be overlooked, and a raft in the splendid isolation of Nature often appears to be a less stressful environment than a competitive urban setting where an individual's blood pressure is liable to surge in the fight-or-flight reaction when confronted with the slightest provocation."

According to Tierney, the major flaw in Twain's thematic treatment of the Nature-versus-civilization conflict is that Huck never made any quantitative measurements of stress on his journey. Huck should have taken blood pressure readings on the raft and in other situations and produced a series of reports such as "The Cardiovascular Toll of Table Manners," "The Influence of Blood Oaths on Diastolic Pressure," and "Slavery As a Potential Promoter of Stress."

Tierney did the Nature-versus-civilization crosscountry fieldwork himself, with a blood pressure kit, as his contribution to social science research. He says that results of social science research always fall into three categories: (1) The results show no pattern at all, and the experiment was a waste of time, (2) The results are just what common sense would have predicted, and the experiment was a waste of time, (3) The results contradict common sense, no one believes them, and the experiment was a waste of time. Tierney's alleged experiment was an utter waste of time, but it filled two pages in an impressive magazine and he was paid for it.

[12] "It is the academic cant of relatively recent origin, that a self-respecting scientist *must* be a bore, that the more dehydrated the style of his writing, and the more technical the jargon he uses, the more respect he will command. I repeat, this is a recent fashion, less than a century old, but its effect is devastating. . . .

"Needless to say, technical communications addressed to specialists must employ technical language; but even here the overloading with jargon, the tortuous and cramped style, are largely a matter of conforming to fashion." Arthur Koestler, *The Act of Creation* (New York: Macmillan, 1964), 265.

[13] D. Bruce Lockerbie, "Schools that Work," *Christianity Today* (Nov. 6, 1987), 60. This essay reviewed *Public and Private High Schools: The Impact of Communities* by James S. Coleman and Thomas Hoffer.

[14] Planting sources is an old trick. The famous British psychology professor Sir Cyril Burt (1883–1971) turned out to be a remarkable source-planter. He apparently invented credentialed researchers and wrote articles by them — with invented statistics, of course — which he published in scholarly journals. Then he cited those creations of his to support his own "research findings" and the conclusions he wanted the scientific community to accept. This was revealed after his death; in his lifetime he was highly honored and his scholarship was not publicly questioned. Ironically, Sir Cyril Burt had the honor of providing the foreword for Arthur Koestler's 1964 tome *The Act of Creation*. Perhaps he chuckled about his own creative deceptions when he wrote that foreword at the age of eighty, basking in the afterglow of a long, successful career.

[15] I highly recommend the entertaining little book *How to Lie with Statistics* by Darrell Huff (New York: Norton, 1954). Huff begins by quoting Benjamin Disraeli: "There are three kinds of lies: lies, damned lies, and statistics." Huff instructs writers about how and how not to "statisticulate," showing that this trend was strong over thirty years ago. In fact, Huff ends with a passage from Mark Twain making fun of thoughtless misuse of statistics a century ago.

[16] Richard Mitchell, *Less Than Words Can Say* (Boston: Little Brown and Company, 1979), 111.

[17] I find that many young adults today do not know Hans Christian Andersen's story "The Emperor's New Clothes." In this story a vain and foolish emperor was tricked by two swindlers who convinced him that they could weave extravagantly fine new fabric for imperial robes. The cloth would be invisible to anyone stupid or unfit for his job, so of course no one would admit that the cloth was invisible. The emperor went out on parade in his imaginary new clothes, and all the people pretended to admire them. Finally one honest child cried out, "But he has got nothing on!" This story illustrates the conspiracy of silence that often surrounds the pretensions of people with rank, and the vulnerable innocence of

those few who object. The term "the emperor's new clothes" applies most obviously to occasional events in the worlds of academia and aesthetics — both worlds that include creative writing.

[18]John Kenneth Galbraith, *Economics in Perspective: A Critical History* (Boston: Houghton Mifflin, 1987), 2.

[19]The father of a friend of mine did an impromptu Dr. Fox performance when unexpectedly called upon to give a report at a conference of sales representatives for the major company where he worked. He happened to have with him a page he had just received from a friend — the "Systematic Buzz Phrase Projector" devised by a man named Philip Broughton who was exasperated with bureaucratic jargon where he worked. The trick is to choose any three-digit number, then combine the three buzzwords from the following columns.

0. integrated	0. management	0. options
1. total	1. organizational	1. flexibility
2. systematized	2. monitored	2. capability
3. parallel	3. reciprocal	3. mobility
4. functional	4. digital	4. programming
5. responsive	5. logistical	5. concept
6. optional	6. transitional	6. time-phase
7. synchronized	7. incremental	7. projection
8. compatible	8. third-generation	8. hardware
9. balanced	9. policy	9. contingency

The random three-word phrases can be dropped into any speech with a ring of decisive, knowledgeable authority. According to Broughton, "No one will have the remotest idea what you are talking about, but the important thing is that they're not about to admit it."

My friend's father strung a bunch of these three-word phrases together on the spot and delivered his report with cheerful confidence. When he finished, he received a standing ovation, and one of the top men in the company told him that this was the best presentation they had ever heard. I think it wisest not to divulge the name of the famous company or of my friend's father.

[20]Jacques Barzun, *Simple and Direct: A Rhetoric for Writers* (New York: Harper & Row, 1975), 18.

Chapter 3

Pitfalls and Pratfalls

It took me fifteen years to discover I had no talent for writing, but I couldn't give it up because by that time I was too famous.

— ROBERT BENCHLEY

Every writer wants to look good.

There are several basic ways for a writer to look good, but there are endless ways for a writer to look like a fool. I will point out a dozen danger areas, with irreverent survival suggestions — pointers about spelling, grammar and punctuation, formal and informal usage, slang and cliches, openers and closings, sermonese, dialogue, and purple prose.

Spelling

"Bad spellers of the world, untie." That says it all.

The first, fastest way for an author to look inept is to misspell (not mispell) words. There is an old story about the man who was arrested for producing pornography. "But Officer," he protested, "I don't even own a pornograph!" Faulty orthography is almost as taboo as pornography in polite society. When an author is caught with some in his manuscript, about all he can plead is, "But Officer, I don't even own an orthograph!"

The amount of time that American schoolchildren spend on spelling is staggering, and the amount of time that American writers and editors spend on spelling is also extravagant (not extravegant). But there is no avoiding it, because spelling errors look so bad. A couple of spelling errors on your page make it look as unappetizing (not unapettizing) as a salad with a couple of flies on it. We've been trained that way. Most writers are mortified when they are caught with misspellings.

Thorstein Veblen explained in *The Theory of the Leisure Class* that conventional English spelling is a perfect example of conspicuous waste (not waist). It is archaic, cumbersome, and ineffective; its acquisition requires much time and effort; and failure to acquire it is easily detected. Good spelling is one of the social graces, and spelling errors are gauche — like wearing socks that don't match or spilling the contents of your purse on the floor. Everything else being equal, good spellers are socially superior to poor spellers. Good spellers are, at their very worst, people of shabby gentility (not gentillity). Unless poor spellers can afford to buy good spelling from someone else, they are in an underclass — the bag ladies of the educated world. It's hard to respect ideas set forth in weak spelling.

Perfect spelling, like perfect grooming, is a sign of success and control. It means status. When ordinary people worked outdoors, pale skin was considered beautiful because it was a sign of leisure (not liesure) spent indoors. Now that most ordinary people work indoors, tan is considered beautiful because it is a sign of leisure spent outdoors. Either way, rich is beautiful. Perhaps buying a tan in a salon is equivalent (not equivelant) to paying for someone else's good spelling, as many businessmen do.

When C. S. Lewis's brother Warren wrote one of his superb books about French history, C. S. Lewis discovered that Warren had spelled "diary" as "dairy" all the way through the manuscript, and told him so.

Warren responded loftily, "I use *simplified* spelling."

That's insouciance. And if you can spell a few fancy words like *insouciance*, you can afford some slip-ups elsewhere. (*Insouciance* means a carefree indifference, the opposite of anxiety and mortification.)

I suggest that writers who are imperfect spellers attack the problem with both effort and insouciance.

1. Pay attention to your spelling, because you want to appear literate and competent to your editors and readers. Try to notice correct spellings of words when you read. (The best readers absorb meanings so skillfully that they don't normally take time to absorb exact spellings as they zip along. The worst readers are probably too confused to absorb them.)

2. Keep your perspective; never forget how silly our spelling customs are. Don't let pesky spelling diminish your love of the words themselves.

3. Use the dictionary often and also check words with your companions who are good spellers. Don't guess in your final draft.

4. Make an alphabetical list of your own weak words, for quick reference. Have copies of that list wherever you write.

5. Get the help of a secretary or personal editor who spells well, if you can, and also get aid from an electronic spelling checker.

6. Remember that most perfect spellers are not gifted writers and that most gifted writers are not perfect spellers — although they wish they were. Perfect spelling goes along with keen visual recall.

7. This is a ploy and may or may not be ethically (not ethicly) permissible (not permisable). Mistype your own first name and some other extremely easy word on your first page to show that you are an imperfect typist and an imperfect proofreader. Then any spelling errors that slip through may be taken for typos. Typos are less embarrassing (not embarassing).

Grammar

I think of the verb as the life of the sentence. It's like the breathing of your baby in its crib. To understand the grammar of a sentence, first you enter the room and look and listen carefully — is the baby alive? You can tell by its breathing. That is the verb. Then you tiptoe to the crib and touch the small body. That's the subject of the sentence. Everything else is extra.

Everything else extra can get rather complicated. It runs from objective complements to appositive nouns, from cognate objects to coordinate conjunctions and subordinate connectives. Unless we are teaching grammar, we tend to forget the terms. My old handbook is Smart's *English Review Grammar*.[1] I see that when I studied that book in 1956 I wrote myself a warning note inside: "Chapter IX confuses true coordinating conjunctions and conjunctive adverbs!" I suppose that's true, and I don't suppose it has made much practical difference to anyone, especially writers. I think that grammar rules describe what good writers do, rather than telling good writers what to do. Furthermore, some rules have been relaxing.[2]

Here are ten of the basic rules of grammar as set forth once by George Feinstein, a California college instructor.

1. Each pronoun agrees with their antecedent.
2. Just between you and I, pronoun case is important.
3. Verbs has to agree with their subjects.
4. Watch out for irregular verbs which have crope up in English.
5. Don't use no double negatives.
6. A writer mustn't shift your point of view.
7. When dangling, don't use participles.
8. Join clauses good, like a conjunction should.
9. Don't write a run-on sentence remember to separate sentences.
10. About sentence fragments.

To those, I would add: "As an English teacher, dangling modifiers are common among writers today. Ugly and awkward, I try to teach students to spot them. Most writers can avoid dangling modifiers, hopefully."

Grammar is far more interesting than spelling, but here again both sincere effort and insouciance are in order. The goal is to keep in step with good writers of our own day. Not out of duty, but because that is what works. Grammar is a delightful study, like geometry, and the terms and rules can come in handy. But writers don't need the terms and rules; they need a good ear. They need to hear what's right and wrong in sentences.

I have often asked my college English classes, "Is God displeased when you use bad grammar?" That always wakes them up. Few dare to say either yes or no, and they wonder what I'm up to. (I grew up hearing and using *ain't* until a second-grade teacher told me that nice girls don't use that bad word.)

The rules of grammar are only descriptive rules, not moral rules. Some of us love good grammar because we love words and ideas; but proper English grammar today is largely the result of historical accidents. It was not ordained by God. There is much beauty and some logic in grammar, but it is nothing absolute and definitive like the logic in mathematics.

Using poor grammar is similar to wearing clothes that are shoddy or unattractive by contemporary standards — "She done it" is a slip that makes a speaker sound out of the mainstream. Writing "She gave the books to Harry and I" makes a writer look inept because the preferred wording today is still "She gave the books to Harry and me." (To check on *I* or *me*, without taking time to analyze it grammatically, just leave out Harry and hear how it sounds: "She gave the books to . . . me." Your ear knows.)

Until recently, the rules about pronoun gender were set and simple. We used feminine pronouns (*she* and *her*) when the gender was female. We used masculine pronouns (*he, him,* and *his*) when the gender was male or a possible mixture of male and female. If there was only one male in a class of female students, it was proper to say, "Each student must bring his book." That might not have been representative, but it was routine.

Then came the revolution. Publishing houses began to change editors' rules for the sake of symbolic equality of the sexes. Some writers could not or would not give up the bisexual use of *he, him,* and *his;* but most cooperated. Some writers switched to "Each student must bring his or her book," and others chose "Each student must bring her or his book." Some switched to "Each student must bring his/her book," and others chose "Each student must bring her/his book." Some writers risked using "Each student must bring their book" (a single subject with a plural gender-free pronoun), and others switched to plurals whenever possible, as in "All students must bring their books." Other writers simply jumped back and forth willy-nilly, as in "Each student must bring his book and keep it on her desk."

I suppose any writer, male or female, is apt to tear his/her hair over this problem at times. I think writers do best to try to keep things in a plural neuter for the sake of their nerves and their readers' nerves.

We used to be taught that we must never split an infinitive, but I found that I was apt *to accidentally split* one sometimes. I think the difference between a fair writer and an excellent writer is that the excellent writer doesn't do such things accidentally. Raymond Chandler complained to a friend once about an editor wanting to correct his split infinitives: "When I split an infinitive, God Damn it, I split it so it will stay split, and when I interrupt the velvety smoothness of my more or less literate syntax with a few sudden words of bar-room vernacular, that is done with the eyes wide open and the mind relaxed but attentive. The method may not be perfect, but it is all I have."[3] Chandler was not recommending split infinitives to other writers, but he was determined to use one when he wanted one.

Once an editor corrected a sentence by Winston Churchill because he had ended it with a preposition, which was then against the rule. (That rule is something we don't have time to go *into*.) Churchill rebuked his editor: "This is the sort of impertinence up *with* which I will not put." That mocking sentence was the death knell for the silly rule that one should never end a sentence with a preposition. As Churchill said, "I got into my bones the essential structure of the ordinary British sentence, which is a noble thing."

James A. Michener claims that he has never thought of himself as a good writer, but that he is one of the world's great rewriters. "I find that three or four readings are required to comb out the cliches, line up the pronouns with their antecedents, and insure agreement in number between subject and verbs. . . . My connectives, my clauses, my subsidiary phrases don't come naturally to me and I'm very prone to repetition of words." Most older writers learned grammar in school and can use it that way. I suspect that most young writers haven't learned much grammar in school but can polish their writing anyway.[4]

Some people simply can't learn much grammar. They can't remember overnight what a preposition is, no matter how hard they try. I came up with a helpful idea for one person like that. "Tell me how *I* would say that," I challenged him when he didn't know how to improve a short sentence. "Imagine hearing *me* say it in *my* voice." He turned on his imagination and listened to me in his mind and it worked. His inner ear told him what my wording would probably be. He was amazed that he had that power. I think that is the power that creative writers use all the time.

And I think that is how we decide when we are going to use *who* or *whom* and *it is I* or *it's me*. We know what the rule says, but then we also listen to our voice or someone else's saying it in our minds.

Real writers wear their grammatical skill rather lightly. Robert Frost said, "You can be a little ungrammatical if you come from the right part of the country." Mark Twain claimed to insert "here and there a touch of good grammar for picturesqueness."

A century ago Thomas Wentworth Higgins said in his preface to a collection of Emily Dickinson's poems, "When a thought takes one's breath away, a lesson on grammar seems an impertinence." True. But the grammar must be in pretty good order if the thought takes one's breath away. What more can we ask *for*?

Punctuation

Unfortunately, our punctuation marks are in perpetual disarray. I have five minor punctuation rules that help writers maintain their dignity:

1. Let your exclamation points be extremely rare, unless you quote someone who is yelling, and never use more than one. (Remember that!!!)

2. Don't set off a nickname, slang term, or odd word in quotation

marks unless for some reason you absolutely have to. (Don't be that "cute.")

3. Remember that a scarcity of commas is better than a surplus, because a careless omission is less distracting than ignorant overuse. (Clauses, that are restrictive, should not be set off by commas.)

4. *It's* always means *it is*. (People forget it's meaning.)

5. You can live a full life without ever using a semicolon. (I like to use all my typewriter keys; I don't like to waste anything I've paid for.)

Of all the punctuation instructions I have read, my favorite overview is that of the rebellious Robert C. Pinckert, "Punctuating by Sound."[5] He calls for simplified punctuation. He claims that punctuation marks are there to tell readers how the words are supposed to sound. The best way to punctuate is to rely upon the sound of your sentences when you say them aloud. First you must train your ear. I summarize his teaching here and add a few ideas of my own that he might not agree with.

Pinckert divides punctuation marks into three groups of four each. The first group he calls the *full stop*. It includes periods, question marks, exclamation points, and semicolons. He describes the sounds of each of these. For the period, the voice distinctly drops and stops. For the question mark, the voice rises in pitch wherever the question is located. For exclamation points, the voice is crying out. For the semicolon, the voice drops and stops just as for a period, but the pause is shorter. Pinckert thinks periods are usually preferable to semicolons.

The second group of punctuation marks is called the *half stop* and includes commas, dashes, colons, and parentheses. The trouble with commas is that they are used for too many purposes, which confuses people. The sound of a comma is the sound of the last word warning that the pause will be short and there is more coming. The voice is stressed, rises in pitch or volume or both, dips a little, and comes back up — then the pause. Listening for the comma pause in your prose can greatly simplify knowing where not to put in commas. No pause, no comma.

The sound of a dash is distinctive because it marks a sharp break in thought — a heavily stressed word followed by an unusually long pause. Dashes often come in pairs — as you can see right here — to set off an interrupting thought. The sound of a colon is the same as that of either the comma or the dash, but one rarely needs it. When used in a sentence, the colon usually means this: *specifically* or *as follows*. The sound for parentheses (or brackets or ellipses) is the voice distinctly dropping down to indicate that the parenthetical matter is less important. In fact, when one uses an ellipsis, the parenthetical material was so unimportant that it got left out altogether. The ellipsis is a series of three pinholes in your manuscript where some words fell through . . . and if it comes at the end of a sentence there are the four holes. . . .

Pinckert calls the third group of punctuation marks *spelling* marks, and they include the apostrophe, quotation marks, hyphen, and slash. They do not indicate any sound and are intended only for the eye. Most languages do not have them, Pinckert says, and he thinks they are more trouble than they are worth. The apostrophe is used for contractions, of course, and for most possessives because of the mistaken idea that "John's book" once stood for "John his book." ("Mary's book" supposedly represented "Mary his book.") Writers must learn to use apostrophes correctly for self-protection because leaving them out makes you look careless, but putting them in where they are not needed makes you look like a nincompoop. The signs in front of people's houses that say "The Smith's" advertise to every passerby that the Smiths who live there don't understand apostrophes. Nor does the company from which they bought the sign.

Pinckert claims that quotation marks are the most difficult marks of all, but I think commas are harder. In the end, the best advice for writers who haven't absorbed the rules and who feel uncertain about either apostrophes or quotation marks is to spend a little time looking for them in books and magazines and copying out samples of how they are used there. Patiently copying out examples gives built-in familiarity with how the arrangement works.

Here is an example I prepared to give out to my students:

"I'm not sure how to punctuate dialogue," complained A.

"We are supposed to indent every time someone new speaks," B answered quickly. Her head was splitting.

"Well, that could mean an awful lot of indenting," A replied doubtfully. "I don't see why we should have to use that much paper."

B slammed her book down on her desk with irritation. "Do it however you choose!" she whispered with contempt. The rest of the dialogue was punctuated with profanity.

According to Pinckert, the stylebook of Oxford University Press says that if you take hyphens seriously you will go mad. They were originally used when a word was split at the right margin. Then they also started to link closely connected words such as *prize fighter*, when these were not yet fused into one word like *starlight*. The fact is that *prize fighter* is written in three ways now, including *prize-fighter* and *prizefighter*. The only way to know standard practice on particular words is to check a current dictionary. Some writers are dropping the hyphens in compound numbers and fractions, such as *twenty one and one half*. Pinckert wishes that they would also be dropped from two-word or three-word adjectives that come before modifier-laden nouns. But they weren't dropped in this last sentence.

Last/least is the shorthand slash, which is used to mean *and/or*. Pinckert thinks we should probably write out the words and skip the slash, saying simply "he and she," "he or she," and "he or she or both."

Formal and Informal

Don Addis drew a cartoon of an academic type thumbing a ride to the university. On his suitcase is the motto "English Department or Burst." That says most of what needs to be said about misuse of formal and informal English. It's a matter of sensing what is appropriate in a given situation.

Choosing formal or informal English is like choosing either dress-for-success outfits or sweats. Either type of clothing and language can be fine for its purpose. When formal English is too stuffy, stiff, and even pompous, it is in poor taste; when informal English is too slangy, silly, and sloppy, it is in poor taste. In contrast, when formal English is used well, it is human — but dignified, reserved, and courteous, like a sympathy card. When informal English is used well, it is intelligent — but relaxed, spunky, and talkative, like a birthday card.

It is learning to use formal English that most often enables readers from humble origins to rise in the world. I once had a community college student who had grown up in Harlem speaking Black English but who didn't let it show unless he wanted to. He had spent a couple of years in the Marines and ended up in California writing a mixture of formal English and academic jargon in the classroom. He was sleeping in his car at that point, but he hoped to work his way through the nearby university and become a medical doctor.

One day in class he started defending Black English, assuming that I had some prejudice against what I would call his heart language — the one he grew up with. I told him he was lucky to be bilingual (Black English is a dialect with its own grammar imported from Africa), and that he can talk in my native English but I can't talk in his. It is mine that will get him through medical school in our country, and I could help him with it. His trouble was not excess informality; it was pretentious formality. I covered his essays with red ink and advised him to continue writing that way for professors who like that style. But I told him he was too intelligent to keep writing that way by accident. When he saw that I was on his side, he started lingering after class to talk.

Within a few weeks he had three styles of written English at his command: Black English from Harlem, pompous Formal, and literate Informal. Teaching him to use literate Informal was almost as easy as teaching a child to eat ice cream, because he had a good ear. All he needed was for someone to point out what works well and that the choice was his.

Excellent informal English can be more demanding than excellent formal English because it has far more possibilities for good and bad. Nietzsche said, "It takes less time to learn to write nobly than to learn to write lightly and straightforwardly." Informal English has a larger and livelier vocabulary, more audacity, more fireworks, more poetry, more surprises, and more pizazz. In contrast, formal English is soothing and dignified. It spells words out instead of using contractions. It does not compete with its subject matter. It shows that the writer is educated and does not let him make a fool of himself by taking risks.

Slang and Cliches

Using slang in literature means taking big risks.

Carl Sandburg said, "Slang is the language that takes off its coat, spits on its hands, and goes to work."

Robert C. Pinckert responds, "The truth is most slang takes off its coat, spits on it hands, and lies down and falls asleep."

Most slang doesn't last long. It looks foolish when it gets old, when it is slightly misused, and when it is used by the wrong people in a futile attempt to sound hip. Except in quoted dialogue or monologue, it must never be used in formal writing and is usually a poor choice in informal writing. However, once it has worked its way into standard informal English, then it can be a good condiment.

I used the word *poppycock* in the title of the appendix to this book. It is an expression of annoyance, often used to ridicule some pretentious nonsense. It sounds rather prim and conservative. In fact, however, this word is good old Dutch slang referring to semiliquid dung. Time can make any word socially acceptable.

Slang dictionaries like the one by Eric Partridge are entertaining, but Raymond Chandler thought they were not dependable because he spotted many slight inaccuracies in them. He claimed that much of the most picturesque slang of crooks and cops was invented by writers and then picked up by the crooks and cops. Genuine underworld slang is more simple and direct.

Chandler gave an example of how one of his own slang inventions got picked up by another author accidentally. Chandler had invented the term *the big sleep*, meaning *death*, and he used it for a book title. Eugene

O'Neill apparently thought it was standard underworld slang for death and used it that way throughout his play *The Iceman Cometh*. It's not easy for writers to distinguish between a genuine crook term and an invented one, Chandler concluded.

It's not always easy to distinguish between lovable old figures of speech and tiresome cliches, either, I think; and much depends upon how skillfully they are used. Orwell's advice about avoiding any figures of speech that you have seen often in print is excellent, of course. But in informal writing a knowledgeable author might upon rare occasion want a cliche. Rose red, home and hearth, bright as a penny, bottom line, lady luck. . . .

The trick with cliches is first of all to discover them and enjoy them as you become familiar with our language. Then you learn not to use them because they have been used too much already. Then you learn to use them in informal writing when you really want to do so and think you won't look foolish. (They can be useful in poetry and are wonderful in wordplay.)

In his essay "How to Write Good," Michael O'Donoghue makes fun of cliches by revealing the ten magic phrases of journalism:

1. violence flared
2. limped into port
3. according to informed sources
4. wholesale destruction
5. no immediate comment
6. student unrest
7. riot-torn
8. flatly denied
9. gutted by fire
10. roving bands of Negro youths.[6]

Of course many readers enjoy the familiar cliches that make them feel at home in the world. Writers of special genres such as romance novels serve up all the cliches that their readers relish. That's what they're paid to do. These writers may look foolish to literary critics, but they can *laugh all the way to the bank*, the favorite cliche of all successful writers.

A special category of cliche is the fad word, which may be new or may be an old word that is suddenly in the spotlight and overused. Fad words are usually vague as well as vogue, and they are highly contagious. It takes effort not to use them. Pinckert objects to the faddish verbs that are constantly made out of nouns in our day, such as *update, implement, data, customize, winterize, destabilize, personalize, polarize, impact, parent, eyeball, dialogue,* and *author.* (Let's not dialogue about impacting people who want to author a book. Let's talk about helping people who want to write a book.)

Melvin Maddocks wrote an essay once about the Cliche-of-the-Month club, where Commitment, Relevance, and Meaningful Relationship are commemorated with bronze plaques on the wall. For each of those there had been two or three Viable Alternatives. In Maddocks' essay author Frank Lee Trendee, always on the Cutting Edge, revealed that the most important new cliche was Restructuring. But that was long ago. *Time flies* for new cliches. For old cliches, *some things never change.*

So there are the dear old *tried-and-true* cliches, and the brash new *with-it* cliches — and neither is any good in formal English.

Openers and Closings

In any prose, the first trick is to get the reader reading. Michael O'Donoghue offers a lesson on "grabbers" designed to arouse the reader's curiosity. "Sylvia lay sick among the silverware. . . ." is one of the suggestions he offers to beginning writers. He makes a magnanimous gift of this sentence to anyone who wants to use it, and I pass it on. He is making fun of the gyrations that writers go through sometimes to try to get an interesting first sentence. The basic rule for first sentences, which O'Donoghue breaks, is that they must not turn the reader away.

In a short story it is usually good if the reader can identify the protagonist right away and if the nature of the plot problem comes out soon. Sometimes it is stated boldly in the very first sentence. The names and identities of the main characters should come through clearly and easily early in the story. The tone or mood is usually best set immediately — ominous feelings, playfulness, ordinary seriousness, suspense, yearning, or despair. After the opening scene, there is usually an expansion of the problem at a more relaxed pace.

Writers tend to make double openers for any prose — a short story, novel, article, factual book, even a personal letter. ("How are you? I am fine. Sorry I haven't written sooner.") The first opener is like clearing the throat or pulling the chair forward or shuffling a few papers. The second opener is where the subject begins. The trick is to get rid of the first opener before submitting the manuscript for publication. There is nothing wrong with floundering awhile when starting to write, gunning the engine before you get the car in gear. That's bad for your car, but it's fine for your writing. It doesn't matter how you get started unless you are writing an essay test and can't edit it.

There are two openers that clever children discover in grade school but that adults should usually avoid. One is the leading question. "Have you ever wondered how to breed guinea pigs?" "Why was David a man after God's own heart?" "When should we vote?" "Will anyone read beyond this dull question?" Opening with a question isn't apt to work well.

The opener that I consider hopelessly naive is the one that cites *Webster's Dictionary.* At its worst, it cites Daniel Webster — who is the wrong man; *Webster's Dictionary* is named after Noah Webster. "As Webster tells us, a home is a shelter, a residence, a place to live." It's bad enough to be told flat out what the dictionary says about something obscure, but it's maddening to be told what the dictionary says about something common. Looking up even the simplest words in the dictionary (ultimately, in the mammoth, authoritative *Oxford English Dictionary*) is a prod and tonic for many writers, but it's not the kind of thing that should be mentioned except in special cases. That's like starting out by telling how you sharpened your pencil.

The most common closing is a little homily — the moral of the story, the philosophical touch, the happily-ever-after ending, the grand observation, the soulful amen. Even the stirring challenge or the authorial benediction. That's nice work if it fits and makes sense. The trouble is that the amateur writer often tries too hard and produces what can be called technically the overinclusive conclusion. This amounts to an exaggeration or meaningless generalization or inappropriate challenge. One of my students ended a six-page literature examination with these words: "Man's choice between heaven and hell is before him every day, which choice will *you* make?" The altar-call conclusion.

Sermonese

The writer of the literature examination quoted above included this sentence on his first page: "The choice of one or the other, no compromise, no deviation, yea, one choice is given to the reader of this book." I just wanted him to answer some test questions in plain English. *Yea* is neither formal nor informal English; it is archaic rhetoric. I suppose that this young man had heard it in sermons and thought it was literary. It's a kind of sermonic purple prose.

Another ex-student of mine recently asked me for advice about the doctrinal book he was writing for young adults. I found this passage in the middle of his first chapter: "Are you tired of your spiritual bankruptcy? Be glad! Jesus has earned God's total acceptance." I find that well-churched college students often tend to carry over common pulpit patterns into their prose. People don't say "Be glad!" in normal English speech and writing now.

Readers are not captive audiences like congregations. Hardly anyone walks out during a sermon, although many drift or doze; but readers often walk out on authors. No one walks out faster than the acquisitions editor you hoped to impress. My friend's manuscript was well organized and competently written, but the material was like an extended sermon setting forth traditional doctrine. Unfortunately for writers, few people are willing to read book-length sermonic material unless it is from a celebrity or is somehow titillating — making alarming forecasts or attacking well-known people. It's amazing how well those books sell.

I told my friend that his manuscript looked as if it would get an A in the classroom, but I didn't think he could get it published because he hadn't aimed at any real reader. If he had taped up the picture of one of his typical readers near his typewriter, I think it would have helped. As a talented stage performer and public speaker, this author knows how to coax and court and entertain his audience as he goes along. That knowledge is in his bones, and I suspect he was born with it. But he hadn't carried that intuitive understanding over into the role of author. As soon as I told him this, he saw what I meant.

Actually, this young author specializes professionally in two of the talents an author needs most — the skill of entertaining and the art of stage illusion. For writers, illusion means doing tricks with words honestly.

The Illusion of Dialogue

The one kind of writing that employs the art of illusion most of all is dialogue. The writer has to concoct conversations that will seem real on the page. Real conversations that are long don't seem real on the page because writing them down verbatim leaves out the voice color and includes so much banality and confusion. Writers have to trim and straighten out what speakers say, highlighting the meaning without the aid of voice and gestures. Yet they have to make the dialogue seem to be what people would really say. This is a bit like a hairdresser working hours to get a model's hair to look as if it hasn't been touched by a hairdresser.

Further, writers have to be highly selective. Beginning writers tend to include routine exchanges that might be included on television programs when the audience is busy watching how the characters look and move. On paper they are deadly.

"Hello. How are you today? Are you new here?" she asked.

"Hi. I'm Randy. I've never been here before. It's hot, isn't it?"

"Yes, sort of hot, I guess. Are you thirsty?" she asked.

"I don't know. What do they have to drink here?" Randy answered.

It is pointless to write out dull conversation that doesn't move the story along or reveal the characters. Professional writers would summarize the encounter and then move on into the story. Or they might slip some important hints into the opening words. Perhaps the point here would be the expression in the girl's eyes or the way she tapped her tennis racket impatiently on the counter. All gestures, all words have to carry freight of some kind because there is no background music to set the tone.

Good writing has no idle dialogue or meaningless description. Every bit should help the reader to tune in to something significant about the characters or the situation. There can be idle characters who make boring conversation and live meaningless lives, but the writer sets even those forth skillfully. The difference between nature and art is selection.

Elmore Leonard says, "I try to leave out the parts that people skip."

Another basic trick of dialogue writing is writing the "he said" tags so the reader barely notices them. Only amateur writers think they have to keep varying their verbs with monstrosities like *interjected, opined, ejaculated, queried, simpered, glowered, exclaimed, questioned, interrogated, complained,* and *observed*. There are many synomyms for *said*, but most of them are intrusive, and the words in the dialogue should do the work. The fewer tags the better, and the simpler the better. Just keep it clear who is speaking.

"Hello. How are you today? Are you new here?" Her voice startled him.

"Hi, I'm Randy. I've never been here before." He put his sack down on the pavement and looked at her. "It's hot today, isn't it?"

"Yes, sort of hot, I guess." She took off her dark glasses and squinted up at him. "Are you thirsty?"

"I don't know," he said. "What do they have to drink here?" He thought his voice sounded raspy with thirst.

This version of the dull dialogue has added some flesh to it and used it to create a bit of tension that could possibly point toward an interesting plot. That is how even dull dialogue can carry some freight and does not waste time if the writer is doing something with it.

These basic principles of dialogue writing are useful in all kinds of articles and anecdotes as well as in fiction and biography, whenever someone is talking. And in any of these, writers who are not Mark Twain or Joel Chandler Harris are wise to avoid the tar baby of trying to spell out accents or regionalism or dialect. It is usually insulting to someone to do that, and few writers know enough to do it well. A hint of a special speech pattern or nonstandard English like "he don't" — less than one small sample per page — is enough to give the idea. Like garlic, a little goes a long way. Which leads us to the topic of purple prose.

Purple Prose

As C. S. Lewis said once, it is easier to prune the jungles of student enthusiasm than to irrigate the desert in students who don't care. Purple prose is a jungle of writer enthusiasm. I think that purple prose is fun for many people and excellent practice for young writers who enjoy it.

I trust that my fine student who wrote the following page won't mind my sharing it with a wider audience. When I saw her first piece of fiction I was surprised — by the seething volcanic vocabulary of her passionate purple prose. She was overwriting.

> In fetters of clinging ivy, a castle kept vigil over the pounding sea as it had done for centuries, sadly doomed to fallen glory by the cruel, inclement moors on which it stood. Below the cliff, on indigo swells, the mist was rolling in; shrouding the peninsula like a ghostly hand maniacally spread across the face of the wintry scene. Night would dust the lonely seascape soon, thought the woman. She was hidden behind a window casement, watching a weak sunset, admiring the snowdrifts that crested eastward. "Land pillows," her Jeoffrey had called them once, fields seamed by cobbled fences that rambled on forever. Against a dappled world the whiteness had taken on a pearly lustre which in the last light was now glistening, almost like veins of gold. The moat beneath the scant window twisted a foul train around the old stone wall. It was clogged with fat protruding rocks, fine reeds and thick slime. Andrea Barnslow was puzzling how cold that dark water might be as she faced the embers of the sunlight. I'll meet my eternity a spinster, she mused. What an ugly sounding word — spinster! But there would never be another Jeoffrey.

This writer has started off with abandon, which is a good way to start. I asked her to rewrite her setting with more control, and she did a good job on it. But I saved her first version anyway.

Although some readers and writers take purple prose seriously, other people laugh at its excesses and the way it seems to entrance those who like it. It shows a kind of youthful infatuation with technicolor words, dramatic settings, and lush, overgrown figures of speech. Sentences are often overloaded in purple prose, like a woman wearing too much costume jewelry. In the first two sentences of the passage above, all these words of enchantment cluster close: *fetters, doomed, cruel, fallen, glory, inclement, moors, cliff, indigo, mist, shrouding, ghostly, maniacally.* This is laying it on rather thick. This is the opposite of minimalist writing, which tends to be bare, like a boy's letter home. Minimalist fiction is fashionable today, like the European cuisine that is high style in the United States — skillfully prepared, impeccably served, and decidedly skimpy in content. In contrast, purple prose is like a thickly frosted wedding cake.

Purple prose is just one category in the annual Bulwer-Lytton bad-sentence contest. This wacko contest was started in 1982 by a California English professor named Scott Rice.[7] He was inspired by Bulwer-Lytton's brief but trite opening sentence made famous by Snoopy in the Peanuts comic strip: "It was a dark and stormy night." Competitors are supposed to write long, sublimely saccharine sentences with labored language, maudlin metaphors, and repetitive redundancies. All entrants receive a card that says, "We've received your execrable prose and it's receiving the treatment it deserves."

Word of the bad-writing contest spread fast, and in the first eight years writers have entered from eighty countries around the world. One ambitious writer has submitted 1,500 entries so far without winning. In 1988 alone, 11,000 entries came in.

Viking-Penguin has published three collections of the worst contest entries so far: *It Was a Dark and Stormy Night, Son of It Was a Dark and Stormy Night,* and *Bride of It Was a Dark and Stormy Night.*

Judges are a panel of California English professors, and in 1988 they awarded an Apple II computer to the first-place winner of the entire contest, an Indiana journalism student. Her entry made fun of writers who try too hard and let an extended metaphor run amok. All the entries are by writers laughing with each other about how writing can run amok.

Winner of the 1988 purple prose category, which got no prize, was "The silent snow fell relentlessly, unceasingly, mercilessly from the sordid sullied surreality of the sky as if some enormous, ethereal diner were shaking grated parmesan on the great, soggy meatball that was Earth."

There is a kind of insincerity in bad writing, Scott Rice explains, an attempt to say more than you mean. Writers who enter this contest turn that fact on its head by meaning to say something about saying more than they mean. It is creative play. Intentionally writing ridiculous sentences and trying to look foolish is a good change of pace. It's a left-handed approach to writing better.

SUGGESTED ACTIVITIES

1. Start looking and listening for cliches, and make a list of the cliches that you love to hate. List any cliches you can find on the front page of the newspaper, the sports page, and the society page. List any cliches you can find in a magazine article, a textbook chapter, and a chapter

in a romantic novel or an adventure novel. What tentative conclusions can you draw about where cliches are common and where they are rare?

2. Two students in the cafeteria have a brief encounter with a member of the opposite sex they have been watching and discussing. Write this short-short story as a slice of life, as a teen romance, as an inspirational piece, or as light social satire. Sprinkle some description of the setting through the dialogue so that your reader gets concrete images of the setting, mood, and characters.

3. Select a current news story or a poem with strong emotion in it. ("Do Not Go Gentle into that Good Night" by Dylan Thomas and "Mending Wall" by Robert Frost would work well.) Convert the main idea into a dialogue between two people. Try writing this dialogue three different ways, and see which of the three you like best. Could this dialogue be used for the beginning of a short story?

4. Write a one-page description of your last birthday in rather highflown sermonese with a strong inspirational slant. Next, rewrite the account in a modestly dignified and formal way, as if it were an essay required of you in a scholarship competition. Finally, rewrite the account in an informal style that appeals to ordinary readers like yourself and your friends and relatives. Note that any of the three styles could be inspirational and any of them could be either happy or sad, but only the third style could be humorous. (When a supposedly formal paper is comical, it is probably in reality an informal burlesque of the formal style. That is like a boy acting silly in his dad's tuxedo.)

5. Try writing four scenes in purple prose. First, describe briefly the place where you live, a store where you shop, and your usual means of transportation. Next, write a death scene in purple prose — then rewrite it starkly, with simplicity and understatement. Which death scene seems more powerful at this point?

NOTES

[1] Water Kay Smart, *English Review Grammar* (New York: Appleton-Century-Crofts, 1952).

[2] The following books about current trends in English do not agree with each other, but they are all interesting: Theodore M. Bernstein, *Watch Your Language;* Edwin Newman, *Strictly Speaking* and *A Civil Tongue;* Arn and Charlene Tibbetts, *What's Happening to American English?;* John Simon, *Paradigms Lost;* and Jim Quinn, *American Tongue and Cheek.*

[3] Dorothy Gardiner and Kathrine Sorley Walker, *Raymond Chandler Speaking,* (New York: Houghton Mifflin, 1962), 77.

[4] *The Elements of Grammar* by Margaret Shertzer (New York: Macmillan, 1986) is a handy guide that gives a very light overview of grammar, punctuation, and usage. I have long valued the alphabetized contents of *Reference Handbook of Grammar and Usage*, first published in 1972 by Scott Foresman. I also recommend *Harbrace College Handbook* by John C. Hodges and Mary E. Whitten, published by Harcourt Brace Jovanovich.

[5] Robert C. Pinckert, *The Truth about English* (Englewood Cliffs, N.J.: Prentice-Hall, Inc., 1981), 56–82.

[6] Michael O'Donoghue, "How to Write Good" in *Laughing Matters: A Celebration of American Humor*, edited by Gene Shalit (Garden City, N.Y.: Doubleday, 1987), 292–300.

[7] Catherine Foster, "Downwrite Awful Winners," *Christian Science Monitor* (May 10, 1988), 1, 6.

7. What is done. Action that demonstrates the essence of the main character.

An author does well to have good ideas about how the main character might respond in these following situations: being lost alone in the mountains with night coming on; finding an injured dog on the doorstep; discovering that a close friend is inexplicably depressed; desiring to meet an attractive stranger on the street; accidentally breaking a precious object; suddenly realizing that old age has arrived; dying; realizing that a beloved belief was wrong; encountering God.

All kinds of character traits might be central to a story, such as physical courage, enduring loyalty, callousness, shrewdness in judging people, lack of purpose, victimization, nurturing, eagerness to grow, destructiveness, or generosity. Key traits are always things the author cares about. I have noticed that in one way or another *valor* is a key element in many outstanding novels. And I have noticed that something about human valor often brings tears to the eyes or quickens the pulse.

Some stories can make eyes wet with tears of laughter, tenderness, pity, grief, or appreciation. Research shows that tears usually come more easily to the eyes of women than to the eyes of men, and in either group tearfulness varies greatly. But most people come across stories that at least give them a catch in the throat or make them feel that they would cry if they had any tears stored up. For example, it seems that few people have got through Sheldon Vanauken's autobiographical *A Severe Mercy* without weeping.

One of my students wrote a very short story about a homebound spaceship with two people on it; the ship was low on fuel. I was reading the story aloud to the class. Most of the story was dialogue between the returning pilot and his brother-in-law manning the space station back on earth. The pilot's copilot was his sister, and he expressed to her husband how tender and protective he had always felt toward her. Suddenly the story ended, and listeners realized that the pilot had bailed out to lighten the ship to make sure his sister got back to earth. There was a moment of silence as the ending sank in. Then a bright, cheerful girl in the second row burst into a brief torrent of sobbing. I turned to the blinking, red-faced author and said, "Congratulations. Whatever future success you have as a writer will just be echoes or amplifications of the success that you have had tonight. Your writing reached deep into someone's heart."

I suggest that we use "wet" for writing that arouses or changes our body chemistry. I imagine that a writer writing about restaurants or recipes would be gratified to learn that a reader's mouth watered over his words and that stomachs started to growl. Horror stories can make our hands moist and make our hearts pound and make us shiver. Soothing writers purposely do just the opposite, relaxing our muscles and calming our pulse with gentle words and pictures. And I suspect that writers of torrid romance would like to make readers blush or breathe heavily. All of these physical changes — flutters, floods, flushes — are quite real and could be monitored by scientists.

Writing that influences body chemistry is not necessarily better than writing that doesn't. But we know that when readers get wet eyes they are not bored. Perhaps "dry wit" is the style of humor which amuses us to chuckles without arousing us to such laughter that our eyes get wet, no matter how clever it is. "Dry" writing, then, can be that which, no matter how interesting, does not affect our central nervous system so that our bodies are changed by it.

Anne Tyler's novel *The Accidental Tourist* gave me the most unusual wet reading experience I have ever had. I had received the book as a gift from one of my students, and I sat alone in my living room reading it one evening, occasionally laughing a bit out loud. I was in the restaurant scene where the bereaved father, a bewildered and naively comic man, had just been rebuffed by his estranged wife. Suddenly I realized I was in my own living room with tears streaming down my cheeks. I found that I was weeping with laughter and sobbing with compassion at the same time, with the same tears — overcome by a mixture of hilarity and grief. That is a strange and powerful sensation. (I have since heard of a little girl who found herself laughing and crying at the same time and asked her parents if that made her face a rainbow.)

Most of us would feel awed if our writing ever caused a reader to shed even one tear for one of our characters. James Hilton, creator of the beloved Mr. Chipps in *Goodbye, Mr. Chipps*, has sometimes been asked how a writer creates a lovable character. He warns writers not to set out to create a particularly lovable character. One might create a dummy with attributes attached to him like labels, or one might produce a mess of mawkishness that nobody will enjoy. The only good trick that Hilton can recommend to writers is to have something to say or some story to tell, and to do that as simply and effectively as possible. A writer should create his characters and let them be lovable if they will.[8]

Sir Walter Scott introduced characters in his novels by starting with the hair and describing the features and clothes all the way down to the feet, but all this visual description isn't often necessary. (Some authors like to figure out every detail about their characters' looks, lives, and possessions, but they don't tell much of that background information to their readers.) Better writers, such as Dostoevsky or Dickens, give you the feeling that you would know the character even with your eyes shut. Hilton says a good writer blows you a petal of meaning instead of felling a whole forest for you. As Logan Pearsall Smith put it, "What I like in a good author is not what he says, but what he whispers."

Unlike James Hilton, humorist Peg Bracken readily passes along half-serious advice for creating attractive and lovable characters in light, reader-flattering fiction. I have modified her advice here:

1. Heroes and heroines must be extremely fine and attractive people, but not too perfect; otherwise they will seem artificial or will make readers feel inferior. The main character has to win the reader's loyalty.

2. The writer must somehow criticize heroes and heroines for "flaws" that are endearing traits the reader wouldn't mind having, such as unruly hair that clusters in shiny curls or extra-long legs or a throaty voice. The character might be a bit too impish or gruff. This makes the reader feel generous and wise for valuing the character anyway. We have all heard of "damning with faint praise." I call this trick "praising with faint damns."

3. Lovable characters may have had ugly-duckling childhoods in which they were too shy or too tomboyish or too gangly or otherwise imperfect. Past imperfection compensates for their being glamorous adults and enables readers to identify with them.

4. The lovable hero or heroine must be free of any flaws that readers won't tolerate in fiction, such as missing teeth, bad feet, acne, or a double chin. The list of intolerable flaws varies somewhat from one type of publisher to another.[9]

Most writers have a keen sense of what is and isn't acceptable in traditional fiction. For example, Hemingway characters may consume hundreds of specific alcoholic beverages in a given novel, eat many meals, sleep, travel, mate, hunt, fight, bleed, and die — yet never once use a toilet.

Experimental fiction and various kinds of nonfiction are another matter, but even there writers and editors conform to certain conventions that are rarely questioned. Some of these conventions are matters of content, and others are matters of word choice.

Word Choice and Choice Words

Frederick Buechner said in an interview once, "I choose my words with crazy care."

I wonder if the main reason so many fine writers fall into alcoholism is that tinkering with sentences and struggling with word choices all the time pushes them over the edge.

For example, there is just no good, strong verb in English that means giving off an unpleasant odor, because *stinks* spoils almost any sentence of serious writing. It is a word with perfectly good credentials (used in the King James Bible), but nowadays people are offended or embarrassed by it. Likewise, we lack a good all-purpose word for older children because *kids* usually seems too informal. We also lack an all-purpose noun that means "similar people." *Peers* sounds sociological, *fellows* sounds antique, and *colleagues* sounds professional. And we also lack an adjective that means that an event provided fun for participants. *Fun-filled* often seems forced, and *fun* as an adjective still sounds rather adolescent.

> "The kids at the fun camp enjoy their peers but are unhappy that the water stinks." "The pre-teen children at the merry camp enjoy their fellow campers but are unhappy that the water smells bad." "The boys and girls at the fun-filled camp are happy with the other children their age, but they are unhappy that the water has a bad odor."

It is useless to go on trying in this case. The sentence was doomed to mediocrity from the beginning. The only thing to do is to break it apart and start from scratch some other way.

It used to be said that piano tuners often became mentally peculiar because of always straining to achieve the perfect pitch for every note; but now they have an electronic device that makes it easier for them. Perhaps seeking perfect words is a kind of stress that is too hard on the nerves. Mark Twain said, "The difference between the right word and the almost right word is the difference between the lightning and the lightning bug."

I noticed the following modest but perfect phrase in an ordinary newspaper article about the desert recently: "creatures that slither and sting." That's Twain's lightning. Sometimes it strikes us when we aren't expecting it.

I think that playing with the words we already know is even more important than expanding our vocabularies. The more we love and handle words, the more apt we are to have the right ones come to us when we need them. I sometimes jot down colorful words or experimental combinations of words, as a kind of word doodling:

> arms akimbo, legs askew
> don't pander to pantheistic panhandlers
> splendiferous and humungous hummingbirds
> this is a momentous memento
> some swashbuckling skulduggery
> an insulting onslought of consultants
> never dilly-dally or shilly-shally in response to flimflam
> institutionalization (8 syllables) vs. being locked up (4 syllables)

Lots of verbal doodling keeps us limber. It doesn't matter whether the doodling is kept or thrown away. It is good to make lists of favorite words, grumpy words, shining words, tender words, thumping words, slippery words. Lists of colorful place-names and people's names. (Read the telephone book for all kinds of surnames.) Lists of words that hiss or growl or mumble.

One of my students noticed that many words that begin with *sn-* are unpleasant: *snitch, snatch, snare, snicker, sniff, snub, snarl, snappish, snout, snuffy, snipe, snippy, sneezewort, sniffle, snag, sneer, snoop, snakey, snort, snub-nosed, snaggle-toothed, snooty, snore, sneak, snail, snivel, snot,* and *snafu.*

I read a teeny-tiny article once titled "Harum-scarum, Topsy-turvy Hurly-burly Words." It listed about sixteen double near-rhyme words such as *mishmash, topsy-turvy, wishy-washy,* and *knickknacks.* I added *zigzag, bric-a-brac, seesaw, steam clean, ticktock, pitter-patter, wigwag, tip-top, rickrack, lickety-split, riffraff, pit-a-pat, shipshape, flip-flop, dingdong,* and *ticky-tacky.* Plus *dilly-dally, shilly-shally,* and *flimflam.*

Some of the double words in the article really rhymed: *hoity-toity, hocus-pocus, higgledy-piggledy, hurly-burly, fuddy-duddy, hurdy-gurdy, pell-mell,* and *hodgepodge.* So I started collecting all the other rhyming double words I came across or recalled. This is what I came up with:

Seabee, jelly-belly, claptrap, ragtag, palsy-walsy, willy-nilly, honey-bunny, boo-hoo, funny-bunny, bowwow, teeny-weeny, teensy-weensy, eensy-weensy, itty-bitty, itsy-bitsy, helter-skelter, yakity-yak, hotshot, fat cat, fan-tan, pow-wow, teepee, namby-pamby, zoot suit, fancypants, super-duper, slam-bam, whang-bang, rooty-toot-toot, slick chick, lovey-dovey, mellow yellow, bluesy-woozy, wingding, kootchykoo, bigwig, silly-billy, falderal, heebie-jeebies, shady lady, muckluck, cool yule, crumb-bum, fender bender, poopy-poop, double trouble, to-do, kowtow, hokeypokey, mumbo jumbo, abracadabra, hustle-bustle, chugalug, oopsy-doopsy, brain drain, chockablock, walkie-talkie, voodoo, fuzzy-wuzzy, eighties ladies, razzle-dazzle, flower power, hi-fi, sci-fi, okey dokey, phony baloney, and *nitty-gritty.*

Oshkosh is in Wisconsin, and London has both Fleet Stree and Pall Mall. There is a grocery store chain named Piggly Wiggly that probably sells Ritz Bits and Reese's Pieces. We hear the names Rintintin, Care Bears, Plain Jane, Tricky Dicky, Action Jackson, Pickwick, and Pee-wee. But no rhymed double name is more beloved than good old Humpty Dumpty.

Word lists can be contagious. Most people are familiar with the terms *a herd of cows, a flock of doves, a school of fish, a covey of quail,* and *a pride of lions.* James Lipton got busy and made up a list of new group names, then published them in a book he titled *An Exaltation of Larks.* Robert

McAfee Brown noticed that Lipton skipped the subject of religion, and he came up with some examples like a "a blaze of martyrs," "an assurance of Calvinists," and "a joy of sects." I read Brown's examples in a magazine.

I was telling my husband about Brown's article, and the only example I could recall was my favorite, "a cloister of nuns." When I checked the article an hour later, I discovered to my delight that this was not Brown's invention, but my own. After that "a batch of monks" was inevitable. My husband answered with "a collection of offering plates."

"A raft of bulrushes," I retorted slowly. "A babble of tongues. A clutch of rosaries, and a plenary of inerrantists!" He left the room.

"A gong of church bells, and a rise of spires," I added for no particular reason. "Also, a sprinkle of fonts and a whole dunk of baptistries. Not to mention an approach of altars." So much for church furnishings.

"A klutz of cults," I found myself thinking. "A wane of Moonies. A union of ecumenicists. A call of evangelists. A cull of expositors." That was enough. I had jotted them all down.

"A prodigal of parables," I scribbled on. "A beg of petitions. A pride of sins. A ward of excellences." It was getting late.

"A fleet of kind thoughts," I mused. "A pave of good intentions. A lent of disciplines." I was trying to stop. "A switch of conversions."

"If witches come in covens," I reasoned, "why can't saints come in havens? A service of deacons. A repast of pastors. A chapter of Bible teachers. An enthusiasm of youth leaders. A go-forth of missionaries. A wave of choirleaders."

The wave of choirleaders swept me on. "An order of liturgists. A soar of anthems. A strum of harpists. A diapason of organists. A render of soloists. An accord of choirs. An urgency of exhortations. An admit of confessions . . . Help! I can't stop!"

It was as if I had put on magic shoes that made it hard to stop dancing. Friedrich Nietzsche spoke of "Dancing with the feet, with ideas, with words, and . . . with the pen." Some of us find after many years of writing that our brains seem to be dancing with words much of the time, even when we are asleep.

Caught in the Web of Words

James Murray's granddaughter knew him as "Grandfather Dictionary." This gentle, self-educated man was from a humble origin, but he eventually became the editor of the fabulous *Oxford English Dictionary*. The original project took fifty years of extremely intense work — with a scholarly crew and far-flung volunteer helpers, but without computers. Murray wrote over half the gigantic dictionary himself, by hand. Sometimes his work on the history and meanings of only one word was more than the work usually required to write an entire scholarly book or two.

After seventeen years of backbreaking work, Murray was still in the letter *C*, at words beginning with *cu-*, and afraid that his publisher was going to cancel the project. One of his friends urged him come to visit for a short Easter vacation: "I could find enough talk to *cumber* you. You could come by a *curvilinear* railway. Bring a *cudgel* to walk with. . . . We have *cutlets* in the *cupboard* & *currants* & *curry* & *custards* & (naturally) *cups* . . . say you'll *CUM!*" But Murray didn't dare to spare the time. He felt he had to finish *C* by the end of 1893, and he did.[10]

His friend sent him the following congratulatory poem then:

> Wherever the English speech has spread
>   And the Union Jack flies free,
> The news will be gratefully, proudly read
>   That you've conquered your ABC!
> But I fear it will come
>   As a shock to some
> That the sad result will be —
> That you're taking to *dabble* and *dawdle* and *doze*
> To *dullness* and *dumps* and (worse than those)
> To *danger* and *drink*
> And — shocking to think —
> To words that begin with d — — !

In our time, Robert Burchfield has been serving as chief editor of new supplements to the *Oxford English Dictionary*, which is still a monument of devotion, pride, and passion. When a geologist objected to the inclusion of an obsolete geological term, Burchfield answered, "I'm going to put it in because it's in W. H. Auden's poetry, and I don't care two figs for your geology."[11]

Chilean poet Pablo Neruda also had a passion for words:

> You can say anything you want, yes sir, but it is the words that sing; they soar and descend. I bow to them, I love them, I cling to them, I run them down, I bite into them, I melt them down. I love words so much: the unexpected ones; the ones I wait for greedily are stalked until, suddenly, they drop. Vowels I love: they glitter like colored stones, they leap like silver fish. They are foam, thread, metal, dew. I run after certain words. They are so beautiful I want to fit them all into my poem. I catch them in mid-flight as they buzz past. I trap them, clean them, peel them. I set myself in front of a dish: they have

a crystalline texture to me: vibrant, ivory, vegetable, oily, like fruit, like algae, like agate, like olive. And then I stir them. I shake them, I drink them, I gulp them down, I garnish them, I let them go. I leave them in my poem like stalactites, like slivers of polished wood, like coal, pickings from a shipwreck, gifts from the waves. Everything exists in the word.[12]

As if in answer to Neruda, English playwright Christopher Fry once made fun of his own love of words and slowness as a writer:

> Sometimes when I am trying to work I think of the picture of myself which emerges from the press-cuttings, and it seems, in a way, very splendid. I see a man reeling intoxicated with words; they flow in a golden — or perhaps pinchbeck — stream from his mouth: they start out at his ears; they burst like rockets and jumping crackers and catherine wheels round his head; they spring in wanton sport at his feet and trip him; but trip him or not, he loves them; let them all come, go where they may; let them strangle sense, flood the stage, break the dams of form; facility shall have its day. His typewriter continues to chatter long after it has been put back in its case. Words will grow out of him, like fingernails, for some time after his death.
>
> Then, having looked at this picture and marvelled, I turn to my typewriter. Like an ancient red Indian chief, I sit for some hours in silence. At last I am ready to speak, and say "How," or perhaps some slightly longer word. My two fingers withdraw from the typewriter and the night wears dumbly on toward the dawn.[13]

Fry was not entirely joking; he was capable of working on one play off and on for twenty years. His plays are written in verse and are what he calls "comedies of redemption" — the joyous experience that comes not from cheerful externals but from internal reconciliation between characters, between past and future, between man and his fate. "I have come to the verge of saying that comedy is greater than tragedy. On the verge I stand and go no further."

S. J. Perelman was also noted for his unusual love of all kinds of words and his slow writing. He wrote some plays, but his resemblance to Christopher Fry stops there. He was an American satirist who published about twenty collections of humorous essays, many of them printed first in *The New Yorker*. His books had titles like *Acres and Pains; The Road to Miltown; Chicken Inspector No. 23;* and *Baby, It's Cold Inside.* He was an entertaining but cynical man, somewhat of a curmudgeon. He enjoyed words with personality, like *flummox, kerfuffle, fiascos,* and *chopfallen.*

Groucho Marx once told Perelman, "From the moment I picked your book up until I laid it down I was convulsed with laughter. Someday I intend reading it."

E. B. White said that Perelman had the greatest and most formidable vocabulary he had ever encountered. It was like an elaborate Erector set, each word attached to others, making a huge structure in Perelman's mind.

Perelman hated Hollywood and hated working with the Marx Brothers, but he was the writer of their funniest films, *Monkey Business* and *Horse Feathers*. Later he won an Oscar for writing *Around the World in 80 Days*. He went around the world at least six times, mainly in later life, collecting odd words and odd experiences and trying to shake depression.

Perelman loved words, but he said he hated to write. "On the other hand, I'm a great believer in money." He had expensive tastes. When he had plenty of money, he didn't write. When he needed money, he wrote in a bare little room. He was not apt to finish one page in a day, and it usually took him over two-and-one-half weeks to finish about ten double-spaced pages. He might rework the same sentence dozens of different ways. He wrote as many as thirty-seven drafts of a single article.

Thomas Merton wondered why it is that some people with no belief in God write so carefully and some of those who believe in God write carelessly:

> If we do not try to be perfect in what we write, perhaps it is because we are not writing for God after all. In any case it is depressing that those who serve God and love Him sometimes write so badly, when those who do not believe in Him take pains to write so well. I am not talking about grammar and syntax, but about having something to say and saying it in sentences that are not half dead.

Having something to say is a very personal matter. But saying it in sentences that are not half dead depends largely upon trying to do what this chapter has been talking about:

1. Activate the five senses.
2. Use details in order to show, not tell.
3. Feel along with people (both your characters and your readers).
4. Contemplate the power of "wet" prose.
5. Collect, fondle, and juggle words. Treasure words.

True ease in writing comes from art, not chance,
As those move easiest who have learned to dance.
'Tis not enough no harshness gives offense,
The sound must seem an echo to the sense.

Alexander Pope, from *An Essay on Criticism*

SUGGESTED ACTIVITIES

1. Think of your happiest moment. Capture it on paper by giving sensory descriptions (sights, sounds, smells, tastes, physical feelings). See if you can communicate the emotions without referring to any abstract quality like happiness or joy. Now try the same exercise with your saddest moment.

2. Write a paragraph describing each of your favorite holidays, including private family holidays. Emphasize the sights, sounds, and smells of each of these occasions, and try to include words that sound like the seasons (e.g., soft snow settling on the window sills; the bang, burst, crack, pop, and sputter of fireworks; long lazy afternoon picnics where sunlight filters through leafy trees and insects buzz and hover). These holiday descriptions might be enjoyed by your children and grandchildren someday, especially if you write the story of your life or your family history for them.

3. Write the first page of a future short story, setting the scene in one of these places: a forest glade, a crowded beach, a cemetery, a moving train, a palatial home. Is this story realistic, mystery, humorous, satirical, gothic, fantasy, inspirational, science fiction, or another type?

4. Tell a story about two traveling companions without invading the minds of any of the characters and without directly interpreting them to your readers. The point of view is that of an outside observer with no inside information. Make the images as clear as a movie camera would, the sound as flawless and distinct as that on a compact disk. The only interpretative comments or explanations in this story should be those spoken naturally by your characters.

5. Write a story from the point of view of Victoria Vance, who finds herself seated next to a distinguished-looking man her age on a jet bound for London. She is a history professor from Occidental College in California, divorced from a science professor. Her son is twenty-two and her daughter is twenty. In London she will do research for her second book, which is to be about medieval pilgrimages in England. Trace the movements and mannerisms of Victoria and her companion as they rustle papers, eat and drink, possibly sneak looks at each other, and barely speak at all. Give her thoughts, feelings, and reflections.

6. Now write an entirely different story — exactly the same sequence of external events from the point of view of Roger McCarthy, Victoria's seat partner. Roger is a sales and development officer for a New York company that distributes sophisticated electronic equipment, and he is

headed for several days of apparently routine meetings in London. Roger is from an ordinary middle-American background; but his wife Joanna is a busy social activist, and their three children are highly successful. Thirteen-year-old Jenny is a swimmer; eighteen-year-old Alan is senior class president and captain of the basketball team; twenty-two-year-old Audrey is working toward a doctorate in microbiology. Writing students who have tried a similar version of these two stories in the past sometimes came up with highly original plot twists reminiscent of O. Henry.

NOTES

[1] In Gilbert and Sullivan's comic opera *The Mikado*, Pooh-Bah told the king grisly details about an execution he and his friends hadn't really carried out. Then they discovered that their "victim" was the king's own son. His friends said, "a nice mess you've got us into," and he replied, "Merely corroborative detail, intended to give artistic verisimilitude to an otherwise bald and unconvincing narrative."

[2] Barbara Tuchman, "History by the Ounce," (first published in *Harper's Magazine*, July 1965), *Practicing History, Selected Essays* by Barbara W. Tuchman, (New York: Knopf, 1981), 35.

[3] Ibid., 39.

[4] Ibid., 38–39.

[5] Barbara Tuchman, "The Historian as Artist," (originally published in *New York Herald Tribune Book Week* March 6, 1966), *Practicing History*, 45.

[6] Tuchman, "The Historian as Artist," 47.

[7] "Mood disorders affect 80% of well-known writers," *Brain Mind Bulletin*, December 1987 (Volume 13, Number 3), 1.

[8] James Hilton, "Creating a Lovable Character," in *Handbook of Short Story Writing*, edited by Frank A. Dickson and Sandra Smith (Cincinnati: Writer's Digest, 1970), 55–57.

[9] Peg Bracken, "The New Mallarky," in *Handbook of Short Story Writing*, 43–46.

[10] K. M. Elisabeth Murray, *Caught in the Web of Words: James Murray and the Oxford English Dictionary* (New York: Oxford University Press, 1979), 273–274.

[11] Christopher Swann, "Finding Just the Right Words," *The Christian Science Monitor* (July 16, 1987), 23.

[12] As quoted by Philip Yancey in "Christian Publishing: Too Many Books & Too Few Classics?" *Christianity Today* (March 2, 1984), 22.

[13] Christopher Fry, "An Experience of Critics" as quoted by Margaret Ramsay in "Christopher Fry: An Immensely Thoughtful, Careful Writer," *The Christian Science Monitor*, September 22, 1971, "Z page" (an insert section with no regular page numbers).

Chapter 5

English, the Marvelous Mess

*So the LORD scattered them from there over all the earth,
And they stopped building the city. That is why it was
called Babel—because there the LORD confused the
language of the whole world.*

— GENESIS 11:8–9, NIV

Yee ben salt of the erthe.

Writing fairly well in English is like cutting a cantaloupe. But writing superbly in English is more like performing brain surgery. It requires extraordinary talent, preparation, and concentration.

Although most people can write fairly well in English, they are still apt to write terrible English by accident; and yet some get to where they can write almost heavenly English. The quality of English runs to extremes. That's because of what the English language really is and where it came from.

Strange as it seems, most people who spend a large part of their lives creating things out of the English language don't have the vaguest idea about what English is and where it came from. They are mighty surprised when they find out.

Guess your way through the following quiz:

True or False

1. English is one of the world's oldest languages.
2. English has more complicated grammar than primitive tribal languages.
3. English is easier to learn than Russian and Chinese.
4. English spelling follows a set of dependable rules.
5. The English language is named after England.
6. Shakespeare wrote in Old English.
7. English has fewer speakers than Chinese.
8. English is descended from Hebrew, Greek, and Latin.
9. English is a logical, orderly, and reasonable language.
10. Our English vocabulary is ideal for our needs, but smaller than the huge, sprawling vocabulary of Chinese.

Most people miss several of these. The correct answer to all ten statements is *false*. English is one the youngest languages in the world, not one of the oldest. English grammar is far simpler than the grammar of many small primitive tribes. English is harder to learn than Russian and Chinese. English spelling rules are undependable. English was not named after England; it was the other way around. Shakespeare wrote in Early Modern English, not Old English. English has more speakers than Chinese or any other language (about 350 million native speakers and about 350 million more for whom it is not native). English is descended from an old form of German — not Hebrew, Latin, or Greek. English is illogical, disorderly, and unreasonable. And English has the largest vocabulary of any language in the history of the world.

There is nothing boring about English; it is full of surprises for everyone. English is the scruffy new kid on the block who turns out to be a world-class artist and athlete and intellect in spite of his patched jeans.

The ABC's of Our Family

There are about 2,800 languages in the world, and English is the only one that has recently skyrocketed in practical value. There is no other language so valuable all over the world. Aside from a healthy body and a good home, the English language is the most valuable birthday gift that a baby can receive. Babies can learn any first language easily, even

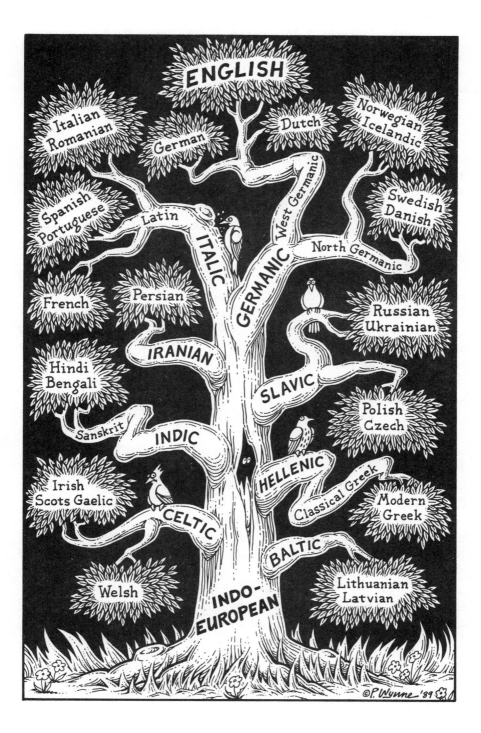

English. A baby who takes the shortcut and learns English at home is starting out in life with the equivalent of a $500,000 bank account. By learning English in his crib, he is saving years of excruciatingly hard work in school, because if he is to be a success in life he will probably have to know English. This is a funny twist in world history, because English itself is just the youngest cousin in the largest language family in the world.

The 2,800 languages of the world fall into twenty-three different families that don't seem to be related to each other. Two of those families have most of the speakers, and the other twenty-one are relatively small. The second-largest language family is the Sino (China)-Tibetan, which includes all the Chinese and some of their neighbors. Of the small language families, the largest are Japanese-Korean, African Negro, Semitic-Hamitic (including Hebrew), Dravidian (of India), and Malayo-Polynesian. The rest are far smaller.

The largest language family of all is the one that includes the languages of about one-third of the human race, including English. Its story parallels the story of Babel. Linguists tell us that five thousand years ago there was a great language in central Europe. We don't know its name, and so we call it Indo-European. It is a mysterious "lost" language because not one sentence of it is left in writing for us.[1]

In about 2500 B.C., when the pyramids were built in Egypt, that great language split up into eight different languages and evidently disappeared off the face of the earth. The eight branches were ancient German, Italian, Greek, Celtic, Baltic, Slavic, Iranian, and Indian. As different as they appear, these branches all bear a family resemblance. For example, our word *brother* in English is *broeder* in Dutch, *Bruder* in German, *phrater* in Greek, *brat* in Russian, *braithair* in Irish, and *bhratar* in Sanskrit.

Sanskrit is one of the two most famous "dead" languages in world history. (*Ginger* is a Sanskrit word.) The old literature of Latin and Sanskrit has survived and is still read, but the languages are stone-cold dead. That means that after hundreds of generations of people who lived and died with those words on their lips, the day came when no babies ever learned those languages from their parents anymore. (They learned Italian or Hindi instead, in most cases.) Latin and Sanskrit are fossil Indo-European languages studied and admired and quoted by scholars, but never again used in daily life.

When asked to name a dead language, American students often guess Greek. That would surprise the ten million people in Greece and neighboring areas who speak Greek to each other all day long and teach it to their babies. To paraphrase Mark Twain, the Greek-speakers might say that their death has been greatly exaggerated.

The New Testament was written in the Greek branch of this Indo-European family, but the Old Testament had been written centuries earlier in the Hebrew branch of a completely different family — the Semitic language family. Ironically, the Greek New Testament caused Hebrew to become precious to English-speaking people, and that is why some of our most common English names (such as John, Ann, David, Joseph, and Mary) are really transplanted Hebrew.

Many people who love their Bibles are shocked when they first hear the claim that world languages are not all descended from Hebrew. It is easy to assume from Genesis 11 that Hebrew was the world's one language before the Tower of Babel, since Genesis was written in Hebrew; but the Bible doesn't claim that Hebrew was the first language, and linguists say it was not. Hebrew writing, however, was the origin of all alphabets (in contrast to ideographic picture-writing like Chinese).

Hebrew was evidently written at least as early as 1500 B.C., the time of Moses. The Phoenicians were ancient seafaring merchants who adopted the Hebrew letters. They passed the letters on to the ancient Greeks. The letters were all consonants — clicking, buzzing, popping, and humming kinds of sounds like our letters, *b, f, k, m,* and *s.* This alphabet was first written from right to left, as Hebrew is still written today. Some of the letters could face either direction. Sometimes early Greek writers would zigzag down the page, changing direction on each line, and they had a word for this that meant "as the ox turns in plowing."

At about the time of the first Olympics, in 800 B.C., the Greeks adjusted the Hebrew letters to their own sounds in such a way that they had letters to represent vowel sounds like *a, e, i, o,* and *u.* This had never been done before. The Hebrews called their first consonant letter *aleph,* meaning "ox"; and the Greek made it a vowel and called it *alpha.* The Hebrews called their second letter *beth,* meaning "house"; and the Greeks called it *beta.* That is where everyone got the word alphabet — from the first two letters of the Hebrew and Greek alphabets.[2]

Some of the creative writing done right away with that new Greek alphabet has never been surpassed in over 2,500 years,[3] and then the New Testament was written with it as well. The Romans soon modified and beautified the Greek alphabet and spread it all over Europe. So our English alphabet wasn't designed for English at all. It is a hand-me-down from other languages, patched and altered many times along the way. We got it from the Romans, who got it from the Greeks, who got it from the Phoenicians, who got it from the Hebrews themselves.

Many Christians feel friendly toward the ancient Greek and Hebrew languages because the Bible came through them, just as many American Christians feel unfriendly toward the Russian language because of discomfort about the U.S.S.R. But we can't ignore the Slavic branch of our language family. It includes, among others, the Russian, Polish, and Czech languages, cousins of English. They have over 250 million speakers who inhabit the very area where scholars think that the Indo-European family probably began.

The branch of our language family that is most apt to charm Americans is the branch that flowered from Latin. Because Rome was the capital city of this branch, these languages are called Romance languages. They include Italian, Spanish, Portuguese, Romanian, and French; and they are spoken by over 300 million speakers. These are considered the pretty cousins of English. English is not considered pretty, but it is often considered wonderful.

Our own branch of the Indo-European family is the Germanic branch, with about 400 million speakers. This branch has two groups in it. The Scandinavian languages (Swedish, Norwegian, Danish, and Icelandic) are like half sisters to English — much closer than cousins. But German and Dutch are the two full sisters to English.

Of all twenty-three language families, the Indo-European family is most spectacular. And of all eight branches in the Indo-European family, the Germanic has now won the lottery of history. That is because of an amazing chain of circumstances that produced English and then caused the world to go crazy over English in spite of its faults. It is a wonderful and terrible language.[4]

Before England Was England

The first member of our language family to get to Britain was not English, but Celtic. It originated in the area of France in about 1500 B.C. — the approximate time of the Exodus from Egypt and the sinking of "Atlantis" (the Minoan island called Thera) into the Aegean Sea. The poetic and dramatic Celts, ancestors of most red-haired people in Britain and the United States, flourished and spread across Europe and the British Isles by 500 B.C. Although other tribes lived in the British Isles before the Celts arrived, the Celts are the first real Britons. But in spite of their passion for independence (still obvious in Ireland today), the Celts were overwhelmed by other tribes; and the Celtic languages survived only in pockets in Britanny (the western tip of France), Ireland, Scotland, and Wales.

Lewis is one of the best-known Welsh surnames, and the most popular Christian author of this century, C. S. Lewis, was in fact descended from a great-grandfather who was a preacher-farmer in Wales. The Welsh are noted for hauntingly beautiful choral singing and for wonderfully lavish use of words. (Dylan Thomas's story "A Child's Christmas in Wales" is a perfect example of Welsh writers' intoxication with their adopted English language.) Wales is bilingual, and one-fifth of its citizens claim to know Welsh as well as English today.[5] Road signs give both Welsh and English place names. One tiny Welsh village is famous among travelers simply because of the length of its Celtic name:

Llanfairpwllghyngyllgogerychwyrndrobwllllantysiliogogogoch!

If no one had conquered the Celts, we can assume that England might be something like Wales today. But in 55 B.C. Julius Caesar landed with his legions and took over, pushing the untamed Celts to the fringes of the land and ruling those who stayed put for about four hundred years. The Romans valued Britain for its agriculture and metals. About fifty years after the Romans arrived, according to tradition, the tin trade brought a ship from the Mediterranean with a young boy on board who came along as guest of his mother's brother, a certain Joseph of Arimathaea. The boy's name was Jesus, and he visited in the region of Glastonbury.[6] Eighteen centuries later, William Blake wrote a poem about that legendary visit:

> And did those feet in ancient time
> Walk upon England's mountains green?
> And was the holy lamb of God
> On England's pleasant pasture seen?
>
> And did the Countenance Divine
> Shine forth upon our clouded hills?
> And was Jerusalem builded here,
> Among the dark Satanic mills?
>
> Bring me my Bow of burning gold:
> Bring me my arrows of desire:
> Bring me my Spear: O clouds unfold!
> Bring me my Chariot of fire!
>
> I will not cease from Mental Fight,
> Nor shall my Sword sleep in my hand,
> Till we have built Jerusalem
> In England's green & pleasant land.

If Jesus visited Britain when he was a boy, which is highly unlikely but historically possible, he didn't hear a word of English; he no doubt heard both Latin and Celtic spoken there. Whether or not Jesus himself visited Roman Britain, Christianity soon did so. In A.D. 314 some church leaders from the British cities of London and York (Celtic names) attended a church conference in Europe, just as they might do today. The Romans kept things safe and orderly as long as they could. Latin was the official language.

In A.D. 410 the Romans had to leave all their fine walls, cities, and roads behind in Britain when their empire collapsed. For forty years the Celtic language continued as before, almost as if the Romans had never come and gone. But then the inevitable happened; savage Germanic tribes from Denmark, called Angles and Saxons, attacked the unprotected Celts and took over Britain. It was like being conquered by pirates. The legendary King Arthur was probably a real Celtic leader who helped to hold the invaders back as long as possible after the Romans left.

The Latin historian Tacitus had already described Germanic tribes, and he said that in their homeland some of them worshiped the goddess Mother Earth in a ceremony performed by slaves. After the ceremony they threw the poor slaves into local lakes. Evidently the lakes were sometimes peat bogs, and peat water has amazing preservative properties. So it was that a century ago some Danish peat diggers discovered perfectly preserved leathery brown bodies of murdered slaves, about fifteen hundred years old. The very stitches in their clothing and hairs of their head are preserved, as well as their fine facial features. They look like extremely skillful sculptures, but they are called swamp corpses or bog people; and they are now on display in various Danish museums. They are an eerie memento of the early speakers of "Anglisc" (English).

In contrast to the highly civilized Romans, few Angles and Saxons could read and write; but they loved clever word use and poetry and riddles:

> I am fire-fretted and I flirt with Wind
> and my limbs are light-freighted and I am lapped in flame
> and I am storm-stacked and I strain to fly
> And I am a grove leaf-bearing and a glowing ember.

They brought to Britain their brooding epic poem about a hero named Beowulf, an ominous story of doom and destiny. "Beowulf" was eventually written down, three thousand lines long, and is our chief surviving example of Anglo-Saxon literature — better known as Old English literature. It is a swashbuckling and spooky tale still much enjoyed, although it has to be read in prose translation today. Part of the charm of it lies in the frequent use of colorful substitutions for common words, such as "battle-flasher" for *sword* and "whale-road" for *sea*.

"Sorrow not," Beowulf urges. "Better is it for every man that he avenge his friend than that he mourn greatly. Each of us must abide the end of this world's life; let him who may, work mighty deeds ere he die. . . ."

Old English looks as foreign as German to us today, and it sounds as foreign as German when read aloud by someone who has studied it. Less than a quarter of our present English vocabulary is from Old English, but all our most common words are from Old English; in fact, every single one of our 100 most common words is from Old English. Old English words include (in modern spelling) *the, is, you, we, our, us, and, name, are, will, become, on, of, here, there, stone, bone, go, fire, how, loud, soul, guilt, right, man, woman, wife, God, forgive, heaven, hell, evil, earth, house, meat, leaf, eat, drink, child, earth, sheep, ox, plough, dog, wood,* and *field.* (Sixty percent of the words in Abraham Lincoln's Gettysburg Address are from Old English.) The heart-words of our language were all brought to Britain by the pagans from what is now Denmark. They include our "four-letter" words. They are short, plain words. They are our life-and-death words.

Many people's last names come to us from the Anglo-Saxons, and there is a verse to remind us of them:

> In *-ford,* in *-ham,* in *-ley,* in *-ton,*
> The most of English surnames run.

Once they had settled into their pleasant new land, the Anglo-Saxons were quickly and easily converted to Christianity by various missionaries. In the most famous story about the conversion of the Anglo-Saxons, a Roman church leader named Gregory noticed two handsome blond boys for sale as slaves in the marketplace in Rome. He asked where they were from and was told that they were Angles. They had angelic faces, he answered (in an intentional pun), and should become coheirs with the angels in heaven. So he sent St. Augustine and a group of helpers to Britain to establish the church there, which they did in Canterbury, and that is the headquarters of the Anglican Church to this day.

Once There Was an England

In about A.D. 700 the first British historian wrote about the "English church and people." The people called themselves Angle-kin (spelled Angelcynn), and they called their language English (spelled Englisc). In another century or two, the country was finally called Englaland, the land of the Angles. We now call their language *Old* English.

This is how the Lord's Prayer looks in Old English (in our modern version of the alphabet):

Faeder ure *th*u the eart on heofonum si *th*in name gehalgod. Tobecume *th*in nama gehalgod. Tobecume *th*in rice. Gewur *the th*in willa on eor *th*an swa swa on heofonum. Urne gedaeghwamlican hlaf syle us to daeg. And forgyf us ure gyltas swa swa we forgyfa*th*urum gyltendum. And ne gelaed *th*u us on costnunge ac alys us of yfele.

(Our father, which art in heaven, hallowed be thy name. Thy kingdom come. Thy will be done on earth, as it is in heaven. Give us this day our daily bread. And forgive us our debts as we forgive our debtors. And lead us not into temptation, but deliver us from evil.)

The English picked up extremely few Celtic words from the people who had lived on their island for many centuries before them (the Romans didn't pick up Celtic words either); but when the English became Christians they picked up many Greek and Latin words from Europe, such as *angel, disciple, apostle, martyr, mass, shrine, psalm, nun, monk, pope,* and *devil.* The Latin term *spiritus sanctus* (Holy Spirit) was used alongside the Old English *Halig Gast* (Holy Ghost), and the Latin term *evangelium* (good news) was used alongside the Old English *god-spell* (gospel). That was the very beginning of the extremely important choice that runs right through much of our English vocabulary — the choice between basic Old English words and their Greek- or Latin-style equivalents.

Old English energy and determination, combined with Christianity and literacy, quickly illuminated England. Then around A.D. 800 Vikings attacked and destroyed the choicest monasteries, which were treasure-houses of learning. In fifty years, the Danes took half the country. Now it was not legendary King Arthur fighting to save the Celts from the Angles; it was history's very real King Alfred fighting to save the Angles from the Danes. Alfred managed to halt the Danish takeover at the halfway point, and then he united the various little kingdoms of England under himself (A.D. 871–901) by persuading the people that all who speak English (in its various dialects) were one at heart. The Danes spoke what we now call Old Norse, which meant North.

Alfred was in love with English, and he saved our language. Once he got the Danish Vikings settled down fairly peacefully among the English, Alfred went on an English-language campaign. He rebuilt the schools and monasteries, and he started translating important Latin books into Old English so that his countrymen could read them in their native language. This was the beginning of English prose literature. King Alfred the Great should be considered the patron saint of everyone who writes in English to this day.

The difference between Old Norse and Old English in those days was much like the difference between Danish and Swedish today; neighbors could communicate only with great difficulty. Old English picked up some Norse vocabulary, including many *sk-* words such as *skirt* and *skin* and *sky*, but of course English prevailed over Norse. In the process, however, a strange and wonderful thing happened to Old English: it was simplified. Old English had eighteen different grammatical forms of the word *the*, for example, and the nouns had complicated endings for speakers to choose from. Since these distinctions weren't really necessary, they were dropped — much as we seem to be dropping the distinction between *who* and *whom* today. (Purists always find these changes painful.) One of the happiest losses for English was the arbitrary genders (masculine, feminine, or neuter) assigned to all nouns. If that hadn't happened, English would still fit Mark Twain's description of German: "In German, a young lady has no sex, but a turnip has."

In England there is to this day a place called Torpenhow Hill. That name shows the four layers of British habitation up to this point in our story. *Tor* is the oldest, a pre-Celtic (possibly Iberian) word meaning "hill." *Pen* is Celtic for "hill." *How* is from the Danish *haugr*, which means "hill." And of course *Hill* is English. So it is that *Torpenhow* Hill means "Hillhillhill" Hill.

Merry Middle English

Less than two hundred years after the Danish Vikings merged cozily into the English countryside and the English language grew in status and simplicity, suddenly all was lost. Or so it seemed. Back when the Danes were invading Britain, other Vikings had been invading what is now called France, across the English Channel. They merged with the French and ended up running Normandy. In 1066 they invaded England, killed King Harold in battle, and pillaged the countryside. On Christmas Day in 1066, William of Normandy was crowned king of England. He and the new leaders he brought over to rule the country spoke French, not English. Overnight, English was the language of the underclass and French was the language of the aristocrats. Good King Alfred must have been tossing in his grave.

Once again England was bilingual. Poor laboring people worked outdoors with English cows, pigs, sheep, and deer; but the aristocrats dined in French style upon beef, pork, mutton, and venison — not to mention gravy, salad, almonds, cherries, biscuits, jelly, spices, confections, cream, sugar, platters, goblets, and a huge array of other table terms — including dinner itself. They loved *fashion* (a French word) and dressed in French garments from cloaks to petticoats, made of satin, taffeta, lace, and furs. They *adorned* (a French word) themselves in jewels and ornaments, diamonds, and pearls. They furnished their homes with curtains, couches, cushions, lamps, wardrobes, and chandeliers. The humble English watched enviously and learned all the French words that went with upper-class style.

The rich Normans also brought in French social words like *sovereign, royalty, prince, count, chivalry, baron, noble, dame, servant, messenger, feast, minstrel, juggler,* and *tournament.* They took over the churches and gave the English such words as *religion, theology, sermon, baptism, communion, prayer, crucifix, trinity, sanctuary, divine, convert, ordain,* and *temptation.* They took over the courts and gave us words such as *crime, judgment, suit, plaintiff, defendant, jury, punishment, imprison, estate, legacy, heir,* and *pardon.*

In many areas of life two sets of words were used, as in the legal term "last will and testament." *Will* is English and *testament* is French, and they were used together so that everyone would understand. Nine-hundred years after the Normans conquered England, lawyers are still using double terms such as "last will and testament," and hardly anyone remembers why.

Another kind of mixing of French and English words also took place. In 1225 English use of the French word *gentle* was first recorded. In 1230 it was combined with the English word *woman* to give us *gentlewoman.* In 1275 we had *gentleman* (*man* is English), in 1300 we had *gentleness* (*-ness* is English), and in 1330 we had *gently* (*-ly* is English). In the same way the English turned *faith* into *faithful* (*-ful* is English), *faithfully,* and *faithfulness.* I would call these mixed words "Frenglish" words.

Although the English were a subjugated and humiliated people, they were the majority, and they spoke an especially strong, vigorous language. They continued to eat, drink, sleep, sing, speak, play, walk, run, ride, and swim in English. They consumed bread, butter, fish, milk, cheese, salt, pepper, wine, and beer in English. They lived in houses with rooms, doors, windows, floors, steps, and gates in English. They used their head, hands, arms, legs, feet, eyes, ears, nose, and mouth in English. Many of these basic English bodies were attractive to their new French overlords too. Within a century, the French aristocrats and English subordinates were mingling their families as well as their words. In another century French had become like a foreign language to many upper-class people. English simply swallowed up French, adopting at least 10,000 French words but not taking on any of the French grammar.

To this day, Frenchified spelling suggests high style, high quality, and high price to English-speaking consumers. Where do you expect to pay a higher price for movie tickets — at the theater or the theatre?

Which seems to be a more elegant cosmetic — cream or creme? Even a recently arrived immigrant to the United States is apt to catch on to the *par excellence* still implied in a bit of French spelling on an American label, 920 years after the Normans took over England, halfway around the world. French still looks and sounds toney to speakers of English. People still think that French spelling spells class.

French meant the end of Old English. Next came what we call Middle English, which lasted only from A.D. 1066 to 1500. One of the cleverest and most amusing authors of all time was Geoffrey Chaucer, an Englishman who managed to associate with the powerful elite in London of his day. He was lucky enough to avoid dying in the black plague; and he often entertained the king, who was a personal friend of his. Chaucer is best remembered for his poem *Canterbury Tales*, left incomplete at his death in A.D. 1400. English was extremely changeable at that time. Chaucer's English was all too soon the language of yesterday, but his observations about human beings are still as fresh as next week's *Time* magazine. That is the major reason why many people have made the effort to master Middle English for five hundred years — to read Chaucer.

Middle English is easier to learn than Old English, but it is still like learning a foreign language — perhaps equivalent to beginning Spanish in difficulty. The grammar is more complex than Modern English, but simpler than that of Old English. Here is the opening of *Canterbury Tales:*

> Whan the Aprill with his showres soote
> The droghte of March hath perced to the roote. . . .
> Thanne longen folk to goon on pilgrimages. . . .
>
> (When April with his sweet showers
> Has pierced to the root the drought of March. . . .
> Then people long to go on pilgrimages. . . .)

Many libraries have recordings of Chaucer's *Canterbury Tales* read by experts who know about how it should be pronounced. It is worth hearing. It is far more lilting than Modern English.

John Wycliffe translated the Gospels from Latin into Middle English just when Chaucer was writing his tales, and this is how Wycliffe wrote Matthew 5:13:

> Yee ben salt of the erthe; that yif the salt shal vanyshe away, wherynne shal it be saltid? (A.D. 1389)

As a by-product of his Bible translation, Wycliffe brought more than a thousand Latin words into the English vocabulary all at once. An opponent of his complained, "This Master John Wyclif translated from Latin into English — the Angle not the angel speech — and so the pearl of the Gospel is scattered and trodden underfoot by swine." "Swine" were people who read English instead of Latin.

To see how relatively easy Middle English is, try reading the same verse in Old English instead:

> Ge synd eorthan sealt; gyf thaet sealt awyrth, on tham the hit gesylt bith? (A.D. 995)

We have to strain to remember that for people living in England in A.D. 995, this language was perfectly clear; and if they could have had a sample of our Modern English, it would have struck them as a bizarre foreign mishmash that is no longer true English at all.

Old English and Middle English were both thrust upon Britain by invasions. But the shift into Modern English came about more peacefully and naturally as the speech patterns of the country changed in various important ways. Pronunciation changed, and the grammar inside words became increasingly simple. Thus we came to the point where the position of words in a sentence usually determines the meaning, not changes within the words themselves. In English we say "The lion ate the man" or "The man ate the lion," and we know which ate which without any spelling changes in the words lion and man. We can plan a table or table a plan, book a place or place a book, and lift a thumb or thumb a lift. The words don't change in looks or sound, just in their order. That is radical streamlining for any language.

William Tyndale translated Matthew 5:13 into this streamlined Early Modern English at its very earliest:

> Ye are the salt of the erthe; but and if the salt be once unsavery, what can be salted ther with? (A.D. 1526)

Eighty years later, in the days of Shakespeare, the all-time favorite English translation of the Bible used these words:

> Ye are the salt of the earth: but if the salt have lost his savour, wherewith shall it bee salted? (A.D. 1611)

The King James Version of the Bible is in Modern English, but it is in Early Modern English, which is a far cry from today's Modern English. Here is the same verse in today's New International Version:

> You are the salt of the earth. But if the salt loses its saltiness, how can it be made salty again? (A.D. 1973)

It is hard for most of us to make ourselves realize that William Tyndale's version was as clear and direct for his readers as this one is for us. There was nothing quaint about any of those translations in their own day. The sanctity or charm that we tend to enjoy in older styles of English are often a matter of misunderstanding. Thus, "Ye Olde Tea Shoppe" may be more inviting than "The Old Tea Shop"; but they are really the same. (The apparent *Y* at the beginning of *Ye* is just an old way of printing the sound *th*.) The quaint spelling is merely a throwback to the time when everyone was welcome to spell words according to whim — as Shakespeare did. Today free spelling may seem as irresponsible as free love, but when free spelling was standard practice, it was neither naughty nor charming. It was business as usual.

Modern English Muddle

Simplified grammar and the invasion of French vocabulary were the biggest changes in English until the end of Middle English. (We had 50,000 to 60,000 words in Old English, and the Norman Conquest in 1066 brought in about 10,000 French words.) Since Modern English began, standardized spelling and exploding vocabulary have been the two biggest changes. By the time the King James Version of the Bible was published in 1611, English had grown to almost 150,000 words, and we kept adding. We have about a half-million English words in the *Oxford English Dictionary* (our most comprehensive dictionary), but it is commonly said that there are at least 750,000 words in English now.[7] (French has fewer than 100,000 words, and it is a rich and sufficient language.)

Most English words won't ever be needed or wanted by most readers and writers, of course. (A spectacular word-whiz with a working vocabulary of 50,000 words would know half the words in French; but in English, about 6 percent.) About 35 words make up half our talking, and 70 words make up half our ordinary writing. In a week of ordinary light conversation a person might use only 2,000 different words. The average person who reads a fair amount probably knows about 20,000 words well enough to use them easily at any time, and would probably recognize twice that many. It is staggering to think of how many words an American brain has to select and reject, juggle and sort, in order to write a paragraph.

The superabundance of English words may be daunting and even confusing sometimes, but it gives writers an extraordinary flexibility in sounds and sense and shades of meaning. It is not much of an exaggeration to claim that in English we have a double load of synonyms. We can say what we have in mind in common (Old English) words, literary (French) words, or academic (Latin) words — and all in English. It is easy to see and hear the difference.

I *asked* my teachers about *goodness*. (Old English)
I *questioned* my teachers about *virtue*. (French)
I *interrogated* my teachers about *probity*. (Latin)

It was a *time* when one could *rise* easily. (Old English)
It was an *age* when one could *mount* easily. (French)
It was an *epoch* when one could *ascend* easily. (Latin)

I felt *fear* when I saw the *holy fire*. (Old English)
I felt *terror* when I saw the *sacred flame*. (French)
I felt *trepidation* when I saw the *consecrated conflagration*. (Latin)

Some people laugh out loud when they hear the last sentence, but others love it. There's no accounting for tastes (that is an old Latin proverb translated into English), and people have argued for centuries about the relative value of French and Latin in the English vocabulary. Although there are always writers who like the Latin words best, Bishop Reginald Pecock wanted to stamp them out in the 1500s and replace them with newly invented compound words from native English. For example, he would have replaced *inconceivable* with *not-to-be-thought-upon-able*, and *he* would have replaced *impenetrable* with *ungothroughsome*. A later scholar named Freeman longed for pure English and declared, "This abiding corruption of our language I believe to have been the one result of the Norman Conquest which has been purely evil."[8] (The words *language* and *purely* are from French. The words *corruption, result,* and *conquest* are from Latin. From 1867 to 1879 Freeman published eight enormous volumes about the Norman Conquest, in spite of his disapproval of the corrupted language he did it in.)

Whether one is a purist and calls the problem *spelling* (from Old English) or one is a pedant and calls it *orthography* (from Latin), the problem of getting the right letters in the right order is one of the most frustrating aspects of English. This first became a problem when William Caxton started printing books in England in 1476 and had to make choices about dialect and spelling for the thousands of books he brought out. Hand-copied books had been a luxury for the wealthy, and most were in Latin; but now ordinary English people could buy mass-produced books in Latin or English, and most preferred English. Publishing boomed. English words were trapped in print however they were caught at the time. Then dictionaries came along (Samuel Johnson's was completed in 1755) and made everything official.

There are several reasons why spelling plagues us. To begin with, our alphabet doesn't fit our language exactly. Some sounds can be written in more than one way, and some letters have more than one sound. In addition to that, after the Norman Conquest, French writers and secretaries sometimes carried over French spelling habits into English, where they didn't fit. The next major contribution to spelling chaos was the shifts in pronunciation that have often occurred in English. Many spoken letters eventually went silent, like the *k* in *knight*. The words *right*, *light*, and *night* were trapped in print when they were commonly pronounced with a soft *gh* before the *t*. The sound disappeared, but the *gh* remained. Later, some busybody inserted a *gh* into *delight* and *tight* simply for looks, although they were never pronounced with the extra sound. Meddlers fond of Latin changed the spelling of some English words to make them look more Latin — adding the silent *b* to *debt*, for example. And of course we have added words from hundreds of languages, keeping the foreign spelling or changing it as someone saw fit at the time. Some piecemeal spelling reforms in the United States never caught on in England and Canada, causing differences such as *honor* and *honour*. The best to be said for the spelling of the English language is that it has boundless variety.

We have such arbitrary and chaotic spelling that many highly intelligent and gifted writers are imperfect spellers, to their chagrin. (There seems to be no correlation between correct spelling and writing talent.) The one way to be sure of how to pronounce a written word in English is to hear it read correctly, and the one way to be sure of how to spell a heard word in English is to see it spelled out correctly. Then one needs a good memory for that kind of detail.

Some anonymous versifier set forth the lack of coordination between our spelling and pronunciation especially well:

> I take it you already know
> Of tough and bough and cough and dough?
> Others may stumble, but not you
> On hiccough, thorough, slough and through.
> Well done! And now you wish, perhaps,
> To learn of less familiar traps?
>
> Beware of heard, a dreadful word
> That looks like beard and sounds like bird.
> And dead — it's said like bed, not bead.
> For goodness sake don't call it deed!
> Watch out for meat and great and threat.
> They rhyme with suite and straight and debt.
>
> A moth is not a moth in mother
> Nor both in bother, broth in brother.
>
> And then there's dose and rose and lose —
> Just look them up — and goose and choose.

And cork and work and card and ward,
And font and front and word and sword.
And do and go and thwart and cart.
Come, come, I've hardly made a start.

Obviously, English is not "user friendly." Some people laugh fondly at English and some agonize over it, but no one ignores it. English is the largest, most widespread, most economically valuable, and most difficult language in the world today. Anyone who invented a language and made it this overgrown and confused would be a maniac. But no one invented English. It came about by a series of historical accidents. It is a jumble of contributions, traditions, and accommodations from all kinds of sources. The following anonymous verse points out a few of the inconsistencies we have to cope with:

We'll start out with box. The plural is boxes.
But the plural of ox should be oxen, not oxes.
One fowl is a goose, and two are called geese,
But the plural of moose should never be meese.
You may find a mouse or a whole nest of mice,
But the plural of house is just houses, not hice.
If the plural of man is always called men,
Why shouldn't the plural of pan be called pen?
Cows in the plural may be called cows or kine,
But a bow, if repeated, is never called bine.
And the plural of vow is vows, never vine.
If I speak of a foot, you show me two feet;
If I give you a boot, would a pair be called beet?
If one is a tooth and a whole set are teeth,
Why shouldn't the plural of booth be called beeth?
If the singular's this and the plural is these,
Why isn't the plural of kiss always kese?
And the one may be that and the two may be those,
Yet hat in the plural would never be hose;
And the plural of cat is just cats and not cose.
We speak of a brother and also of brethren,
Then speak of a mother, but never of methren.
The masculine pronouns are he, his, and him,
But the feminine never are she, shis and shim.
So English appears, and I think you'll agree,
The funniest language that we'll ever see.

The verse is someone's way of turning the confusion inside out and making a pattern from it. Writing is a way of creating order and beauty or humor in the midst of chaos. That may be why writing well is one of the world's most difficult and rewarding skills.

Life is not orderly.

The English language is not orderly.

Thought is not orderly.

People wish to believe that the world is well organized, that the English language is well organized, and that our own thought processes are well organized. But reality is not like that. Human life and the great English language and our own thinking processes are not tame and tidy. They are wild and random and rich and wasteful, like oceans and forests and human history. In that tumult and variety we sometimes catch glimpses of a deep inner order and meaning in everything anyway, including ourselves. Then some of us write about it.

SUGGESTED ACTIVITIES

1. What is your own language heritage? What languages did your parents, grandparents, great-grandparents, and more distant ancestors speak? Are you aware of any regionalisms in the area where you grew up (such as "you-all")? Have you picked up any regionalisms from far away because of the entertainment industry and changing fashions? Hawaii has a special surfer-related pidgin English, California has Valley-girl slang as well as Silicone Valley high-tech slang, Texas has "Texan," Pennsylvania has "Pennsylvania Dutch" sayings, and Michigan has a few people who still call each other "Kid." Minnesota residents are teased in the good-humored book *How to Talk Minnesotan* by Howard Mohr (New York: Penguin books, 1987). Analyze your own language roots and how they influence your writing.

2. Try inventing some poetic word combinations of your own similar to the old Anglo-Saxon use of "whale-road" for *sea*, "battle-flasher" for *sword*, "wave-traveler" for *boat*, and "triumph-tree" for *cross*. (These old constructions are called kennings.) Try to think of colorful compound words for today to stand for *motorcycle, electric guitar, power saw, jet plane, microwave oven, dishwasher, video cassette, foster parent, cocaine, freeway, pacemaker, refrigerator, freezer, telescope,* and *peanut butter.* Your kennings might work well in poems.

3. In 1980 Russell Hoban published a grim novel, *Riddley Walker*, written entirely in the strange English of a distant and barbaric future. ("On my naming day when I come 12 I gone front spear and kilt a wyld boar. . . .") Write a paragraph in the English of A.D. 2300 as you choose to imagine that it might be then. Don't depend upon the subject matter to show that this is in the future; concentrate upon

changes in grammar, vocabulary, or sentence structure, and add a note telling what those changes are. For example, you might pretend that there is no more gender in pronouns and also that the present popularity of the letter *X* in marketing has permeated our general vocabulary. Or you could pretend that in a backlash against everything unisex, we have put gender back into all our nouns and pronouns and into our verbs as well. You could pretend that in reaction against modernity, we have adopted a quasi-Elizabethan English much like that of the King James Bible. You could also pretend, as James Thurber did in *The Wonderful O*, that a dictator (pirate) has outlawed certain letters of the alphabet.

4. Write a brief poem expressing your feeling about the English language. (This is like a painter making a picture of the very paints and canvas with which he makes the picture.)

5. Wachamacallit? Although English has a gigantic vocabulary, we still lack words for many common things. Rich Hall finally made up a word to stand for words that are made up for little things that have no names: *sniglets*. Once there was a word for these newly minted words for ordinary things, they caught on. Now there are books full of sniglets, many contributed by the public. *Dillrelict* is the last pickle in the jar, which can't be captured by your fork. *Downpause* is the moment of dry weather when you drive under an overpass during a storm. *Sturtz* is the torn corner of any pages where a staple used to be. *Stuple* is the used staple that got separated from its papers. Look around and think a bit, and invent a dozen sniglets of your own.

6. Start keeping a list of real words that you particularly enjoy because of their looks, sound, or meaning.

NOTES

[1] The two poems by Greek farmer-poet Hesiod from about 720 B.C. are the earliest surviving Greek literature, and some scholars believe that they are a good example of Indo-European oral poetry. (For an overview of the Indo-European culture, read Colin Renfrew's *Archaeology and Language: The Puzzle of Indo-European Origins* from Cambridge University Press.) About twenty-seven centuries ago, Hesiod had this to say about rivalry between writers: "Both potter is jealous of potter and craftsman of craftsman; and poor man has a grudge against poor man, and poet against poet." There were no novels back then, so Hesiod did not mention rivalry between novelists.

[2] Thomas Pyles, *The Origins and Development of the English Language* (New York: Harcourt, Brace & World, 1964), "Letters and Sounds: A Brief History of Writing," 21–49.

[3] Homer's *Odyssey* and *Iliad* were written circa 700 B.C. The dramas of Aeschylus, Sophocles, and Euripides were written between 450 and 400 B.C. They are beloved today, even in translation.

[4] Recommended reading: *A History of the English Language* by Albert C. Baugh (New York: Appleton-Century Crofts, 1935).

[5] In 1921 Welsh was more widely spoken than today, but seemed to be fading fast. That is when the University of Wales launched a literary and historical dictionary project that is thriving still and is scheduled for completion in 1997. Two of the three large volumes are now finished; editors have completed words beginning with the unique "ll" sound that comes between l and m. But this is not the dictionary of a dying language. Today there is a Welsh-language TV channel and a subsidized Welsh-language publishing industry that issues hundreds of books yearly. A best-seller in Welsh is a book that sells 3000 copies, so there is little financial profit for Welsh authors; but there is an intimacy with the small reading public. Lovers of Welsh think its survival is "rhywbeth rhyfeddol" — something wonderful.

[6] C.C. Dobson, "Did Our Lord Visit Britain?" in *Jesus Through the Centuries*, edited by Manuel Komroff (New York: William Sloane, 1953), 180–203.

[7] For a survey of English today as well as its backgrounds, see *The Story of English* by Robert McCrum, William Cran, and Robert MacNeil (New York: Viking, 1986).

[8] E.A. Freeman, *History of the Norman Conquest*. Vol. V, 547.

Chapter 6

A Foot in
Your Mouth

If you can't be funny, be interesting.

— HAROLD ROSS

Through thousands of years of human history, most poetry was meant to be spoken a-loud. And most poetry had a rather regular beat that could be marked with a tap of the foot. The regular beat helped people to memorize and recite the poems. To this day, when lines of poetry have a regular beat, we call each accented syllable a foot. As I see it, prose walks and runs and jumps, but poetry is the writing that dances.

Most people who care about words would say that poetry is the finest form of writing.[1] Using a completely different measuring stick, some people would say that sermons are more important. Both poetry and sermons are often assumed to be the most inspired and inspiring, the truest, the loftiest, the most humane, and the most audacious kind of writing.

It is an odd situation. Every week in our country hundreds of thousands of poems and sermons are written, but we have few people who are willing to read any of them. Even the people who write most of them don't usually read any except their own. And few people will buy books of poems or sermons to use for gifts.

"Publishing a book of poetry," according to Don Marquis, "is like dropping a rose-petal down the Grand Canyon and waiting for the echo."

We tend to think of Britain as more literary than the United States, but even there poetry books account for under .5 percent of the £2-billion-a-year book market.

Poet Robert Graves summed up the problem philosophically: "There's no money in poetry, but then there's no poetry in money either."

Art Poetry

When people say that they write some poetry, that is as ambiguous as saying that they play some music. There are basically two kinds of poetry, what I like to call art poetry and folk poetry. (I assume that these are two ends of a spectrum.) They are often called serious poetry and verse. Serious poetry is the poetry that literature professors and other sophisticated people take seriously. It is subtle, complex, and often surprising in the way it is crafted.

Jacob Rabinow is the inventor of our mail-sorting machines and automatic headlight dimmers, among other things. He mentioned art poetry when he wrote about the creative process. "An invention is really putting together things that normally don't go together. A really good invention, in fact, is a work of art. A good piece of poetry, for example, is old words put together in a way that a sophisticated audience understands as good art."[2]

Art poetry is what Robert Frost was talking about when he said that poetry takes life by the throat.

Robert Penn Warren, our first Poet Laureate, tried to describe what is missing in weak poetry: "A poem you don't feel in your toes is not a very good one." Then he added, "But it also takes a person who knows how to feel to his toes to read a poem." We are short on responsive readers.

These facts are illustrated in the single best book about poetry that I know of, *The Bat Poet* by American poet Randall Jarrell.[3] It tells the story of a soft little brown bat that once stayed awake in the daytime and fell in love with the poetry of the mockingbird's song the first time he heard it. Then he tried to write a song like that of the mockingbird and discovered that if you get the words right, you don't need a tune. He made up poems in his head and memorized them, but other bats didn't understand anything about poems.

"The trouble isn't making poems," he decided, "the trouble's finding somebody that will listen to them." He admired the mockingbird so much that the mockingbird finally felt obligated to listen to the bat's first poem. But his response was pedantic; he merely analyzed the poem's technical features for the bat. The bat thought, "What do I care how many feet it has?" The poem was about life and death, not about its meter and rhyme scheme. Fortunately, the new little poet found a chipmunk who could understand (who felt to his toes, in Warren's words).

This bare summary doesn't hint at the poignancy and depth of Jarell's statement about poetry. His book is in my opinion the ideal first primer for poets of any age.

At Williams College a seminar called "Bad Poetry" is based upon the idea that better poetry readers make better poetry writers.[4] Students analyze unsuccessful poems (bad poems or early versions of poems that were later improved by their writers) to better appreciate successful poems. The idea is that understanding the qualities of other people's poetry will help students to improve their own poetry.

My own favorite example of bad poetry is an elegy for three turkeys written by six-year-old Marjory Fleming in 1809.

> Three turkeys fair their last have breathed,
> And now this world forever leaved;
> Their father, and their mother too,
> They sigh and weep as well as you.
> Indeed, the rats their bones have crunched,
> Into eternity they're launched.
> A direful death indeed they had,
> As would drive any parent mad:
> But she was more than usual calm,
> She did not give a single damn.

Some of the dangers that ambitious little Marjory did not know to avoid were lachrymose style, laughable incongruities, pretentiousness, forced rhyme, choppy couplets, trite flourishes, ridiculous images, and suddenly deflating shift of tone. These earned her a measure of literary immortality by giving pleasure to her readers for almost two centuries now. Some writing is so bad that it is good.

But a little girl's grief over the death of humble fowl can be the stuff of good poetry, even when it includes disconcerting shifts of tone. John Crowe Ransom showed that in his poem "Janet Waking," which tells tenderly how his tiny daughter went out to greet Old Chucky the hen and found her dead from a bee sting on her bald head:

> So there was Janet
> Kneeling on the wet grass, crying her brown hen
> (Translated far beyond the daughters of men). . . .[5]

An old hen is challenge enough, but could there ever be a serious poem about the death of an animal as stupid as a turkey? Richard Wilbur's "A Black November Turkey" is just that.

> Shuddering its fan and feathers
> In fine soft clashes
> With the cold sound that the wind makes, fondling
> Paper-ashes.[6]

Anyone serious about writing serious poetry should sample Ransom and Wilbur and scores of other major poets. Understanding some of our heritage of good poetry helps us to create good poetry.[7] Reading good writing is an aid to good writing. That truism has been somewhat out of style for the past twenty years, with the emphasis upon poetry as therapy; but now things are changing back. Graduate degrees in poetry at Stanford University will eventually require as many literature classes as writing workshops.[8]

Poet Robert Siegel has tried to describe what it is like to create art poetry. It is a rarified intellectual and spiritual, even mystical experience.

> Whether things are common or secret (and all things are both common *and* secret), I wish to call them up by the power of words — or rather, *as* words. A sensation, impression, or image will step out from its surroundings and demand my total attention. The thing itself will appear to rise up in words. Here is the wonder of the magic, what Keats called "natural magic": as the image reaches up toward the words, the words become the image, the thing itself. For one happy moment they are fused. . .
>
> When such a moment comes, I go to my typewriter, careful to preserve the fragile image riding, as it were, on the front of my brain. Sitting down at my desk, I feel the image spring living roots through fingers and keys until the poem is rooted, however tenuously, on the page. From this point on the poem either grows or does not. A certain tact is necessary to avoid trying too hard, to avoid forcing what should not be forced — a wise passiveness. Yet the experience is not at all like automatic writing. If anything, awareness is increased at these times, as in Coleridge's description of the poet at work: "The poet . . . brings

the whole soul of man into activity . . . a more than usual state of emotion, with more than usual order; judgment ever awake and steady self-possession, with enthusiasm and feeling profound or vehement." The moment of creation brings a heightened sense of consciousness. In this consciousness, the critical faculty does not work slowly and laboriously, as it will during revision. Rather, it is part of a whole-souled activity. The mind follows the direction of the poem by a kind of intuition, all that one has learned by example and practice working seemingly by reflex. "Like a piece of ice on a hot stove, the poem must ride on its own meaning," Frost wrote. The poet must also ride that piece of ice — an impossible feat, of course. There is always something miraculous about a poem's coming into being at all.

When a first draft arrives this way, I feel completely happy as a maker. I won't know until later whether what I've written is as good as I feel it is. (It rarely, or never, is.) The intensity of what I experience while writing is no guarantee of a poem's quality. Some of my best experiences have turned out to be failures as poems — failures often difficult to abandon. Another poem, written with less feeling and full of gaps to be filled in later, may eventually turn into something good. An idea for a poem came while I was reading a newspaper article. I then read a hopelessly dull article in an encyclopedia to gain more information. Only later, in the process of writing, did strong feeling come. All that dry information provided a kind of tinder.

Occasionally, the good poem springs forth whole. It seems, as Emerson believed, to have been "written before time was." The poet is merely the transmitter. Most often, though, the transmitter is hampered by static and the whole poem doesn't come through. The trick of revision is to restore this imperfect transcription. Sometimes the most important parts come through only during revision.[9]

Folk Poetry

Art poetry and folk poetry can spring from the same creative source. Robert Siegel once studied with the great poet Robert Lowell at Harvard, and he has been published in *The Atlantic* and other sophisticated periodicals. But I have seen the same general observations about inspiration and creativity expressed briefly by Eddie Espinoza, a minister who has written a few simple worship songs. Although songs sometimes come into Espinoza's mind as if he is taking dictation, they usually need polishing and rewriting. "A common mistake that many songwriters make is treating their songs like their offspring. One would never think of doing plastic surgery on a baby, but our songs are not babies. An eraser comes in very handy."[10]

Espinoza mentions greeting cards in relation to his songs, and indeed folk poetry or people's poetry is sometimes referred to as greeting card verse. Folk poetry is easy to read and understand. It has broad appeal. I know of no more popular folk poem than "The Night Before Christmas," which a distinguished seminary professor wrote for his family in four hours on Christmas Eve in 1822 and later published in a newspaper.

Edgar Guest was another competent and clever newspaper poet, who became extremely popular after the First World War. Today's most successful folk poets include Rod McKuen and Susan Polis Schutz. Schutz began by going to stores in small towns to sell cards designed by her artist husband. This led to a multimillion dollar business, Blue Mountain Arts, Inc., and Schutz became the first lady of American folk poetry. I suppose that people like her verses because they are just like the verses that other people across our country write every day — ordinary words about ordinary feelings set in broken lines on the page, with nothing distinctly poetic about them. When a friend innocently gave me Schutz's book *I Want to Laugh, I Want to Cry*, all I could say to myself was "I want to laugh, I want to cry." I wanted to laugh and cry over someone making a fortune off such inept cliches. (I wished I had done it.)

I wanted to laugh and cry over a simple poem of mine once also. It was verse I had written in college and submitted to *Ideals* magazine. Fourteen years later *Ideals* responded, informing me that they had just accepted and published it. They sent me a check for ten dollars and one free copy of the magazine. This is the poem they had stored for fourteen years:

GROWING UP

There once was a time
    That is hard to recall
When high was a bird
    And round was a ball.

When long was an hour
    And big was a tree,
And there wasn't a thing
    More important than me.

Now high is in light years
    And round is the world,
And Long is eternity's
    Ages unfurled.

Now big is the universe
    Dwarfing our sky. . .

I think everything's growing
Much faster than I.

It was obvious that I would never support myself by writing verse. Hardly anyone ever does. Poetry rarely pays for a poet's paper, postage, and typewriter repair.

Shel Silverstein has surpassed all other folk poets in popularity. His book of verses called *A Light in the Attic* hit the top of the *New York Times* bestseller list in 1981 and eventually became the all-time best-selling hardcover book. The book is an intelligent collection of preposterous verses and drawings for children of all ages.

In well over one hundred delightful bits of doggerel, readers are exposed to an amazing array of anecdotes about cannibalism, dismemberment, disfigurement, bizarre fatalities, and other excitement. In most of the verses there is a broad wink and a conspiratorial tone; it's obviously Silverstein and his readers against the establishment. Silverstein is relentlessly funny and interesting. Tossed in with all the fun and vinegar one finds a few dollops of pathos or unexpected sweetness. There is rarely a dull moment.

I wrote two stanzas in the Silverstein word-style to review his book:

This is a laugh-and-screamish,
   Moonie-beamish, sour-creamish,
Winning-teamish, stop-and-look,
   Extra-squeamish kind of book.

An up-and-downish, silly-clownish,
   Inside-outish, round-aboutish,
Snicker-snoutish, stop-and-look,
   Brave-Boy-Scoutish kind of book.

Versed Aid

Louis Untermeyer once wrote a ridiculous essay, "Versed Aid to the Injured," in which he pretended to be telling readers how everyone can write publishable verse.[11] With his simplified instructions as a guide, all that is needed is the desire to write and patience — but not much of the latter.

Untermeyer gives a sample stanza about spring that is perfect because everything in it is completely familiar, and the lines could be rearranged in any order without its making any difference at all. Originality isn't needed or wanted. The secret is "to keep to the perennial and expected essentials" — a euphemism for banality. I followed his advice and quickly came up with this stanza:

Christmas now returns at last,
    With gifts for every girl and boy.
Warm memories of winters past;
    The season brims with peace and joy.

And it works as well backward:

The season brims with peace and joy,
    Warm memories of winters past;
With gifts for every girl and boy,
    Christmas now returns at last!

Every phrase is familiar. The lines can be read in any order at all. Readers can drift through the stanza without stirring a brain cell.

Untermeyer's next advice is about the writing of sonnets in honor of something or someone. First one chooses the title, "To_____." Then one begins the sonnet with the words *O thou*.

Using a rhyming dictionary, fill in the ends of fourteen lines with rhyming words in a standard sonnet rhyme scheme, and place a possible word or two at the start of every line. Then fill in the skeleton structure at your convenience. Here is a typical patriotic sonnet before the lines are filled in:

TO _____

O thou . . . . birth
Great . . . . land,
Stern . . . . command
Wisdom . . . . mirth,
Noble . . . . worth,
Future . . . . planned,
All men . . . . understand
Throughout . . . . earth.

Inscrutably . . . . designed,
Glorious . . . . sea to sea;
Foes . . . . blind
Nations . . . . free —
Lover . . . . mankind,
Thy fame . . . . eternity.

An even speedier method of composition is to skip all the words except the final word of each line when writing a familiar-sounding poem. A slumber song should always make good use of the word *rest*. Untermeyer calls his sample lullaby "Sunset Croon."

. . . . dies,
. . . . west,
. . . . skies,
. . . . Rest.

. . . . calls,
. . . . nest;
. . . . falls.
. . . . Rest.

. . . . alarms,
. . . . breast;
. . . . arms.
. . . . Rest.

. . . . love;
. . . . best.
. . . . above —
. . . . Rest.

Untermeyer is making fun of unoriginal poetry by lazy writers, but the constructions he suggests can be used as practice exercises for beginning writers. All writers had to start as beginners at one time or another. All writers' beginnings are humble.

Puzzles, Tricks, and Word Stunts

Poetry and puzzles often make sound and sense interact in special ways. Many poems are kinds of puzzles, and many word puzzles are almost poems. Both poetry and word puzzles tend to be full of literary special effects. Playing with them is valuable practice for writing.

Here are two popular word riddles:

What's the difference between ignorance and indifference?
I don't know and I don't care.

Are you still vacillating?
Maybe I am and maybe I'm not.

Here is a traditional old riddle in verse:

WHO IS SHE?

In the garden there strayed
A beautiful maid
   As fair as the flowers of the morn;
The first hour of her life

> She was made a man's wife,
> And was buried before she was born.[12]

Oxymorons are inherently contradictory statements used by mistake or for effect, such as icy fire, the sound of one hand clapping, and making haste slowly. A graduate student recently asked me to look over the first draft of her dissertation for her, and on page one I spotted this oxymoron: "Ages ago, people wrote about God in prehistoric documents." Her advisors hadn't noticed the error yet, and she and I had a good laugh over it.

I think of the odd jokes called "Irish bulls" as expanded oxymorons. (I've been told that "Irish bulls" are pregnant bulls.) C. S. Lewis recounted a typical "Irish bull" from his childhood: A man bought a new kind of stove that cut his fuel consumption in half, so he bought a second stove in order to use no fuel at all.

Tautologies are verbal redundancies used by mistake or for effect, such as seeing with your own two eyes, whispering quietly, or seeking a wealthy philanthropist. "The water was very wet indeed." Cutting out accidental tautologies is a way of trimming off excess verbiage; but some tautologies provide a useful kind of emphasis.

Malapropisms are accidental misuses of words. "I took the subscription to the drug store." "To understand English, you have to learn about Semitics." "He went on a drunken bing." "You could have knocked me down with a fender." "Her baby was late, so her doctor seduced her." The world is full of malapropisms, and they are fun to collect.[13]

Palindromes are words or phrases that spell the same thing whether read forward or backward. Here are three classics:

> What was the first thing Adam said to Eve?
> "Madam, I'm Adam."

> What did the visitor to T. S. Eliot's editorial offices ask later?
> "Was it Eliot's toilet I saw?"

> How did the Panama Canal come to be?
> A man. A plan. A canal. Panama.

These are all a kind of mirror-image writing, playing with letter patterns. Here are some of my humble efforts to create more:

> How much butter did the farmer sell?
> Not a ton,
> But a tub.

> What's the palindrome that means "block a swallow"?
> Plug a gulp.

What's a friendship rule for children?
Pals never even slap.

What's a basic rule of moral living?
Live on no evil.

What's the bad news since Adam and Eve?
Sin is.

What advice do Robert's parents send to him at college?
Dear Bob, Read.
Mom
Dad

What does the old British butler say in the morning?
Rise, Sir.
Tea! Heh? Eat.

What color is a palindrome sunburn?
Redder.

What does a palindrome-hater do when he reads these?
Gag.

Word puzzles and writing games come in many forms, including acronyms (Biola University got its name from an acronym for the old Bible Institute of Los Angeles), acrostics, puns, triolets, limericks, conundrums, tongue-twisters, clerihews, anagrams, lipograms, cryptograms, rebuses, wit-twisters, and Espygrams. These are all good brain aerobics for writers. I particularly recommend Willard R. Espy's collection titled *The Game of Words*.[14]

Preachments

One of the writing games that people enjoy most is parody, and in the Lewis family papers at Wheaton College in Illinois there is a long-forgotten parody by the mother of C. S. Lewis. Flora Hamilton Lewis was the daughter of an Anglican preacher in Belfast and dutifully went to church all her life. According to Lewis himself, Belfast sermons were not always very edifying. A century ago Flora parodied the preaching style with a mock sermon based on the nursery-rhyme text "Old Mother Hubbard."

> Brethren, the words of my text are:
>> Old Mother Hubbard, she went to the cupboard
>> To get her poor dog a bone.

> But when she got there, the cupboard was bare,
> And so the poor dog got none.

Mother Hubbard, you see, was old; there being no mention of others, we may presume she was alone, a widow — a friendless, old, solitary widow. Yet did she despair? Did she sit down and weep, or read a novel, or wring her hands? No. She went to the cupboard, and here observe, she *went* to the cupboard, she did not hop or skip or jump, or use any other peripatetic artifice; she solely and merely *went* to the cupboard.[15]

The rest of this sermon, a footnote to history, is located in the footnotes of this chapter. Flora was not making fun of the Bible or the church. She was just making fun of a tedious preaching style. (Seven years later she would give birth to C. S. Lewis, and fifty years later he would write and preach sermons that were never tedious.) Actually, part of the definition of the words *preachment* and *preachy* is "tedious." That is because all too often the writers of sermons make some basic mistakes. Cornelius Plantinga, Jr., of Calvin Theological Seminary, suggests "a shot to the heart" for sermon writers.

Like a Shot to the Heart

A friend recently told of hearing a sermon that began roughly like this:

> Have you ever seen . . . a *train*? Have you ever *seen* a train? Have *you* ever. . . .?

And so on.

Because he was harried, or lazy, or merely unaware, this preacher had tried a greasy old recipe: You ask an outstandingly uninteresting question. Then, using a pattern of alternating emphases — the homilist's hamburger helper — you ask it repeatedly till you enrage all listeners not already numb.

Preachers err when they suppose such devices charm everybody but snobs. My grandfather was a devout farmer who loved the church and the things of the faith. One Sunday noon he complained angrily of a sermon he found insulting. Jesus, the preacher assured the congregation, had healed a blind man:

> He was *blind*, beloved! He could not see. His eyes were dark. Things were hard for him to spot. His optic nerves were shot. Blind, beloved!

I know that a preacher can sabotage his own sermons in ways beyond meaningless repetition. Some sermons run on tangents to their texts. Many lack point or force, even if adorned with cute alliterations or blusteringly delivered. Some suffer from predictability more in concept than in language:

> A man was born two thousand years ago. He preached and worked miracles and went around doing good. But his followers abandoned him in the end, and when he went to his death he nearly despaired. But three days later an astonishing thing happened that changed the course of history.
>
> Perhaps by now you've guessed that. . . .

Oddly, pretentious sermons often pack the same sedative power as humbler ones. In my own tradition, the three-points-and-a-poem variety has often appeared in the sort of heavy, Latinate language that rises to an almost genius level in its ability to fetch a yawn:

> The Prodigal Son: Three points, beloved, under the general heading, "Election of Guilty Sinners." First, election's predestinate origin in the eternal decree. Second, its forensic accentuation in the justification of sinners. Third, its vindication in eschatological glorification.

Whatever happened to the *story?* Where's that heartbroken word *lost* ("My son was lost and is found again")? Why can't we see the *picture* of grace — a parent running out like some finishing sprinter, arms splayed, robe flapping, beard crushed against that familiar rebel who is sheepishly trying to recall his memorized confession?

Pulpit language undisciplined by apt reading, good models, and careful preparation tends to become flat or puffy. In either case it may suffer from terminal banality. Given how much preaching matters, the struggle for cure is worth trying.

My own reflections on pulpit language have recently had two sources. First, I've been noticing my own pastor's mastery of it. His sermons are lean and meaty, full of insights into Scripture and outsights onto human life. But what especially impresses is how much gets said in twenty minutes. The style is so efficient as to be almost epigrammatic.

Second, a few years ago I wrestled with an assignment to write a doctrine book for thirteen-year-olds. This is a difficult audience not only because their interest in, say, the Second Coming is typically mild, but also because an author cannot hope even to arouse interest unless he uses a particular voice. The language has to be right. On the one hand, theological jargon would be worse than useless, smothering whatever low fires got kindled. On the other hand, patronizing simplicity ("He was blind, beloved; he could not see") is just as insulting to teens as to grandfathers.

So where's the middle of the fairway?

C. S. Lewis once said it exactly: "Any fool can write learned jargon; the test is the vernacular." And Lewis had in mind a certain sort of vernacular — the sort of artful, sparkling vernacular that, at least as he used it, never thinned down to routine prose. Lewis, in fact, passed his test of the vernacular so transcendently that his place as the best Christian author of the twentieth century is probably forever secure. As nearly everyone knows, Lewis's vernacular could often be so tight, spare, and evocative that, like a change in a Mozart score, the replacement of only a few words would mean diminishment:

> Many people are deterred from seriously attempting Christian chastity because they think (before trying) that it is impossible. But when a thing has to be attempted, one must never think about possibility or impossibility. Faced with an optional question in an examination paper, one considers whether one can do it or not: faced with a compulsory question, one must do the best one can. You may get some marks for a very imperfect answer: you will certainly get none for leaving the question alone. Not only in examinations but in war, in mountain climbing, in learning to skate, or swim, or ride a bicycle, even in fastening a stiff collar with cold fingers, people quite often do what seemed impossible before they did it. It is wonderful what you can do when you have to.

The quoted passage is from *Mere Christianity* and was written for adults. But Lewis's children's literature is probably an even purer recording of this simple and yet redolent voice that at once instructs and delights:

> They say Aslan is on the move — perhaps has already landed. Aslan isn't *safe*, but he's good. He's good and terrible at the same time.

> "And now," said Aslan, "to business. I feel I am going to roar. You had better put your fingers in your ears."

Of course none of us who preach will ever be as good as Lewis. We are all Saliere to his Mozart. But we can learn from him and others. One of the most important lessons I myself learned from trying to write for teens is that the kind of language you want — Anglo-Saxon nouns, vivid, active verbs, sparing use of adjectives — is exactly the kind of language needed in the pulpit. Educated pulpit language is not that of *The New York Times Magazine*; it's the language of *The Wind in the Willows*.

After all, why (apart from length) are adults more interested in their preacher's children's sermons than in his regular ones? They are delighted by images instead of arguments, by plots instead of outlines, by crisp language instead of some other kind.

Thus two suggestions. First, all preachers should steep themselves in good children's literature (Lewis, Tolkien, Madeleine L'Engle, E. B. White, Kenneth Graham, A. A. Milne, Ursula Le Guin, Katherine Paterson, Paula Fox, etc.). The best children's literature has a quality of language that is equally potent for adults and that therefore transfers naturally to sermons. I mean, especially a kind of deceptive simplicity. In between flat and puffy banality is the sort of simplicity that sets off depth charges in us.

You can often find it in music. As one of my friends likes to point out, the five-note descending motif in the slow movement of the Mozart *Clarinet Concerto* is eloquent not just because harmonically and thematically it is perfectly set up. The eloquence comes just as much from the sheer simplicity of the motif itself. There it is: just five notes going down a scale, and yet the notes seem to be struck "at a depth not of years, but of centuries."

In great children's literature one finds this same deceptive simplicity. The words look ordinary, and yet they are freighted. It's a simplicity of essence, of concentrate, of distillate.

In a wonderful little book (*How to Read the Bible as Literature*), Leland Ryken makes a similar observation about biblical poetry. For example, on God's care, the earnest, but uninspired, authors of the Westminister Confession instruct us thusly:

> God the Creator of all things doth uphold, direct, dispose, and govern
> all creatures, actions, and things, from the greatest even to the least,
> by his wise and most holy providence. . . .

Inspired poets say this: "The Lord is my shepherd. I shall not want."

Second, where necessary, church councils ought to take quality control of their pulpits by writing a reading requirement into their preacher's job description. Then they ought to appoint a small, friendly committee (including perhaps a librarian and an English teacher) whose task is, twice a year, to furnish their preacher with a thoughtful list of recommended reading. Moreover, twice a year this committee would report to Council on the minister's conquests in the field of reading.

For preachers the test is always the vernacular. The supreme test is the dignified and deceptive vernacular — terse, spare, apparently simple, but cocked and loaded and ready to pierce the people of God like a shot to the heart.[16]

131

Write Up, Not Down

When Plantinga speaks of the value of reading great children's literature, he is on sure ground.[17] Some beginning writers think that they can start out writing for children and then work their way up to writing for adults. But wiser writers are apt to start with adults and work their way up to writing for children. E. B. White, one of the best writers of our century, put it this way:

> Anybody who writes down to children is simply wasting his time. You have to write up, not down. Children are demanding. They are the most attentive, curious, eager, observant, sensitive, quick and generally congenial readers on earth. They accept, almost without question, anything you present them with, as long as it is presented honestly, fearlessly and clearly.

And Katherine Paterson[18] has described what she presents to children (all of us) this way:

> That the good life, far from ending in childhood, barely begins there. That maturity is more to be desired than immaturity, knowledge than ignorance, understanding than confusion, perspective than self-absorption. That true innocence is not the absence of experience but the redemption of it.[19]

SUGGESTED ACTIVITIES

1. Do your words most often limp, drag, march, swagger, waltz, pirouette, polka, jitterbug, or stumble? Try describing yourself in one paragraph in your normal prose. Then describe yourself in three of the styles suggested above. For example, you might try to describe yourself in dragging words, waltzing words, and jitterbugging words. (This is good practice for writing in different moods and voices.) Take your choice, and see how different the descriptions turn out. I think that break-dance words are what Shakespeare wrote at his wittiest and wildest.

2. Tom Swifties are sentences in which an adverb describes the way something was spoken so that there is a coincidental overlap of meaning. Here are several I made up in a rush to include here. "I want my parka," she said coldly. "I should join Weight Watchers," he said heavily. "I have a knife," she said pointedly. "I prefer to eat at McDonald's," he said archly. "My battery is leaking," she said acidly. "Shut the window," he said airily. Sometimes the coincidental adverb modifies an adjective, as in "I have a relatively large family." "That

was a ridiculously silly clown." (Sometimes the verb itself creates the coincidence. "I live in Florida," he stated. "I'm getting dressed," she snapped. "Stop hounding me," he barked. "I play a piccolo," he piped.) Using the following adverbs and others that occur to you, see how many Tom Swifties you can come up with: *limply, brokenly, offhandedly, dolefully, sharply, doggedly, cattily, sheepishly, gamely, saucily, testily, lamely, stiffly, fittingly, loftily, hotly, crisply, frankly, fruitlessly, softly, sweetly, diplomatically.*

3. Using Louis Untermeyer's plan for a preconstructed sonnet, put the name of some friend or relative into the title and think of an adequate number of rhyming words for ending the lines. Then get the poem written with as much appropriate meaning as possible. Proper sonnets have five heavy beats to each line (with a light beat before each heavy beat), but most people find proper rhymes and sense more urgent than the metrical pattern. Proper sonnets are serious and even lofty in tone, but under the circumstances yours may not turn out to be entirely serious. Nevertheless, the person you chose to write it for may enjoy it.

4. What are your favorite children's books? Do you still read children's literature? Write a one-page opening for a children's book that you would like to read. It could be for any age from preschoolers to young adolescents. Summarize two or three alternative courses that the story might take if you write it in its entirety.

NOTES

[1] Katherine Paterson, writer of realistic fiction, began her essay "The Perilous Realms of Realism" by admitting "deep down within myself I believe that the *real* writers are the poets and that crowding the poets in the hierarchy of literature are the fantasists. You'll notice that when my characters read books they tend to read fantasy — fairy tales or C. S. Lewis or Tolkien." Katherine Paterson, *Gates of Excellence* (New York: Elsevier/Nelson, 1981), 68–69.

[2] Kenneth Brown, *Inventors at Work* (Redmond, Wash.: Microsoft, 1987).

[3] Randall Jarrell, *The Bat Poet* (New York: Macmillan, 1963). Illustrations by Maurice Sendak. Jarrell died at the height of his career, shortly after publication of this book. The bat's story can be read as Jarrell's statement about his own life work and approaching death.

[4] Michael C. M. Huey, "Giving Budding Poets Roots," *The Christian Science Monitor* (February 26, 1988), 19.

[5] John Crowe Ransom, "Janet Waking," in *Exploring Poetry*, edited by M. L. Rosenthal and A. J. M. Smith (New York: Macmillan, 1955), 6–7.

Beautifully Janet slept
Till it was deeply morning. She woke then
And thought about her dainty-feathered hen,
To see how it had kept.

One kiss she gave her mother,
Only a small one gave she to her daddy
Who would have kissed each curl of his shining baby;
No kiss at all for her brother.

"Old Chucky, Old Chucky!" she cried,
Running on little pink feet upon the grass
To Chucky's house, and listening. But alas,
Her Chucky had died.

It was a transmogrifying bee
Came droning down on Chucky's old bald head
And sat and put the poison. It scarcely bled,
But how exceedingly

And purply did the knot
Swell with the venom and communicate
Its rigor! Now the poor comb stood up straight
But Chucky did not.

So there was Janet
Kneeling on the wet grass, crying her brown hen
(Translated far beyond the daughters of men)
To rise and walk upon it.

And weeping fast as she had breath
Janet implored us, "Wake her from her sleep!"
And would not be instructed in how deep
Was the forgetful kingdom of death.

⁶Richard Wilbur wrote to me, "I am delighted by Marjory Fleming's bad turkey poem, and also by the fact that you offer my 'Black November Turkey' as a *good* turkey poem." "A Black November Turkey," in *The Pocket Book of Modern Verse*, edited by Oscar Williams (New York: Pocket Books, 1954), 613–614. Permission for reprinting this poem was granted by Harcourt Brace Jovanovich.

Nine white chickens come
With haunchy walk and heads
Jabbing among the chips, the chaff, the stones
And the cornhusk-shreds.

And bit by bit infringe
A pond of dusty light,

Spectral in shadow until they bobbingly one
　　By one ignite.

Neither pale nor bright,
　　The turkey-cock parades
Through radiant squalors, darkly auspicious as
　　The ace of spades.

Himself his own cortege
　　And puffed with the pomp of death,
Rehearsing over and over with strangled rale
　　His latest breath.

The vast black body floats
　　Above the crossing knees
As a cloud over thrashed branches, a calm ship
　　Over choppy seas,

Shuddering its fan and feathers
　　In fine soft clashes
With the cold sound that the wind makes, fondling
　　Paper-ashes.

The pale-blue bony head
　　Set on its shepherd's-crook
Like a saint's death-mask, turns a vague, superb
　　And timeless look

Upon these clucking hens
　　And the cocks that one by one,
Dawn after mortal dawn, with vulgar joy
　　Acclaim the sun.

[7] I recommend *Sound and Sense: An Introduction to Poetry* by Laurence Perrine (New York: Harcourt, Brace and Company, 1956). This overview, richly illustrated by many poems, includes chapters on the nature of poetry, how to read poetry, denotation and connotation, imagery, figurative language, allusion, meaning and idea, tone, musical devices, rhythm and meter, sound and meaning, pattern, and degrees of excellence.

[8] Huey, "Giving Poets Roots," 19.

[9] Robert Siegel, "Participation," *The Generation of 2000: Contemporary American Poets*, edited by William Hayen (Princeton, N.J.: Ontario Review Press, 1984), 280–283.

[10] Eddie Espinoza wrote his popular worship songs "I Only Want to Love You," "Change My Heart Oh God," "You Are the Mighty King," and "Blessed Be Thy Name" as if by dictation. But others, such as "Lord, I Love You," "Lord I'll Seek After You," and "Every Breath" required much rewriting. Espinoza discusses the writing of simple worship songs in his article "Songwriting: An Act of Love," in the spring 1988 issue of *Worship Update* (pp. 9–10), a quarterly publication of the Worship Resource Center of Vineyard Ministries International.

[11] Louis Untermeyer, "Versed Aid to the Injured," *Heavens* (New York: Harcourt, 1922), 113–118.

[12] The answer to this riddle is Eve. She lived in the Garden of Eden, she was married to Adam when she was created, and although she died and was buried, she had never been born.

[13] The word malapropism came from the name of Mrs. Malaprop, a character in Sheridan's play *The Rivals* in 1775. She misapplied words constantly.

[14] Willard R. Espy, *The Game of Words* (New York: Bramhall House, 1972). I also recommend John G. Fuller's *Games for Insomniacs* (Garden City, N.Y.: Doubleday, 1966).

[15] Flora Lewis completed her sermon parody as she had begun it:

We have seen that she was old and lonely, and we now see that she was poor. For, mark the words, *the* cupboard. The one humble little cupboard the poor widow possessed. And why did she go to the cupboard? Was it to bring forth golden goblets or glittering precious stones, or costly apparel, or feast on any other attributes of wealth? *It was to get her poor dog a bone*. Not only was the widow poor, but the dog, the sole prop of her old age, was poor too. We can imagine the scene. The poor dog, crouching in the corner, looking wistfully at the solitary cupboard, and the widow going to that cupboard in hope, in expectation maybe, to open it, although we are not distinctly told that it was not ajar or half open, to open it for that poor dog. "But when she got there, the cupboard was bare, and so the poor dog got none."

"When she got there." You see, dear brethren, the persistence in doing right. She got there. There were no turnings and twistings, no slippings and slidings, no leanings to the right or falterings to the left; with glorious simplicity, we are told that she got there. And how was her noble effort rewarded? "The cupboard was bare."

It was bare. There were to be found neither oranges nor cheesecake nor penny buns nor ginger bread, nor crackers nor nuts, nor lucifer matches. The cupboard was bare. There was but one, only one in the whole of that cottage, and that one, the sole hope of the widow and the glorious lodestar of the poor dog, was bare. Had there been a leg of mutton, a loin of lamb, a fillet of veal, or even an ice from Gunter's, the case would have been different, the incident would have been otherwise. But it was bare, my brethren, bare as a bald head, bare as an infant born without a caul.

Many of you will probably say, with all the pride of worldly sophistry, — "The widow no doubt went out and bought the dog a biscuit." Ah! No! Far removed from earthly ideas, these mundane desires, poor Mother Hubbard, the widow, whom many thoughtless worldlings would despise, in that she owned only one cupboard, perceived — or might I even say, saw — at once the relentless logic of the situation, and yielded to it with all the heroism of that nature which had enabled her without deviation to reach her barren cupboard.

She did not attempt, like the stiff necked scoffers of this generation, to war against the inevitable; she did not try, like the so-called men of science, to explain what she did not understand. She did nothing. The poor dog had none. And then at this point our information ceases. But do we not know sufficient? Are we not cognisant enough?

Who would dare to pierce the veil that shrouds the ulterior fate of Old Mother Hubbard — the poor dog — the cupboard, or the bone that was not there? Must we imagine her still standing at the open cupboard door, depict to ourselves the dog still drooping his disappointed tail upon the floor, the sought for bone still remaining somewhere else? Ah! my dear brethren, we are not so permitted to attempt to read the future. Suffice it for us to attempt to glean from this beautiful story its many lessons; suffice it for us to apply them, to study them so far as in us lies, and, bearing in mind the natural frailty of our natures, to avoid being widows; to shun the patronymic Hubbard; to have, if our means afford it, more than one cupboard in our house, and to keep stores in them all.

And Oh! my dear friends, keeping in recollection what we have learnt this day, let us avoid keeping dogs that are fond of bones! But brethren, if we do; if fate has ordained that we should do any of these things, let us then go as Mother Hubbard did, straight, without curvetting or prancing, to our cupboard, empty though it may be — let us, like her, accept the inevitable with calm steadfastness, and should we, like her, ever be left with a hungry dog and an empty cupboard, may future chroniclers be able to write of us in the beautiful words of our text,

"And so the poor dog got none."

(This sermon is found on pages 213–214 of the Lewis family papers donated by Warren Lewis to the Wade Center at Wheaton College in Illinois. It is published here with permission.)

[16] Cornelius Plantinga, Jr., "Like a Shot to the Heart," *The Reformed Journal* (January 1988), 4–5.

[17] For an overview of the brief history and rich highlights of children's literature, I recommend my own survey *How To Grow a Young Reader* coauthored with John Lindskoog (Wheaton, Il: Harold Shaw Publishers, 1989).

[18] In prizewinning children's author Katherine Paterson's moving keynote speech that launched 1989 as the Year of the Young Reader for the Library of Congress, she called for the United States to start to take more seriously the children entrusted to our care. She also affirmed the naturalness of writing: "The poet William Stafford, when asked when he decided to become a poet, says: 'My question is, When did other people give up the idea of being a poet?' You know, when we are kids we make things; we write, and for *me* the puzzle is not that

some people are still writing; the real question is 'why did the other people stop?' "

"The Year of the Young Reader is a year for us all. We can learn from the young how once again to come to the printed page with wonder and excitement and a humility which allows delight and compassion to flourish." (As reported in "Sticking to a Dream: Year of the Young Reader is Officially Launched," *Publishers Weekly*, (December 23, 1988), 34.)

[19]Katherine Paterson, "A Song of Innocence and Experience," *Gates of Excellence*, (Elsevier/Nelson Books: New York, 1981), 52.

Chapter 7

A Foot in
the Door

*Writing is the only profession where no one considers you
ridiculous if you earn no money.*

— JULES RENARD

"Aha! Then why do you spend so much of your life writing?" We were relaxing over coffee and dessert, and when Sven found out that I was earning very little money from my books he pounced on me.[1]

We had run into Sven and Elisabeth and their husky baby boy a few months earlier when they arrived at Los Angeles International Airport and no one came to meet them. We became their first American friends. We heard about how Sven had exchanged homes and engineering professorships with an American for one school year, and month by month we heard about unexpected problems they ran into.

The apartment here was in bad condition. We had freak weather that year. The baby had constant health problems. They missed the free medical care and helpful grandparents they had left in Sweden. On top of everything else, they heard that their possessions were being damaged by the family that was using their home in their absence.

But Sven was satisfied anyway. He was already planning their next trip abroad, and his face glowed when he told us of the many different countries he had visited when he was single. Then he turned his attention back to me.

"Why do you spend so much of your life writing?" The question was obviously an accusation that I was an impractical person. Elisabeth's current hobby was quilting.

I had to pause a moment. Then I looked him right in the eye.

"I write for the very same reason you travel," I answered. "To explore the world and enrich my mind."

He saw what I meant and broke into a smile. We understood each other after that.

But I hadn't given him a full answer. For one thing, I think that if a child's attempt to create something good is cherished by a loving parent, then it stands to reason that an adult's attempt to create something good is cherished by God. And as John Ruskin said, "The highest reward for a man's toil is not what he gets for it, but what he becomes by it." In that sense any writer can be successful, whether the writing is published or unpublished, read or unread.

Writers often insult as well as praise their own profession. The marvelous playwright Molière was being witty and irreverent as usual when he gave us his tongue-in-cheek explanation of why writers write:

> Writing is like prostitution.
> First you do it for the love of it.
> Then you do it for a few friends.
> And finally you do it for money.

Winston Churchill made writing sound even worse: "Writing is an adventure. To begin with, it is a toy and an amusement. Then it becomes a mistress, then it becomes a master, then it becomes a tyrant." No one should take Molière and Churchill too seriously on this point; they are basically warning writers not to slip away from love and adventure into too much commercialism or drudgery.

Personally, I would rather spend my time teaching and reading — or taking trips and making quilts like Sven and Elisabeth — unless my writing really pays off. The payoff might be inner or outer, mental, physical or spiritual. It might be service to others or harmless amusement.

The apartment here was in bad condition. We had freak weather that year. The baby had constant health problems. They missed the free medical care and helpful grandparents they had left in Sweden. On top of everything else, they heard that their possessions were being damaged by the family that was using their home in their absence.

But Sven was satisfied anyway. He was already planning their next trip abroad, and his face glowed when he told us of the many different countries he had visited when he was single. Then he turned his attention back to me.

"Why do you spend so much of your life writing?" The question was obviously an accusation that I was an impractical person. Elisabeth's current hobby was quilting.

I had to pause a moment. Then I looked him right in the eye. "I write for the very same reason you travel," I answered. "To explore the world and enrich my mind."

He saw what I meant and broke into a smile. We understood each other after that.

But I hadn't given him a full answer. For one thing, I think that if a child's attempt to create something good is cherished by a loving parent, then it stands to reason that an adult's attempt to create something good is cherished by God. And as John Ruskin said, "The highest reward for a man's toil is not what he gets for it, but what he becomes by it." In that sense any writer can be successful, whether the writing is published or unpublished, read or unread.

Writers often insult as well as praise their own profession. The marvelous playwright Molière was being witty and irreverent as usual when he gave us his tongue-in-cheek explanation of why writers write:

Writing is like prostitution.
First you do it for the love of it.
Then you do it for a few friends.
And finally you do it for money.

Winston Churchill made writing sound even worse: "Writing is an adventure. To begin with, it is a toy and an amusement. Then it becomes a mistress, then it becomes a master, then it becomes a tyrant." No one should take Molière and Churchill too seriously on this point; they are basically warning writers not to slip away from love and adventure into too much commercialism or drudgery.

Personally, I would rather spend my time teaching and reading — or taking trips and making quilts like Sven and Elisabeth — unless my writing really pays off. The payoff might be inner or outer, mental, physical or spiritual. It might be service to others or harmless amusement.

Chapter 7

A Foot in the Door

Writing is the only profession where no one considers you ridiculous if you earn no money.

— JULES RENARD

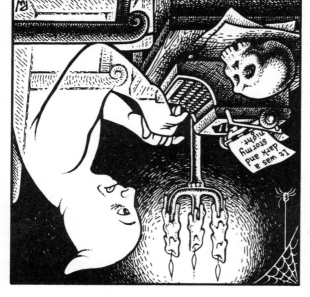

"Aha! Then why do you spend so much of your life writing?"

We were relaxing over coffee and dessert, and when Sven found out that I was earning very little money from my books he pounced on me.[1]

We had run into Sven and Elisabeth and their husky baby boy a few months earlier when they arrived at Los Angeles International Airport and no one came to meet them. We became their first American friends. We heard about how Sven had exchanged homes and engineering professorships with an American for one school year, and month by month we heard about unexpected problems they ran into.

(formerly Kenny David) assured Dr. Glynn that he would be granted full immunity from prosecution.

In 1988 an unusually short whimsical letter appeared in the *Christian Science Monitor* in reply to an essay about the evolution of paper clips. The writer announced, "My research proves conclusively that the paper clip is merely the larval stage of the wire coat hanger." British novelist P. G. Wodehouse struck that same droll style when he claimed, "Every author really wants to have letters printed in the paper. Unable to make the grade, he drops down a rung of the ladder and writes novels."

Fillers are an even humbler form of publication than letters to the editor, but they usually bring a small payment, if only ten dollars. They are the potato chips of journalism. Many people submit special kinds of fillers to *Reader's Digest* according to directions in the magazine, but only a few of them are chosen. Various periodicals buy handy hints, bits of verse, parenting tips, anecdotes, little-known facts, jokes, riddles, puzzles, or aphorisms. (My favorite aphorism at this stage of life is by Sheldon Vanauken: "God gives us many gifts, but never permanence: that we must seek in His arms.") A writer is wise to collect all kinds of snippets in a notebook and keep them on hand for possible use.

The wife of a public relations man once combined her mother's list of handy hints with her own and spent $25,000 of her own money to publish 50,000 copies of a spiral-bound booklet she called *Mary Ellen's Best of Helpful Hints*. She was so good at promotion that in six years she had sold seven million copies. By that time her first book and two sequels offering more of the same had earned her over $2.3 million. Needless to say, her shortcut publishing success makes many serious authors exasperated. They might call her books non-books, but her fortune is not a non-fortune.

Don Marquis claimed, "If you want to get rich from writing, write the sort of thing that's read by persons who move their lips when they're reading to themselves." It is true that the easiest books to write and to read are often the easiest to sell. The general public prefers snack reading, not steak reading.

Jo Petty hasn't made as much money as Mary Ellen Pinkham, but she didn't invest $25,000 and do her own marketing. And she didn't do her own writing. She simply clipped and collected other people's wise quotations. In 1964 the C. R. Gibson Company published her collection in a ninety-page book called *Apples of Gold*.[4] With no advertising and no reviews, the book sold 7000 copies in its first month and then 75,000 per year. It has sold well over three million copies so far. (Sales between 5000 and 10,000 are normal.) Petty's first sequel, *Wings of Silver*, has now sold two million copies, and there are also four later sequels.

excellent writing practice. It is fairly easy to get a letter into a school paper or a hometown paper, but there is great competition when it comes to saying your say in response to items in a national periodical. *Newsweek* gets well over a thousand letters to the editor every week.

If you really want to influence readers who do not know the facts or hold your opinion, concentrate on clarity and brevity and use catchy wording or a powerful punch if you can.

According to Melvin Maddocks, writing whimsical letters to editors is a traditional sport in England, and in play or in earnest those letters often take trivial things seriously. (Virginia Graham claims that English papers are full of silly letters from the middle of July to the end of August.) When Americans copy the huffy English style, as they do in most literary or academic journals, all the outraged sniffing and snorting seems a bit out of place. The best American correspondents, according to Maddocks, are a bit brusque, aggrieved, moralistic, and belligerent. They give the impression that what the writer really wanted to do was to punch somebody in the nose. Unfortunately, today the letter columns of major American newspapers are increasingly given over to pronouncements from officials and lobbyists, squeezing out many of the entertaining letter writers who used to fill those columns. Where can squeezed-out writers go to get a hearing? To the call-in talk shows, maybe.[3] But that isn't the same at all.

I have only once been on a call-in talk show (asking a Los Angeles expert about some science fiction), but through the years I have had brief letters published in *Newsweek*, *Human Behavior*, the *Christian Science Monitor*, *Saturday Evening Post*, *Insight*, *Prevention*, the *Los Angeles Times*, and other secular periodicals, as well as in periodicals such as *Christian Century*, *Christianity Today*, *Eternity*, *His*, *New Oxford Review*, and *Reformed Journal*. I only wrote when I had something I really wanted to say, and it was always fun to get a hearing. It makes sense to notice in advance what kinds of letters are usually selected in a given periodical and to send timely letters in as quickly as possible.

One of my all-time favorite letters appeared in the *Los Angeles Times* in 1987 in response to an article about a former state senator who was changing his first name to Senator. The letter writer said that now his fifteen-year-old son David Glynn had decided to change his first name to Doctor and his last name to Ph.D. Although this might seem legally questionable, the boy's fifteen-year-old friend Attorney Kenneth Burdick, J. D. (formerly Kenny Burdick) assured him that it was legal. And in case Burdick was mistaken, fourteen-year-old President Joseph Kim (formerly Joe Kim) and fifteen-year-old Chief Justice Kenneth David five words or less why she liked Plymouth automobiles. If she lived out her normal life expectancy, this would come to about $12,000 per word for her entry.

Writing contests are a tantalizing project for aspiring authors, although they lead to lots of disappointment for optimistic enterers. (A million people entered the contest that Deborah Schneider won.) I won prizes in a couple of twenty-five words or less contests and a few essay contests when I was a girl, but for all the effort I put into various contests the average profit was nil. Then many years later my old dreams came true when I won a $1000 first prize in a national 300-word essay contest. I earned an incredible $3.33 per word for that essay. Since no one published it, I was free to use it myself later in one of my books. I can guarantee that it is far more fun to win a contest than to go on losing, and it is also far more fun to be read than to be unread.

Solomon warned us that the race is not always to the swift, and certainly writing awards from the Nobel Prize on down are not always won by the best writers. I saw a vivid example of that once when some of us English instructors required our students to enter a college essay contest. A small team of judges chose three winners, presented handsome gift books to them at a private reception, and printed the three winning essays in a souvenir booklet.

The first-place essay was by one of my students and was only fair. The second-place essay by another of my students was only fair. But the third-place essay by a stranger was outstanding. In fact, it was so outstanding that I recognized the very first sentence and all the rest of it. I had read those exact words a few months earlier when this essay appeared in the "My Turn" column in Newsweek. The student who had submitted this essay failed to come to the reception to claim her prize, and no wonder. She was guilty of plagiarism. Yet the unsuspecting judges had ranked her sparkling professional-quality essay lower than two very ordinary student entries. The judges hadn't known a first-class essay when they saw one.

Contest losers are apt to doubt that judges have perfect judgment. They are right. And that is true wherever writers compete for pay or publication. Chance is a major factor in all of life.

Breaking into Print

Goodman Ace was only joking when he said, "I won't buy a magazine that will publish what I write." I advise people to try writing letters to the periodicals they read. A letters column is usually one of the most popular features in a magazine. Brief, pithy opinion letters are

It might be self-fulfillment or fame or friends or fortune. But without enough payoff, writing strikes me as a miserable way to pass the years. It means too much isolation and too much typing.

That is why I like to help people who feel bound to write. The world has enough suffering in it without unsuccessful writing, which is a bit like unsuccessful farming. I wouldn't want to farm unless it gave me health and joy or else I got a decent crop of some kind. Serious farming is hard and risky work in the long run, and so is serious writing. In the sweat of our brows we farm or write, and we are bound to hope for some harvest.

Going Public

The harvest that most writers want most is reaching readers. Some writers are content in not being published and read, but they are the minority. Even reclusive Emily Dickinson tried to get some poems published. Most writers long ardently for publication. Some feel as strongly as the successful but depressed poet Sylvia Plath: "Nothing stinks like a pile of unpublished writing." Unless one is content to be a private writer, one needs to consider various ways of going public.[2]

Sinclair Lewis advised young writers to work hard and start at the top if possible. "It's utterly true that to learn to write one has to write and write and *write!*" he said to his friend Charles Breasted. "And if you can possibly avoid it don't waste your energies on short stories and stuff for ephemeral publication. Write *books.* Write at least eight hundred words a day, if possible a thousand — work in a bare room with nothing in it but a table, a chair, and a typewriter, and enough light — but *no view!* I wrote *Our Mrs. Wrenn* while commuting on Long Island Railroad trains to my blurb-writing job at Doubleday, Doran's. One competent full-length book will do more to establish the prestige of a potential writer than a flood of short pieces."

Sinclair Lewis's advice is all good, but much good advice about writing contradicts other equally good advice. There are many ways to get happily or unhappily published — although beginning writers don't usually believe that any kind of publication could ever be unhappy. The fact is that some writers are so disappointed by flaws in their publications that they wish they had never been published after all, and certain unknown writers who are never published feel highly successful anyway. I refer to contest writers. I knew a journalism teacher who supplemented her income by making contests into a part-time career. She won all kinds of appliances and other prizes including a boat.

The highest-paid writer in history is a woman named Deborah Schneider who in 1958 won $500 per month for life for telling in twenty-

If Petty didn't use the following quotation, she should have: "Next to the originator of a good sentence is the first quoter of it." — Ralph Waldo Emerson. Books or articles made up of other people's words can be creative in themselves. A man I knew once wrote his first article for a national magazine that way, and he was thrilled when it was published. But the article was made up entirely of C. S. Lewis's passages, and he didn't realize he had to get permission and pay a fee. He got caught. When I asked him what happened, he was too embarrassed and depressed to tell me.

Writers can quote freely as much as they want from older works of literature which are in the public domain and, according to the law of fair use, brief excerpts from more recent prose.[5] In specific cases, fair use sometimes has to be decided in court. Up to at least fifty words of prose is usually free for quotation without permission, although people often ask the author as a courtesy. Hardly any recent poetry or verse can be quoted in print legally without permission, especially from the lyrics of popular songs.

Songs are jealously guarded. For example, Birchtree Ltd. music publishing company owned 50,000 copyrighted songs, including "Happy Birthday to You." Although the ditty was written by a pair of kindergarten teachers in 1893, it was not copyrighted until 1935; and it remains the property of copyright holders until 2010. In 1988 Birchtree was able to sell that particular song to Warner Chappell for twenty-five million dollars, because annual royalties for any commercial use of the song come to one million dollars a year. (Beware of having people sing that traditional song in anything you write for publication.)

Writers of prose are sometimes appalled by the fact that they can't quote snatches of well-known songs unless they get permission. Columnist Jimmy Breslin says, "I can remember standing in the snow in front of Irving Berlin's house in a snowfall on Christmas Eve and everybody was singing 'White Christmas' and all I wanted to do was see Irving Berlin's face so I could yell at him that I didn't like him." That was because Jimmy Breslin once had to make costly changes in the galleys of a book when Irving Berlin refused him permission to quote three words from a song.

Judging the Competition

Literary egos and literary feuds never fail to amuse and intrigue the public. Perhaps that is partly because writers so often enjoy praising their favorite books by other writers. Readers are fascinated on those rare occasions when writers turn into mud wrestlers bashing each other's books:

Ernest Hemingway on Norman Mailer: "The whole book's just diarrhea of the typewriter."

Ernest Hemingway on William Faulkner: "He can't write without a quart of rye at his elbow."

Norman Mailer: "Hemingway has never written anything that would disturb an eight-year-old."

Oscar Wilde on Henry James: "Mr. Henry James writes fiction as if it were a painful duty."

Vladimir Nabokov on Fyodor Dostoevsky: "A claptrap journalist and a slapdash comedian."

Charles Baudelaire on George Sand: "She is stupid, she is heavy-handed, she is a gossip."

George Bernard Shaw on Homer and Shakespeare: "With the single exception of Homer, there is no eminent writer, not even Sir Walter Scott, whom I can despise so entirely as I despise Shakespeare when I measure my mind against his."

Book authors have an everlasting love-hate relationship with book reviewers. Over a century ago James Russell Lowell expressed this exasperation in verse:

Nature fits all her children with something to do;
He who would write and can't write, can surely review.

More recently Kenneth Tynan, a literary critic who studied under C. S. Lewis, admitted, "A critic is a man who knows the way but can't drive the car." And author Jim Bishop approached the subject from the other direction: "A good writer is not, per se, a good book critic. No more than a good drunk is automatically a good bartender."

But of course many good writers make good book reviewers.[6] Editors are often awash in free review copies of books which they are glad to send to competent reviewers. Unfortunately, this kind of assignment is extremely time-consuming if it is done right (I don't understand how people can be so unkind as to write reviews without reading the books thoroughly, but it happens all the time), and there is often no pay beyond the free book. A well-written review can aid the book author; it can warn, advise, inform, inspire, or entertain the magazine readers; and it can please the magazine editor — who may later buy articles from the book reviewer.

Authors are immensely grateful when they feel understood by reviewers. On rare occasions they call or write to express their thanks. A wonderful surprise came to an ex-student of mine when she reviewed a book by John Updike in *Radix*. He actually reviewed her review in response:

> Be it not for a writer to judge his critics. But Lucy Sullivan's review of *Problems* (Jan.–Feb. '81) seemed on the mark to me, though I'm not sure a stiffer dose of St. Augustine is what I'm prescribing. Indeed, I'm not prescribing anything, just trying to describe what of the Lord's world comes within my ken. I have faith that whatever is real is probably holy and certainly useful, and within that sense of things feel free from any need to press any specifically Christian point home.
>
> John Updike
> Georgetown, MA[7]

Assorted Articles

It is one short step from book reviewing to other article writing, and indeed some book reviews merge right into other categories. There are many overlapping ways to label articles: reviews, interviews, anecdotes, editorials, columns, think-pieces, devotions, inspiration, humor, how-to, first-person narrative, personality sketch, nostalgia piece, consumer advice, problem solving, information, instruction, and indoctrination, among others. I tend to put all articles into two groups: (1) those that help, delight, teach, amuse, motivate, or inspire, and (2) those that don't.

Interviews with people who have unusual positions, experiences or accomplishments are especially popular today. Because interviews put writers on the spot in a special way, I gathered some pointers for beginners. Since then I was interviewed in English by a graduate student visiting here from Italy, and she followed all the rules without having heard of any of them. They are just good common sense.

1. Identify yourself extremely clearly and say exactly why you are requesting the privilege of interviewing your subject.

2. Set the exact time and place, including the time when you expect to leave. One hour is reasonable for an interview. Be definite, and stick to your plan unless your subject changes it. Arrange to check again before the appointment to make sure that it is still suitable to your subject.

3. If you want to use a tape recorder, ask for permission in advance, explaining that a tape recorder eliminates any possible misquotations. Abide by your subject's preference.

4. The subject's home is ideal for the interview. If that is not

available, try to choose a private spot. A meal makes interviewing difficult.

5. Learn what you can about your subject in advance. If your subject is a writer, read some of her published writing.

6. Arrive in modest, appropriate attire, equipped with writing tools and tape recorder ready for use. Establish your appreciation and friendliness immediately.

7. Face your subject directly, at a comfortable distance of three or four feet if possible.

8. Begin with easy questions (avoid questions with yes/no answers), and expect the subject to lead the way once she gets started. Listen eagerly, nod in encouragement, and don't interrupt if you can help it. Let the subject do the talking.

9. Make doubly sure that you understood everything correctly. An interview is a friendly conversation with increased accuracy.

10. Be agreeable and save any touchy questions for the end. Then make sure that your subject feels good before you part.

11. Be ready to catch things that pop out after the interview has formally ended. Afterthoughts are often the choicest statements.

12. Never use information if your subject warns you not to do so before she tells it to you. Keep any promises you make about confidentiality. Distinguish between the four levels of confidentiality:

a. *Off the record* means that you may not tell the facts or the name of the person who wants the facts kept secret.

b. *Deep background* means that you may tell the facts but may not mention anything at all about your source.

c. *Not for attribution* means that you can refer to the source vaguely but not so the source can be identified.

d. *Not for direct quotation* means that you can name your source but may not use any of her exact words.

13. Ask for permission to call back and check on details if necessary.

14. Offer the subject a copy of the tape recording, a copy of your article before publication, or a copy of the publication.

15. Don't hesitate to rearrange your material when writing it up. Put it into any order that will work well.

16. Turn the casual spoken English into standard written English when you directly quote your subject, leaving out meaningless confusion and repetition. Correct any little slips of the tongue or other accidental but insignificant errors as a courtesy to your subject.

Interviews can be written up in a variety of ways, from question-and-answer format to personality sketches. It is usually best to evoke the reader's senses early in the interview by giving an impression of the physical setting and some clothing or gestures of the subject. Ideally, this will reinforce the tone and content of the interview.

Although interviews are a popular way to break into print, personal articles are by nature quicker and easier to produce. They require no appointments and little or no research. All they require is the ability to draw upon your own inner and outer life in order to inform, challenge, entertain, or inspire readers. And, as Marjorie Holmes points out, these articles are natural springboards to creative nonfiction books.[8]

The Truth about Fiction

Just as articles sometimes grow into nonfiction books, short stories sometimes grow into novels. But it is vastly harder to get short stories published than to get articles published. And it is harder to get novels published than nonfiction. In fact, only fifteen percent of the books in print now in our country are adult fiction; the same number as our science and technology books. There are reportedly only about 2000 new novels and 2000 new short stories published here annually. No matter how few short stories and novels get published, however, people won't stop writing them. They are a favorite art form.

Some fiction writers get good ideas from their dreams and consciously expect help from them. Many get ideas from real events they hear about, just the way Flaubert got the plot of *Madame Bovary*. All writers draw from their own lives; Flannery O'Connor said about writing fiction, "Anybody who has survived his childhood has enough information about life to last him the rest of his days." Willa Cather claimed, "There are only two or three human stories, and they go on repeating themselves as fiercely as if they had never happened before."

Someone has made up a list of these ten basic plots that most short stories embody:

1. The sympathetic protagonist overcomes obstacles and setbacks to achieve a difficult goal with his own efforts.

2. The destructive protagonist seeks to harm a sympathetic character and almost succeeds, but at the last minute he is defeated and perhaps punished.

3. A sympathetic protagonist makes a choice that surprises him by causing a bad crisis; he must surmount this setback and succeeds.

4. A sympathetic protagonist almost achieves a destructive goal and then sees that it is wrong and changes his course, becoming a better person.

5. A sympathetic protagonist is suffering, but a new point of view

or sense of meaning helps him to accept his life situation with peace or gratitude.

6. A protagonist with some negative way of living undergoes a trauma that causes him to reform.

7. A degenerating protagonist comes to a point where he might start to improve, but he wastes the opportunity and resumes his downhill course.

8. A sympathetic protagonist pursues a worthy goal, but he is defeated in spite of his goodness.

9. The evil protagonist pursues a bad goal and achieves it.

10. A morally or mentally deficient protagonist remains unimproved in spite of appeals or opportunities for growth. This is a common theme in literary fiction, not in more popular fiction.

Short stories vary from one page to about forty typed pages (10,000 words) in length, but most of them are between twelve pages (3000 words) and twenty-eight pages (7000 words) in length. Typical books today are 50,000 words or 200 typed pages in length, at about twenty-five 60-character lines or 250 words per page. Obviously, the average book is apt to be about as long as ten average short stories. This rule of thumb is of no great value except for helping authors to evaluate Sinclair Lewis's advice about concentrating on books instead of floods of shorter pieces.

The easiest way to get a short story published is to tailor it for a special-interest periodical that you have read, such as a horse-lovers' magazine or a Baptist youth paper. The easiest way to get a novel published is to write genre fiction — romance, adventure, spy thriller, science fiction, horror, western, war, gothic, fantasy, or mystery.

It is common for literary people to sneer at genre fiction, assuming that it is made up of cardboard characters, formula plots, and cliches. But as genre writer Richard Matheson likes to point out, some genre fiction is excellent. It is not fair to condemn genre fiction and then to pretend that the excellent genre stories are not genre stories at all. Whether they involve love, murder, cowboys, or Mars, all stories should be about *people*. We write about people and their lives and relationships. The three basic types of plots are a person against nature, one person against another, and a person against himself. That is true in any fiction.

Lawrence Block, author of *Telling Lies for Fun and Profit*,[9] has published many detective novels as well as other books. In his short story "One Thousand Dollars a Word" a fictitious author of detective stories had been writing quality stories for twenty years and was still getting the pay he had started with — a nickel a word. During that period candy bars had gone up from a nickel to forty cents. The detective story magazine had gone up from a quarter to a dollar. Even typing paper had gone way up. Only the price of authors' words did not go up.

The magazine editor received so many stories from eager young writers that he didn't have to pay more; he could always publish less professional stories. So one day the despairing author decided to change his career and go from a nickel a word to one thousand dollars a word. He typed out something short and to the point. It started, "I've got a gun. Please fill this paper sack with thirty thousand dollars. . . ."[10] Then he went to the bank.

Block reportedly told Charles Wrong that his story exaggerates nothing in its description of what happens to people who write for mystery magazines. Low pay has driven most serious story writers away. Instead of robbing banks, however, I guess that they are ghostwriting.

Ghostwriting Horror Stories

Our nation is haunted by ghostwriters. They used to be considered literary sharecroppers, but some of them live like courtiers now.

William Novak was already the author of three books of his own when he was hired to write the autobiography of Lee Iacocca for $45,000. Bantam rejected it halfway through because it was too well written and didn't sound like Iacocca, so Novak tried again and succeeded. The book was such an extraordinary bestseller that it made its ghostwriter famous and led to far more extravagant contracts. Now he is called the King of Ghosts. He chooses only a few of the rich and famous people who ask him to write for them for enormous amounts of money.

Samuel Johnson claimed, "Sir, you may be a king or a chimney sweep, but if you cannot write, you are nobody." Today it seems that if you don't pretend you can write, you are nobody. It appears that half the people in the country have ghostwriters or hope to get one. Kings, chimney sweeps, politicians, executives, entertainers, college presidents, preachers, newscasters, pilots, prostitutes — anyone newsworthy or wanting to be newsworthy wants a ghostwriter. I think this is part of the celebrity cult we live in. A friend of mine served so well as ghostwriter for an unknown man related to a movie star that the man and his interesting book were written up in *People* magazine — although the ghostwriter wasn't mentioned.

Here is the most recent proposal that I've received:

> Kathryn, I have a scenario in my head for a book — one that would make a fabulous movie. Really it is a story, incorporating many life styles I've witnessed. Years ago my dad and I agreed that he and I

151

should write a book (mostly about his Social Security people experiences) and I would have to provide the "SEX". Well, I'll tell you Kathryn, providing the SEX reading then and now and I would not have qualified then, so how can I offer you help on a novel? Certainly not from an intellectual aspect, nor a literary knowledge, nor — well — well if you could put words to my feelings — oh I have words — How would it work Kathryn, could it? Did you ever consider writing a Bestseller novel — potential movie script? Would it, should it be 1st person? There are sexy parts of today's Bestsellers that I cannot bear to read to myself — I don't think THAT sort of Bestseller sex is necessary. I don't believe a true creative story teller has to resort to-to-to. I don't know what to call it. Anyhow, are you already overflowing with inspiration?

I was not. This person did not mention money, but many innocent people expect to provide some ideas or feelings, let the ghostwriter write the book and find a publisher, and then split gigantic royalties. I was delighted when I saw the opposite approach once. In the personal ads in a respectable national magazine I saw an unpublished author seeking a backer who would support him while he produced books and novels, in exchange for half his future royalties. That reminds me of Thomas Costain's statement, "I'm convinced that all writers are optimists whether they concede the point or not. How otherwise could any human being sit down to a pile of blank sheets and decide to write, say, two hundred thousand words on a given theme?"

I should write a book about people who have wanted me to write books for them. When I had surgery once an eccentric nurse decided that I must ghost a ghost story for her to make her rich, and she kept coming in to argue with me about it. A tragic woman in my church who was dying from drug abuse got the idea that I should write her tale of triumph over drugs. An executive of a world-famous charitable organization called me twice appointing me to write a book about social responsibility, then stood me up for lunch and never called again. I tried my hand at writing (for hourly pay) a psychiatrist's addled ideas about our Freudian Bible and a glamorous millionaire's life story full of politics and famous names. It turned out that the psychiatrist had been lining up new writers every few weeks for years, and the millionaire was too sick with alcoholism to carry through.

One friend of mine did worse; she was lured into a nonpaying plan by an ex-witch with multiple personalities who wanted to tell how she became healed and whole, but the woman was so erratic that she kept missing interview appointments at her own house. My friend finally got scared off. She is the same friend who created outlines for a series of booklets she was asked to write for a famous international evangelist — only to find that after her detailed plans were warmly accepted none of her calls or letters were answered anymore.

A faraway friend of mine tried to write someone's life story and then begged me to take over the book and write it for her and get it published under her name. I would have been the ghostwriter's ghostwriter. Another friend of mine really was an unsuccessful official ghostwriter's successful secret ghostwriter. It is not unusual today for an official ghostwriter to be someone on the inside track rather than a professional writer who can produce a publishable manuscript. I have not yet heard of a ghostwriter's ghostwriter's ghostwriter, but I'm sure there are some around by now.

One of the most peculiar things about ghostwriting is that from Gary Hart on down, many celebrities or would-be celebrities avoid contact with their own ghostwriters. Perhaps they look down on ghostwriters as their social inferiors, as members of the servant class. I know of one case where a famous preacher showed no interest in meeting his highly qualified new ghostwriter who happened to live about ten miles from his church. She had been selected by his publisher on the other side of the country and was supposed to write his book from material he had taped.

She signed the contract and dropped her other projects as requested, but every time she asked the publisher for the completed contract with the preacher's signature making it valid, she was told that he had too many papers on his desk and hadn't got to it yet. She never found out what was really going on. After several months, she refused to go on working any longer without a signed contract and then entered into a long, bitterly unsuccessful struggle to try to get paid for her time. Ghostwriters need a union or an agency equipped to handle their problems.

A basic risk for ghostwriters and biographers is that people can be flighty or skittish about what they want said and how they want it said. This costs the writer weeks or months of unexpected, unpaid rewriting. I have a friend who was paid a modest salary for a year while writing a woman's story, and when she canceled the book without warning at the last minute he had a temporary breakdown from the shock and disappointment. I have another friend who was halfway through a book about a Christian leader when the leader lost his post because of some scandal. Fortunately, that ghostwriter already had a hefty advance from the publisher for his time and effort. Otherwise he would have been out of luck, as some ghostwriters are.

My first venture into ghostwriting started just before Halloween in 1987. (I will thinly disguise the names to protect the guilty.) One evening while I was doing the dishes I had a call from Mr. Church at a prominent charitable organization with a booming book business. He said that he was in desperate need of a ghostwriter for an optometrist named Tiny Daniel and that I was highly recommended. If I would drop everything to produce a practical and inspirational book about eye care for Tiny in three months, I would get a $2000 advance when I started, and I would receive the final $4000 within thirty days of mid-January book completion. I was already swamped, but he informed me that this organization with an annual budget of $30 million had just moved into new corporate headquarters in my area. Perhaps I would end up doing lots of easy ghostwriting for them for $6000 or more per book. (My book on eye care proved one thing: that hindsight is better than foresight.)

When Mr. Church learned that I still used a typewriter, he said I must buy a computer immediately for this job. I told him to call me back in a few days, but he threw me off guard by informing me that he had to report my final answer at a major executive meeting early the next morning. He urged me to say yes. That seemed like an odd way to do business, but I gave in and agreed. He pointed out that we now had a binding oral contract.

I regretfully dropped a class I was taking, postponed writing a textbook and other projects, bought my first computer, and devoted a tough month to ocular research and preliminary writing. I turned my first chapter in on schedule, and it was warmly accepted. No advance arrived, but by then I felt I could not afford to quit.

When I called week after week to try to set up appointments to interview Tiny, his wife was sweetly evasive at first ("I'm so sorry, just call back again tomorrow") and later hostile ("Tiny has no time for you"). If I were glamorous and flirtatious, I could understand her insecurity. My editor was as bewildered as I, because Tiny kept assuring her that he was willing to be interviewed. During the second month I strained my own eyes by studying seventeen books about eyes and working day and night at the computer screen. Still no interviews and no advance.

This particular company has a superb public relations program and tells prospective donors that it pays all bills in thirty days, out of courtesy to other people. That reminds me of philandering preachers who praise strict morality from the pulpit. They know just what donors like to hear. It's "talk the talk," not "walk the walk."

Although I was never granted one interview with Tiny, even by telephone, I was given bulky transcriptions from garbled reflections he tape-recorded from time to time. (The company spent hundreds of dollars for stenographers' services for Tiny. When Tiny dropped in to visit, the president took him out to lunch.) I met every deadline and fulfilled every new request along the way, partly as an experiment to see how far things would go. As I see it, in order to get the $6000 I had been promised, I ended up doing $24,000 worth of work on the book. With every revision, the book said less and Tiny liked it better. He decided that his real purpose in the book was — in his words — to explore his personality. (He was perfectly happy to explore his personality at my expense.)

Almost one year after I took the job I succeeded in persuading the company to send me my final check, but they made me promise to go on with revisions of the revisions. When Halloween came around again, my study was still piled with Tiny Daniel clutter demanding attention. I had just received fifty more pages of goofy memoirs to turn into a whole new chapter he decided he wanted. I decided I could write my own book about my year as an indentured servant.

What can be learned from this particular ghostwriting tale?

1. The emergency recruitment ploy and rush start is a common scam used by some publishers to get ghostwriters heavily invested, because most writers don't feel they can afford to back out once they have poured weeks of full-time work into a job. This is not only my own conclusion; I have heard the warning from two entirely separate sources in recent months. Your editor may sincerely assure you that the business department is working on the check while you get started, but my safety rule for writers in this: "Never use an electric typewriter while you are soaking in the tub, and never do a minute's ghostwriting until your check has arrived."

2. Do not agree to an oral contract; it is theoretically valid, but for a ghostwriter it is not worth the paper it should have been written on.

3. A company's book plan may satisfy a would-be celebrity until the book is written; then he is apt to think of a counterplan. The unwary real writer can be trapped in the middle — unpaid — until all are satisfied. (In my case the editor wanted an ordinary book about eye care and wanted it out of her way as soon as possible; Tiny seemed to want a book that would turn him into TV's next Andy Rooney; Tiny's highstrung wife admitted that she wanted to play around with the book project for a few years before agreeing to publication; and the publisher evidently wanted Tiny and his wife to be kept happy no matter what it took to satisfy them.)

4. Ghostwriters don't always know why they were hired. I finally figured out that Tiny's father must have left a trust fund that is significantly benefiting this company, and the idea of "a book by Tiny" must be part of the arrangement. (Indeed, Tiny's book heaps lavish praise upon his wealthy father, who took an interest in this particular company.)

Sometimes ghostwriters are called in merely to sustain illusions or to subsidize other people's hidden agendas.

Ghostwriting looks like the easiest way for a beginning author to get a book written and published today. It offers wonderful opportunities for service to others, writing experience, and publication. But all too often it ends up a messy business. I could not resist writing a satire about it based on 1 Kings 3 in the Old Testament.

The Way of the World

Once King Solomon had to decide which of two prostitutes was the real mother of Baby X; each woman claimed it as her own. He pretended he was going to cut the baby in half and divide it between them. The woman who preferred killing the baby to losing her claim obviously failed to really love it; but the woman who chose to give up the baby to save its life thus proved herself the real mother and won the judgment. This case was headlined in the *Jerusalem Inquirer*, and mother and baby became instant celebrities.

Six months later, Mother X returned to King Solomon with a new complaint. She had arranged with a publisher to bring out her whole story in book form. The book was written, and it was terrific; but now the ghostwriter was insisting upon a byline. Mother X was determined to have the book under her name alone. Two pittances and a crock of barley, but no byline.

"It's my pain and my fame that make this book what it is," Mother X reasoned. "This other woman simply wrote down what I would have said if I had taken time to be a writer myself. A glorified typist is trying to muscle in on my story. If I can't have my name alone on the book, I'll cancel it and find a humbler scribe."

Solomon saw that the real author was the one who wanted the good book to survive and flourish. So the ghostwriter, a certain Withso Andso of Tyre, won the case; but the book was canceled because of a papyrus shortage that season.

One year later Withso Andso came back to King Solomon's court. She had become disillusioned about renting out her brain as a surrogate author, so next she tried renting out her womb as a surrogate mother. But once the baby was born, she decided to keep it; and the sperm-donor couple would not agree. Whose baby was it?

Solomon lit up. "We'll cut it in two and you can each take half?"

"No, no," both parties cried. "Even if I lose the baby, please spare its life!" Solomon was crushed.

But he was the wisest man in the world. He called Withso Andso in for a long private conference, and then awarded the baby to her. She felt much obliged.

Six months later, he published his first book, *The Song of Solomon*, which became a runaway bestseller. His friends were all surprised. They never knew he could write that well. He also published a sequel called *Ecclesiastes* before Withso Andso sold her typewriter and moved to Goshen. She used to always throw up her hands and say, "Vanity, vanity, all is vanity! There is nothing new under the sun!" And maybe she was right.

Clawing Your Way

Greed is nothing new, but it does take some new forms. In this day of multimillion dollar publishing deals and what is called the blockbuster complex,[11] publishing and bookselling in the United States have changed drastically. Although we have more small publishers than ever, only 14 percent of the publishers control 90 percent of all book titles. That is bound to have an effect on writing and the people who want to be known as writers whether they really write or not.

For example, a successful Minneapolis businessman named Harvey Mackay decided recently that he wanted to become an author. He had vast amounts of time, money, and energy to invest in becoming a best-selling author. Mackay's subject was already available in several popular books — how to survive in the corporate jungle by outselling, outmanaging, outmotivating, and outnegotiating competition.

First Mackay reportedly spent eighteen months visiting bookstores and consulting authors around the country. He discovered what experienced authors all know only too well — that most books don't sell well because they are not available in the bookstores. Authors can't get them there.

Mackay made sure that wouldn't happen to him. He enrolled in a publishing course at Stanford University and persuaded the director of the program to make his first draft required reading. (I don't know if he claims to have actually done his own writing or not.) That got him free feedback from eighty-five professional editors and publishers. Then he sold his revised manuscript to William Morrow. He offered to conduct a motivational seminar for Morrow's sales force and to pay for a twenty-six-city promotional tour out of his own pocket; that helped him to persuade Morrow to run a gigantic first printing of 100,000 hardbound copies. Mackay paid a product-naming company $6000 to choose his title: "Swim with the Sharks without Being Eaten Alive." He went to meet the man who runs the Waldenbooks chain and talked him into quintupling his prepublication order.

Mackay talked almost fifty famous Americans, from Gerald Ford to

Robert Redford, into writing blurbs for his book. He flew to the international Frankfurt Book Fair and from the Morrow booth there sold his distribution rights for thirty countries and twelve languages. Then he began his lengthy American tour, visiting dozens of bookstores in each of twenty-six major cities. That is one way to become a successful author today. It is the art of self-promotion.

A quite different American author, Henry David Thoreau, started out quite differently with his first book. The first printing was 1000 copies, and only 294 of those sold. In 1849 Thoreau retrieved the remaining copies from his printer and wrote ruefully in his journal, "I have now a library of nearly nine hundred volumes, over seven hundred of which I wrote myself." Thoreau was the writer who said he had traveled far in his small home town of Concord. He wrote about quiet living and good ideas.

The publishing world has vastly more Thoreaus than Mackays when it comes to sales, but the public only hears about the big sellers, the top 8 percent of all American authors who make over $200,000 annually. These are like the lottery winners of the book world. The median annual income of writers is estimated at $7,900. In 1978 a survey of PEN (International Association of Poets, Playwrights, Editors, Essayists, and Novelists) members showed that 39 percent of established professional writers earned less than $3000 on their writing that year.

Humorist Dave Barry has mocked Mackay's kind of advice in his own book *Claw Your Way to the Top: How to Become the Head of a Major Corporation in Roughly a Week*. Then he has mocked his own success as a writer in an article titled "Dave Barry Claws His Way to the Top."[12] Barry tells how he works seven days a week on his writing, whether he is inspired or not. He is constantly gathering ideas, wherever he is. Robert Benchley was his inspiration, but he thinks it is fatal to imitate anybody. He tries to make his writing look as if he tossed it off quickly, but in fact he works extremely hard and rewrites constantly.

On the other hand, Barry gives hopeful writers some exclusive insider advice about how to succeed. First of all, sit down and type out a brilliant novel, a classic. Give this first book a current hot-topic title, perhaps relating it to computers, fitness, beauty, and finance. Sell it to a publisher who does not realize it was written long ago by someone like Melville. Once you are a successful author, try writing a book of your own. Be patient, because it might take weeks to write your book. When you have it completed, put it into a self-addressed, stamped envelope and drop it in the mail.

Submission to Fate

Book submission might as well be made into a laughing matter, like many other painful topics. The respected author Marchette Chute has said, "I just finish a book and if the publisher doesn't like it, that's his privilege. There've been many, many rejections. If you want to write it your own way, that's the chance you take."[13] Irving Stone had his first novel *Lust for Life* rejected by seventeen publishers. Many authors refuse to complete an entire book until some publisher has responded to a proposal with a contract and an advance, and that is a businesslike way to function. But there are still many authors who write their books before marketing them. As some writers say, "How do I know what I think until I read what I've written?" So they risk rejections of completed books.

Fledgling author Bill Gordon expects to appear in the Guinness Book of World Records for receiving the most rejections for a book that has finally been published. His compendium of quotations for writers titled *How Many Books Do You Sell in Ohio?* was rejected 217 times by a total of 176 publishers before he published it himself. Then he started his second book, remarking "I'm already a publishing legend." The record for the most rejections for a yet unpublished book is held by Gilbert Young of Bath, England, who wrote *World Government Crusade*. It has been rejected 242 times.

There are hundreds of true stories about multiple rejections of good books that eventually succeeded. The saddest is the success story of John Kennedy Toole, who could find no publisher for his first novel, *A Confederacy of Dunces*. In 1969 Toole committed suicide. In 1976 his mother got the distinguished New Orleans novelist Walker Percy to read the manuscript. Percy recommended it to a publisher, and it sold 750,000 copies and won the 1980 Pulitzer Prize.

A happier success story is that of William Kennedy. By the time his novel *Ironweed* was making the rounds, his two earlier novels that told the first part of the story were already out of print. Thirteen publishers rejected *Ironweed*. Then Nobel laureate Saul Bellow took an interest in the book and scolded Viking into publishing it and also promoting it. Three years after Toole's *Confederacy of Dunces* won a Pulitzer Prize, *Ironweed* did the same. Then Kennedy saw his earlier novels republished, wrote the film version of *Ironweed*, and also won a valuable MacArthur "genius" grant to support him in style while he continued his writing.

It pays not to lose heart as the years slip by and rejection slips accumulate or sales are low. One of the best-selling and richest authors in America, Dr. Seuss, went through all that early. His first novel, *The Seven Lady Godivas*, was a flop. His first book for children, *To Think that I Saw It on Mulberry Street,* was rejected by almost thirty publishers. The next publisher took it, and Dr. Seuss has been a winner ever since. Now rare old copies of *The Seven Lady Godivas* sell for $3000.

Primo Levi was a young Italian chemist who was sent to Auschwitz during the Second World War and survived to tell the tale. He submitted his book, now titled *Survival in Auschwitz,* to several publishers who all rejected it. Finally a small publisher printed 2,500 copies and the book had good reviews, but the public completely ignored it and it died. Nine years later, after Levi got an enthusiastic response to a speech about his experiences, he offered the book again to one of the big publishers who had rejected it. It was accepted and republished in 1958, and it has been selling ever since. Levi became a full-time award-winning writer. He finally put up a chart in his study to keep track of the translations of his books into many languages.

Toole, Kennedy, Seuss, and Levi are giants, and their successes are gigantic. I once copied down this sentence by a student and saved it because it speaks awkwardly and honestly for most of the rest of us: "I want very much to be a smooth, classy, witty writer of huge fame and immense wealth, but I will settle for readable and middle-class."

The resurrection of Primo Levi's ten-year-old book foreshadowed a peculiar publishing experience of my own. My book about children's literature, which the publisher titled *How To Grow a Young Reader,* was published in 1978 with an inappropriate format and without its much-needed index. Such disappointments are common, but there followed ethical misconduct too outlandish for me to recount here. Besides that, all too soon my book needed updating it never got, the price went up, the paper quality went down, and sales evaporated. I sent polite inquiries and called long distance in vain. This is nothing unusual; I know of another author who called that same publisher seventy-seven times and never got through to anyone who would tell him what was happening to his book.

Finally in 1988 I discovered by accident that a year earlier my publisher had planned and brought out a similar book with almost the same title. That new book was sent to my local bookstore instead of mine, as "a replacement." Mine was dropped without my being notified or given the chance to buy up the hundreds of leftover copies at cost according to my contract. I was left with two old copies on hand.

I had been forced to start to sue another publisher who had broken contract and deprived me of profits by secretly selling thousands of my books to a remainder outlet, and in that case we settled out of court. But in this case I could not convincingly threaten a cross-country legal case. I got no answers to my polite appeals. It was depressing.

Just then I got a call from a quality publisher. Was it true, I was asked, that my children's literature book was finally out of print? They had had their eyes on it for years. Would I consider updating it and adding an index and letting them republish it for me in better format? Just like Primo's masterpiece, my own little *How To Grow a Young Reader* was getting a new birth after ten years of disappointment. It felt like spring, like joy, like resurrection. It felt like love.

Life is full of surprises, both good and bad. First a writer just wants to get something written well; next he wants a contract, he wants the book published without unreasonable delay, he wants people to buy it, he wants to be paid fairly for it, he wants people to read it, and he wants people to understand it and remember it. For Primo Levi and the rest of us, not all these wishes are apt to come true according to our initial expectations. As John Steinbeck said, "The profession of book-writing makes horse racing seem like a solid, stable business."

Certainly an agent can be a great help to an author, taking care of all his publishing worries for ten or fifteen percent of his royalties. The agent tries to find a publisher, negotiate a superior contract, and make sure that the contract is honored. But there are not many qualified agents around, and it is usually easier to get accepted by a publisher than to get accepted by an agent. So most authors give up and slide along acting as their own agents. To paraphrase an old adage about lawyers, the author who acts as his own agent may have a fool for a client. Getting to know lots of other authors is an enjoyable and practical way to become more knowledgeable about publishing, and as a bonus it sometimes helps in the search for an agent.

When things are going well any author is apt to feel euphoria. Sir James Barrie, the author of *Peter Pan*, recalled "For several days after my first book was published I carried it about in my pocket, and took surreptitious peeks at it to make sure the ink had not faded." But when rejections and other setbacks hit us, we may need to have several projects going so that not everything seems to be failing at once. The ultimate setback for some authors is running out of current projects.

Long ago I read an author's half-serious complaint that our government pampers oil well owners and gravel pit owners by giving them a depletion allowance. They get a significant tax break because they are using up a limited natural resource in their property that can't be replaced. Yet writers aren't given any depletion allowance for using up the limited fund of ideas and information in their heads. After all, once James Barrie invented the story of Peter Pan, he had used up that part of his creative ability. There weren't any more Peter Pans in him. It seems to me that the idea of Peter Pan is even more irreplaceable than a ton of gravel. But the world isn't set up to pamper writers.

So writers often befriend and help each other. Many writers feel that one of the best things about being a writer is getting to have interesting writers for friends. And many writers also enjoy helping beginners who come around.[14] Raymond Chandler had bad luck that way, though. He claimed that he had done everything from giving would-be writers money to plotting and rewriting their stories for them, but that it was all a waste. None of them turned out to be writers after all, only people who wanted to be writers. Real writers somehow manage to get ideas and to get some writing done for themselves.

In contrast to Raymond Chandler, I have met fledgling writers who went on to eventual publication and success. In fact, one friend whose book I believed in many years ago finally found a publisher for it in 1987 and then won an award of excellence from *Campus Life* magazine in 1988. The book was made up of inspirational anecdotes from his short career as a zookeeper.

When hopeful writers asked, "Where do you get all your ideas?" a friend of Lawrence Block used to answer soberly that he subscribes to an idea magazine for writers. He said he selects about six story ideas from the latest issue and registers them to reserve them for his use alone; then he uses them up and gets more plot ideas from the next issue. Gullible listeners would often believe this man and wanted to subscribe to the magazine themselves, but he regretfully told them that subscribers have to be professional authors with several sales already to their credit. I can't decide whether Lawrence Block is telling the truth about his friend or telling us a tall tale about his friend's tall tale.

Since there is no idea magazine for writers, here are some wise quotations and handy hints that I subscribe to instead:

1. "All art is autobiographical. The pearl is the oyster's autobiography." — Federico Fellini

2. "The next thing most like living one's life over again seems to be recollection of that life, and to make that recollection as durable as possible by putting it down in writing." — Benjamin Franklin

3. "Unlike God, the novelist does not start with nothing and make something of it. He starts with himself as nothing and makes something of the nothing with the things at hand." — Walker Percy

4. "I've given my memoirs far more thought than any of my marriages. You can't divorce a book." — Gloria Swanson

5. "*Lost Illusions* is the undisclosed title of every novel." — Andre Maurois

6. "Why do people always expect authors to answer questions? I

am an author because I want to *ask* questions. If I had all the answers I'd be a politician." — Eugene Ionesco

7. "I never desire to converse with a man who has written more than he has read." — Samuel Johnson

8. "Every writer needs to be well-read." — Dean R. Koontz

9. "I do borrow from other writers, *shamelessly!* I can only say in my defense, like the woman brought before the judge on the charge of kleptomania, 'I do steal, Your Honor, only from the very best stores.'" — Thornton Wilder

10. "I write what I should like to read — and what I think other women would like to read." — Kathleen Norris

11. "There are no dull subjects, only dull minds." — Raymond Chandler

12. "A writer's materials lie in whatever stirs his imagination, touches his heart, excites his mind." — Jessamyn West

SUGGESTED ACTIVITIES

1. You are on trial for writing without reason. The jury is made up of people in your life, but the judge is yourself. If found guilty, you will be confined to an isolation chamber and given no more writing materials or books. Defend yourself against the charge, gentle writer, in three hundred words.

2. Start your own collection of favorite quotations right away. Don't hesitate to raid *Bartlett's Familiar Quotations* and other collections, as well as noticing quotations in your reading and everywhere else. Copying quotations out will make them more a part of you, and when you take them out of their settings you may discover that a few of them are not so good as you had thought. Many successful writers collect quotations regularly and post favorites over their typewriters. Take time every month to savor some of your favorite quotations.

3. Write letters to the editors of two or three of the periodicals that you read fairly often. Choose timely subjects, make your letters brief and lively, and tailor them as much as you can for the periodicals you have in mind.

4. Write brief reviews of new books you have read recently. Remember that a review is more like a consumer product rating than a book report. Consider places where your book reviews might be used. Notice in the books that you review which strengths you want in your own writing and which weaknesses you want to avoid.

5. Recall a situation in your life which turned out to be a learning experience or a source of growth for you. Write a personal account

that can provide insight, hope, comfort, or pleasure to readers as they think of similar situations in their own lives.

6. It is handy to have a special address book full of your writing contacts — writers, editors, bookstores, book publishers, and periodicals. Make a list of all the places where you might try to get published, with their addresses. (Be sure to include publications of organizations that you belong to and care about.) Make it a habit to notice whether periodicals buy from free-lance writers or not, and keep on the lookout for possible markets.

NOTES

[1] For a detailed history of the business of authorship, I recommend *Authors by Profession*, volumes 1 and 2, by Victor Bonham-Carter (Los Altos, Calif.: William Kaufmann Inc., 1978 and 1984). This study, first published in England, traces little-known and little-understood developments in the writing profession from 1500 to 1981, including such topics as royalties, copyrights, agents, vanity publishing, writers' organizations, book sales, and distribution. Bonham-Carter cites figures showing that few successfully published authors in the past or today have been able to support themselves with their meager book earnings.

[2] *Writer's Market* and *The Writer's Handbook* are useful to writers who hope for publication; they are available in most large libraries. I also recommend two magazines that advise writers about what to write and where to send it: *The Writer* and *Writer's Digest*. These are available in most large libraries also.

[3] Melvin Maddocks, "A Letter to Readers about Letters to the Editor," *The Christian Science Monitor* (December 4, 1987), 19.

[4] Katherine Paterson, prize-winning author of *Bridge to Terabithia* and other outstanding books, has admitted, "When I finally began to write books, it was not so much that I wanted to be a writer but that I loved books and wanted somehow to get inside the process, to have a part in their making."

[5] For information on the current copyright laws, send for circulars 1, 16, 20, and 99, available from the Copyright Office, Library of Congress, Washington, DC 20559.

[6] I recommend John Updike's *Hugging the Shore: Essays and Criticism* (New York: Vintage Books, 1984) for superbly literate book reviews by a major novelist.

[7] "An Author's Response to a Book Review," *Radix* (May/June 1981), 29–30. Elsewhere Updike has elaborated: "It's an area I don't talk about with great fluency, and I don't want to present myself as a Christian writer in the same way, say, C. S. Lewis was. I am a writer who goes to church and is a Christian in the sense of somebody willing to stand up and profess the Apostle's Creed. But when I write, certainly not only the Christian, but the un-Christian in me speaks. That is, I think it is my basic duty to God to write the most truthful and fullest books I can."

[8]Marjorie Holmes, *Writing the Creative Article Today* (Boston: The Writer, Inc., 1986).

[9]Lawrence Block, *Telling Lies for Fun and Profit: A Manual for Fiction Authors* (New York: Arbor House, 1981). I recommend this collection of Block's columns from *Writer's Digest*.

[10]Lawrence Block, "One Thousand Dollars a Word," *Sometimes They Bite* (New York: Arbor House, 1983), 101–107.

[11]*The Blockbuster Complex: Conglomerates, Show Business, and Book Publishing*, by Thomas Whiteside (Middletown, Conn.: Wesleyan Univ. Press, 1981) discusses how the book-publishing business has become part of the communications-entertainment complex of show business. Whiteside traces how conglomerates have taken over the publishing industry and the drastic changes that are resulting.

[12]Dave Barry, "Dave Barry Claws His Way to the Top," *Writer's Digest* (June 1987), 28–30.

[13]As Victor Bonham-Carter pointed out graphically in *Authors by Profession*, volume 2, most writers, even the writers of undistinguished genre novels, feel called to a vocation and want most of all to be read; but publishers are almost exclusively interested in the perceived marketability of products and the financial profit inherent in those products.

[14]Editors for magazines and publishing houses do not usually have time to give encouragement and advice to writers. Many aspiring writers therefore approach experienced writers for free editorial advice. This has sometimes led to happy results, but helpful writers often feel drained by requests from strangers; some have finally offered editorial services at standard hourly rates. I highly recommend that unpublished writers take writing courses, attend conferences, and locate or organize free critique groups where there are people available to read each other's manuscripts and offer constructive advice.

Chapter 8

Writer-Types (How To Type Yourself)

If writers were good businessmen, they'd have too much sense to be writers.

— IRVIN S. COBB

Most good writers and other artists are not business types. Mark Twain was a glaring example of that. He not only managed to snatch debt out of the jaws of success, but he somehow managed to lose a fortune by investing in a new invention for writers called the typewriter. Twain's books had great sales, and his lectures were often packed; but Twain didn't end up rich. Why did such a bright man have such bad luck?

Almost everyone enjoys simple explanations of life's human puzzles. Hundreds of thousands of people read astrology charts in the daily papers for that reason. (Many know that the charts are silly but read them anyway.) This is a lazy way of trying to understand ourselves and other people. "No wonder I write this way; I'm a Gemini." Astrology invites us to peek into the secret recipe that makes us what we are. If offers easy bits of advice for living well. Hence the appeal.

There are many ways to describe human differences besides astrology. The Greek father of medicine, Hippocrates, divided all people into four different temperament-types called choleric (hot-headed), sanguine (cheerful), phlegmatic (sluggish), and melancholic (sad). People can be sorted out physically into endomorphs (soft and plump), ectomorphs (thin and energetic), and mesomorphs (strong and muscular). Now someone has kindly given those three basic body builds clear English names: muffins, birds, and horses.

A popular color analysis in our day divides all people into four categories handily labeled spring, summer, fall, and winter, with rules about colors that look best on each type. This four-season color chart was invented recently by a San Francisco woman, but portrait painters have always known about skin tone. It's a fact of life, like height.

Most people are curious about what groups they do and don't fit into. They like to see how they are unique but know that there are plenty of other people like them for company. That is one reason why young people look into mirrors so often.

The Myers-Briggs Types

After six thousand years of human history, we have a new way to sort people into groups, a way that is immensely practical for self-understanding and for understanding others. Since creative writers are usually preoccupied with the world within or else perceptively watching other people, this new tool is a windfall for writers. The old Greek system was nothing in comparison.

Learning about the Myers-Briggs temperament differences will help writers to better understand themselves; to better understand the fictional characters they create; to better understand different kinds of readers, writers, and editors; and to be more sensitive to people in interviews.

Katharine Briggs and her daughter Isabel Briggs Myers, a prize-winning mystery novelist, spent most of their lives developing the Myers-Briggs temperament sorting system. Their purpose was to help us to love ourselves and others better by understanding our differences, because we are more different than we usually assume. Their work included a survey of 5000 medical students. By the time Isabel died in 1980, their product was published in standard academic and professional style for the psychological establishment.[1] But relatively few people had access to it.[2]

In Fullerton, California, a couple of psychology instructors named Bates and Keirsey worked hard on a popular adaptation of the Myers-Briggs discoveries, adding their own theories and insights. Before publication of their book, Marilyn Bates suddenly died of cancer. David Keirsey published the book under both their names, and after a slow start it gradually caught on across the country.[3] It was not particularly well written from a writer's point of view, but the content excited an eager public.

Ironically, the original writers of the material were almost forgotten in the excitement. Keirsey left out Katharine C. Briggs entirely and only mentioned Isabel Myers once in passing, with her name misspelled. (That is the kind of thing that sometimes happens to pioneers.) The Bates-Keirsey book includes a handy 70-question test with directions for scoring; it is an abbreviated version of Isabel Myers's 126-question test. The latter is more dependable, but the Keirsey adaptation works well enough for casual use.

As I like to describe it, the test divides people into four big human tribes that see life differently and live life differently. (Each tribe is divided into four clans, so there are sixteen clans in all.) Unlike ordinary tribes and clans, these are intermingled in neighborhoods, schools, churches, and even in families. No wonder that we are so often bewildered by our closest relatives. Myers-Briggs helps us to see and appreciate our tribal differences. These differences are mainly inborn, like right-handedness and blue eyes or brown. They are built into our nervous systems.

I came up with a way for people to find their types without having to answer the actual Myers-Briggs questions or the Bates-Keirsey version, which are all copyrighted.[4] In my adaptation the reader makes four choices. If this were a vacation-preference survey, the reader might choose first between a vacation in the mountains and a vacation at the beach. The second choice might be between a July vacation and an October vacation. The third choice might be between using a plane or a car. The fourth choice might be between staying in a big hotel or in a private house. It is the preference that counts, even if it is only a slight preference. By making only four choices, people select one of sixteen different vacation plans. So it is that by figuring out only four life preferences, people divide themselves into sixteen temperament types.

Four Major Preferences

First, imagine all people belonging to two great nationalities that prefer to see the world differently. Three-quarters of our population are called S-people, what I call *Sensible Citizens of Solid Surfaces.* They are down-to-earth and usually glad of it. They are practical and matter-of-fact, and they major in common sense. They "keep the trains running on time." They consider themselves realistic, and they say that life is as plain as the hand in front of your face. They are often satisfied with what they have and are. They are steady and don't mind repetition. They like standard operating procedure. They tend to have a good sense of clock-time. Their tastes and interests are majority tastes and interests. Their critics might teasingly call them Superficial and Simple-minded, no matter how Smart.

The other nationality, only one-quarter of the population, is called N-people. I call them *Navigators to New Worlds.* They are the ones most interested in the Myers-Briggs types. Most writers are in this group, as well as most scientists. They live in the realm of possibility and ingenuity. They tend to be never-quite-satisfied, and they feel a need to grow. They think they sense mysteries. They are imaginative and sometimes make use of a "sixth sense." They get inspirations. They like dreams and symbols, fiction and fantasy; they love ideas. They read between the lines of life. They try to look beneath the surface of things. They get bored with repetition. They tend to have inferior observation skills for everyday details, and some of them lose track of time. They hunger to see meaning. They tend to irritate their close relatives who are S-people. Their critics might teasingly call them Nutty.

Whichever type you are, chances are that most of your teachers and fellow students have been S-people. Most of your community members are S-people. Most of your relatives are probably S-people. Sometimes N- people attract each other without realizing why and find themselves in a network of friends who have common interests or who just click with each other. It feels good to be on the same wavelength with others part of the time, to see things as they do, to flow easily. To be accepted.

The second major division of humanity is between *Thought-process* people and *Felt-values* people. They prefer to draw conclusions differently, and so they see morality differently. Everyone wants to be good at thinking, and most people want to be good at feeling. But when it comes to making decisions, almost everyone depends more upon one of these skills than the other. Thinking is considered a specialty of males in our culture, and feeling is considered a specialty of females. The statistics of Myers-Briggs researchers show that in fact there are more women than men who favor felt-values and more men than women who favor logic. When males and females are added together, T-people and F-people are equal in number.

Thought-process people find their way through life by reasoning, logic, and rules. They analyze, criticize, and judge according to set standards and policies. They value their heads more than their hearts, and value justice above mercy. When it is appropriate, they are quite capable of flunking their students or firing their employees without distress. They can be rather oblivious to other people's feelings, and although they may like harmony, they don't really need it. They may or may not be good reasoners, but they trust their reasoning either way. They try to see things as simple enough that they feel in control intellectually. They are apt to be intelligent and they are apt to be out of touch with their feelings, but that is not always the case. Some of them are dim mentally, and some are warm emotionally. They vary greatly, but they all depend upon rational maps and charts as their guides in life.

Felt-values people, in contrast, go through life following the needle on the compass of love. They prefer to trust their hearts. These people prize harmony and are often full of sympathy. They take the personal approach with people. They live more by the spirit of the law than the letter of the law. They believe in mercy when there are extenuating circumstances. They are humane, and they are often lavishly devoted to others. They would rather persuade than punish, and they care more about doing what is good than doing what is logical. (As Mark Twain said, sometimes you just have to put your principles aside and do what's right.) Some of the F-people are brilliant intellectually; but when they can tell right away what is good, they don't usually go to the trouble to justify it with logic. Why bother?

People tend to be defensive and touchy about their T or F preference, but both can serve well in decision making. The F-people feel that human logic is not a perfect guide, and they see that one reason we often make mistakes in our logic is that we don't have enough data to start with. The T-people, on the other hand, notice how often felt-values lead people into foolishness. In fact, both T-people and F-people can be rational; and both T-people and F-people can be irrational. Both feeling and thinking are good ways of knowing truth and making good decisions, and neither is foolproof. The critics of T-people might teasingly accuse them of being *T*hick-skulled, and the critics of F-people might teasingly accuse them of being *F*uzzy-minded.

The third major division that separates people shows how they prefer to live. J-people are *Job-oriented Jumpers*, and P-people are *Pendulous Postponers*. The public is evenly split between these preferences.

Job-oriented Jumpers like things settled and decided. They love closure. They plan ahead and order their lives, and they often prize efficiency. They are good at decision making. They like to get things organized, and they like to meet deadlines. They say to themselves, "Let's get this show on the road." They feel good when a task is completed, a decision made. If there is no deadline on a job, they often make up their own and try to meet it. (They can't get everything done, because it is humanly impossible; and so they have to decide to put some jobs aside.) They are apt to worry about anything left hanging. They don't often worry once a decision is made and a job done, even if hindsight is better than foresight. They leave it to God and go on to something else.

Pendulous Postponers are the opposite. They are most comfortable when things are open-ended and flexible. They dislike closure. They like to let life happen and to adapt as they go. They usually figure that there's no real hurry, and many of them are apt to miss deadlines without much stress to themselves. They always like to gather more information before completing things. "Let's run that through again." "Let's not rush into anything." They are adaptive and comfortable with options open. They don't like to feel stuck. They always want more data. After a decision is made or a job is done, they sometimes worry that they might have done it better differently. They like to start projects, but they may not finish them.

J-people might be accused of *J*umping the gun, and P-people might be accused of *P*rocrastinating. (Sometimes it's true!)

The fourth major difference is between people who prefer to face outward and people who prefer to face inward. This divides people into Extraverts and Introverts, with the original meanings of both words. This is not the difference between loud and quiet, or bold and shy, or confident and socially awkward. This difference is more a matter of energy.

I call E-people *Extraverts Expending Energy*. They make up three-quarters of the population. These sociable people get their batteries charged by contact with other people. They tend to have quick movements. They are apt to stay late at a party, having more and more fun as the hours pass. They get "cabin fever" easily when they are isolated too much, although they may not know what is wrong with them when that happens. They usually need some solitude, but they need human contact even more than they need solitude. They like to find out what they think by talking to other people. When these people are writers, they have a great need to balance the isolation of writing with some outside stimulus for refreshment. They focus chiefly on the world outside their own heads. C. S. Lewis said that he cherished time alone for his thinking and writing; but if he had to sacrifice one or the other permanently, he would sacrifice solitude for the sake of companionship. Extraverts need the variety and interchange. Their critics might say that they are *E*xcessively *E*xternal.

I-people are the Introverts who make up only one-quarter of the public, and in our society they are sometimes mistakenly thought of as failed Extraverts. They have a great need for privacy. I call them *Introverts Inclined Inwardly and Irked by Too Much Interaction.* They get their batteries drained by too much contact with other people. They are the ones who are apt to leave a party early (if they went at all) because they have less fun as the hours pass. They treasure a few friendships rather than many, but sometimes they are so entertaining and socially gracious that they are mistaken for Extraverts. Introverts usually need human contact, but they need their solitude even more. They are apt to think before speaking (an odd habit). Their critics might say that they are *I*solated.

The marriage of an E-person to an I-person, according to Isabel Myers, presents special difficulties and requires much patience and compromise.

In summary, everyone tends to value more either the need for practicality or the need for a sixth sense; the need to get things settled or the need to keep things open; the need for logic and rules or the need for a sense of what's best; and the need for people or the need for privacy. In all four of these choices, almost everyone leans at least a little in one direction or the other. This reveals a deep-seated preference, even if it is a mild preference. Some preferences seem obvious at first, and some take longer to figure out. (Taking the Myers-Briggs test should settle the matter quickly.) Almost everyone is more S or N, more T or F, more J or P, and more E or I. Thus nearly everyone can be labeled by one of these pairs of initials: S-P, S-J, N-T, or N-F. Those are the markers of the four big tribes.

The Tribes of Growers

The N-F tribe is the most interesting to writers simply because most writers are members of this tribe. If the Growers had a capital, it would probably be Los Angeles. Both Katharine C. Briggs (an INFJ) and Isabel Myers (an INFP) were members of this tribe. (Many of their followers are not.) Members of the N-F tribe are especially apt to take a strong interest in the Myers-Briggs types because they want to know what makes people click.

When I taught a creative writing class at Santa Ana College in 1983, sixteen members were from the N-F tribe, seven were from the N-T tribe, and only eight were from the majority S-J tribe. When I taught the class in 1984, fifteen members were from the N-F tribe, nine were from the N-T tribe, and only three were from the majority S-J tribe. This in no way reflected the make-up of other classes that I taught at Santa Ana College, except for the obvious lack of members of the S-P tribe. It is more than obvious that N-F people are the ones who often feel born to write.

Almost nine-tenths of the population are not in the N-F group and find it the hardest group to understand. The other three groups usually understand each other's characteristics, even if they disapprove; but they say they can't quite figure out the N-F mindset. That is ironic, because N-F people are the ones who talk and write about their mindset much of the time. They are forever reaching out to others with words and hoping to be understood.

I call the N-F group the Tribe of Growers. They make up only 12.5 percent of the population, but they write most of the literature. They are the searchers for meaning. They value possibilities. They yearn to make a difference in the world. Adjectives often used to describe them include creative, artistic, ingenious, inspiring, sensitive, communicative, individualistic, empathic, idealistic, spiritual, appreciative, and people-centered. I call them Personalists because they are often intensely personal and extremely responsive to others. They strongly sense their own uniqueness and greatly long for unity with others. They need harmony, significance, integrity, and important relationships with other people. They are the most romantic and idealistic about sexual love. For Growers, all life is significant; and the key to life is their self-actualization — becoming ever more fully their true selves.

Thus the most basic need among the Growers is their own authenticity. If their sense of authenticity is somehow threatened (if they are accused of fakery or they are dishonest with themselves or they feel out of touch with themselves), they are severely stressed; and if their sense of authenticity is destroyed, they feel destroyed. It has been claimed that they are the most likely to suffer amnesia; whether or not that is true, they might be the most fascinated by amnesia and the most frightened of it.

The Growers are less than 13 percent of the population, but they make up 38 percent of education workers. They tend to be givers. They are great encouragers of others, and they are drawn to the caring professions. They often become ministers, psychiatrists, actors, teachers, and counselors, as well as poets, novelists, and biographers. They are almost always fluent and highly verbal. They tend to pursue extraordinary goals. They often "make things happen" and tend to be at the forefront of reform movements aimed at helping ordinary people. (Many abolitionists who fought against slavery were N-Fs.) Their influence is vastly greater than their numbers would have us expect. Our perfect fictional example of a Grower is Anne of Green Gables. (Was her creator, Lucy Montgomery, a Grower? I'm sure of it.)

The Growers are not perfect, of course. For one thing, they are not easily satisfied. They sometimes promise more than they can deliver. They tend to overload their emotional circuits. They may want to be everything to everybody. They may neglect existing relationships because of their enthusiasm about new relationships. Some Growers move from one "perfect love" to another, leaving deserted families behind them as they move on to new attempts at self-actualization. (The short life of the recklessly romantic English poet Percy Bysshe Shelley is a tragic example of what can happen when an N-F runs wild.)

There are four clans in the Growers tribe. First is the ENFJ clan, which I call *Pastors*. (*Pastor* comes from the word for shepherd.) These make up 5 percent of the population and are outstanding group leaders who care greatly about people. Medical students of this type tend to end up teaching in medical school instead of simply practicing medicine. They find, perhaps to their surprise, that they love to teach young adults. *Pastors* are superb communicators who usually like talking better than writing. They need to be on guard about overextending themselves emotionally, because they can overidentify with others; and they find it hard to say no to any demands for nurture. They are transparently honest, tolerant of others, and naturally cooperative. C. S. Lewis was definitely a *Pastor*. I guess that among today's writers Lewis Smedes and Joyce Carol Oates are both *Pastors* also. *Pastors* are very open people, which makes them easier to spot than some other types.

The second clan in the Growers tribe is the ENFP clan, which I call the *Performers*. These people tend to feel that they are playing a role in life rather than being adequately spontaneous. They are multitalented and dynamic people with little tolerance for routine, boredom, or conformity. They can excel in entertaining, selling, reporting, or many other challenging fields. In my 1983 creative writing class, one-third of the students were members of this clan, although only 5 percent of the population is in this clan. They not only like to express themselves creatively, but they also like to get out and mix with other people. They tend to be optimistic and enthusiastic, and they don't always force themselves to follow through on their many projects. It seems likely to me that Shakespeare was one of these, and Chaucer before him. In our century, almost surely G. K. Chesterton and perhaps Maya Angelou.

The third clan in the Growers tribe is the INFJ clan, which I call the *Poets*. They make up only 1 percent of the population. (Then why do I know so many of them?) They usually make dedicated students, take their values and their work very seriously, and want to contribute to the welfare of others. They are extrasensitive and complex people, with great powers of intuition. "Still water runs deep." They are basically reserved and discreet, although they may be warm and giving with their friends. They find conflict difficult to cope with. They tend to enjoy quiet humor. They are often highly talented writers, and they make good professional editors. I might be wrong, but I suspect that T. S. Eliot was a *Poet* and that Frederick Buechner is a *Poet*.

The fourth clan in the Growers tribe is the INFP clan, which I call the *Priests*. They make up only 1 percent of the general population. They are reserved people with a rich and independent interior life, often highly creative. They may seem otherworldly and impractical in contrast to most people. They are intensely idealistic. They are mild-mannered until something involves their deepest values; then they are apt to make any sacrifice for what they believe in. I think that J. R. R. Tolkien was a *Priest*.

The Tribe of Knowers

The N-T tribe is of special interest to writers because it is the tribe that is closest to the Growers. If the Knowers had a capital, it might be Cambridge, home of the Massachusetts Institute of Technology. Knowers can be highly creative, intuitive, and imaginative, with large vocabularies; but they do not usually invest much in developing their writing skills. Although they get published fairly often in academic journals or technical manuals, many of them are verbose or else terse and impatient with the English language. They often lack empathy for their readers. Knowers are apt to enjoy using words from Latin or other specialized vocabularies, and they are not apt to translate them clearly into common English. But some Knowers have superb writing talent and make the most of it. They can be outstanding writers. Martin Gardner and Isaac Asimov are probably Knowers.

The basic hunger of Knowers is for competence, and if their sense of competence is lost they feel stripped. They have an immense underlying need to feel in control of their inner and outer worlds through knowledge and analysis. They like to see the world as orderly and predictable. They need to "get the whole picture." Their never-ending quest is not for meaning (the quest of the Growers), but for power over the world of nature and ideas.

Adjectives that describe the Knowers well are innovative, skeptical, independent, logical, abstract, knowledgeable, capable, perfectionistic, and skillful. They focus largely upon their mental and career pursuits, which often fill their lives. They are sometimes so stimulated and satisfied by their mental work that they don't bother with personal entanglements.

Like the Growers, the Knowers traffic in ideas. Many of them are book-buyers. The Knower tribe includes most ardent computer enthusiasts. Although the three other tribes include every level of intelligence and natural talent, the Knower tribe actually lacks people with low intelligence. That is important, because the Knowers focus on their intelligence. Not all Knowers are intelligent enough to get into MENSA, but most people who choose to join MENSA are probably Knowers.[5]

Knowers make up 12.5 percent of the population, but only 6 percent of education workers. Even female Knowers rarely teach elementary school if they can avoid it. Numbers of Knowers increase slightly in junior high school, high school, and junior college teaching. But they cluster mainly at the top of the academic ladder, where they often serve as graduate school professors and researchers. David Keirsey, who researched and popularized the Myers-Briggs material, is a Knower and proud of it.

Someone has said, "Scratch an N-T and find a scientist." Knowers often go into science, technology, philosophy, mathematics, logic, design, engineering, management, criminology, manufacturing, or research and development. They love analysis. If they write anything besides nonfiction, it is most likely to be science fiction — because they enjoy it so much. Chess and bridge champions are apt to be from the Knower tribe, and so are devoted players of other strategy games such as "Dungeons and Dragons." Our perfect fictional example of a Knower is Sherlock Holmes. Was his creator, Arthur Conan Doyle, a Knower? I think it highly possible. (Conan Doyle was a science buff, and there is circumstantial evidence that he perpetrated the Piltdown hoax to embarrass some scientists he did not respect.)

The first Knower clan is the ENTJ clan, which I call the *Leaders.* These make up only 5 percent of our population, but they provide far more than 5 percent of our leadership. They are outgoing organizers and planners who tend to move in and fix things wherever they are. They love to get things done, often by or for other people. Supremely self-confident and energetic, the *Leaders* aren't apt to take time to be writers; but they don't doubt that they could do it if they wanted to. I suppose that Winston Churchill was a *Leader,* and perhaps William Buckley is one also.

The second Knower clan is the ENTP clan, which I call the *Entrepreneurs.* Like the ENTJ clan, they make up 5 percent of the population and are full of interests and enthusiasm. They love to come up with unusual ideas and projects, and they love to talk to people — from a stage, sometimes. One of them got excited about the Myers-Briggs types, started an educational company to promote the ideas, hired artists to produce a Myers-Briggs comedy with music, and gave many professional performances (at professional rates) all over Orange County, California.

No shrinking violet, he played the lead in his own show. The ENTP people are apt to be entertaining and ingenious. They like to stay one-up on the other people.

Members of the third Knower clan, the INTJ clan, are what I call *Executives*. They make up only 1 percent of the population, and they are not highly visible; but they often rise to highly responsible positions. They are idea-people who specialize in research and practical applications, masters of the practical logic of human institutions. They like strategy. *Executives* are extraordinary because they are the most intellectually independent and self-confident of all sixteen types. Their confidence in their own thought processes is unmatched. I have wondered if the multitalented Arthur C. Clarke, author of *Childhood's End* and inventor of the communications satellite concept, might be an *Executive*.

Members of the fourth Knowers clan, the INTP clan, are what I call *Professors*. They are apt to be somewhat like the stereotype of the absent-minded professor — brilliant and deeply absorbed in their specialty, but not always highly practical or highly skilled in communication. Some of them would prefer to communicate in efficient mathematical formulas rather than English words, if they had their choice. They tend to be rather reserved, withdrawn, and shy; and they care more about grasping everything intellectually than using what they know. They quickly tire of routine details and too much talk. They sometimes appear impatient or condescending to their intellectual inferiors, even if they are not, and they are always automatically on the lookout for contradictions or errors. They have outstanding powers of concentration. I suppose that Albert Einstein was one of these.

In the realm of the ridiculous, I think that Earl Peckham, protagonist of the Peter DeVries comic novel *Peckham's Marbles*, is a *Professor*. Peckham is an unemployed instructor of writing and literature whose first novel, *The Sorry Scheme of Things Entire*, has sold only three copies. He goes in search of two of those copies to autograph them because he thinks that autographed copies can't be returned to the publisher. There is a happy ending; Peckham, a Knower in love with his own words and ideas, marries a well-endowed woman who can support him in style while he writes and publishes more books. That woman is a Keeper.

The Tribe of Keepers

The S-J tribe includes 38 percent of all people, far more than all the Growers and Knowers combined. If the Keepers had a capital, it might be Grover's Corner, New Hampshire — the fictitious setting of *Our Town*.

Keepers are often referred to as the salt of the earth. They are the American-flag and apple-pie people. Adjectives that describe this tribe include practical, sensible, dutiful, responsible, traditional, conservative, stable, punctual, and predictable. Keepers are the majority members of the PTA, the Scouts, the Rotary clubs, and most other clubs and lodges of our country. They are our great "belongers." They tend to fit into school comfortably when they are young, because public schools are run by people of their own tribe.

Keepers have an immense need to fit into the mainstream. They hunger for inclusion, and this requires social stability and tradition. It requires continuity. Keepers need customs, possessions, rules, and procedures that they are used to, that give them their place in the world. They are uncomfortable with too much innovation, and they don't go adventuring in the realm of ideas. They watch the television programs that most other people are watching and look at the magazines that most other people look at. They are the holders of the fort and the holders of the savings accounts. They like the middle of the road. If they ever kick over the traces in their personal lives and become irresponsible or immoral, which sometimes happens, they are sure to do it in what they consider traditional American ways.

Keepers provide us with 56 percent of our education workers. They provide most of our elementary teachers, nurses, bankers, accountants, clerks, draftsmen, secretaries, physical therapists, managers, preachers, and insurance workers. They are good down-to-earth caretakers and decision makers. They are the people most likely to serve on committees and to go along with the status quo. Their reading is apt to be light and easy or strictly practical. They sometimes think, "I could write a book about things I've seen," and indeed many of them could. But no matter how talented they are verbally, they aren't often in love with words and ideas, and so they aren't apt to try to be writers — if it isn't apt to put bread on the table.

The first clan of the Keepers is the ESTJ clan, which includes 13 percent of our population. I call them the *Managers*. They like to get practical things done efficiently and correctly. They are good with finances. They usually work hard and often rise to responsible positions. They tend to radiate good cheer, to add a light touch to traditional social gatherings, and to support civic organizations. They are responsible and enthusiastic community members. Any novel with a cross section of the populace in it will have some *Managers* in it, and in my opinion *Babbitt* by Sinclair Lewis (our first winner of the Nobel Prize for Literature) is the heavy-handed satirical skewering of the *Manager* by an author who was probably an irritated *Entertainer*.

The second Keeper clan is the ESFJ clan, which also includes 13 percent of the populace but has more females than the ESTJ clan. I call this clan the *Seller*. This is the most sincerely sociable clan of all — usually focused on the family or church or neighborhood rather than on wider circles. In Sinclair Lewis's novel, Mrs. Babitt was like this common female type. If *Sellers* are actually selling products, they personalize every transaction. This is the clan with the greatest need for cooperation from other people, and they are much concerned about what others should and shouldn't do. Family traditions and holidays are extremely important to them, and they often start traditions and carry them on for the rest of the family (whether the family likes it or not). They are apt to write lots of family letters and traditional diaries to keep track of ordinary events.

The third Keepers clan is the ISTJ clan, which I call the *Accountant* clan. It contains 6 percent of the population. These people are practical and dependable; and when they are highly talented, they modestly accomplish remarkable things with their diligence and attention to detail. They can excel in many vocations that call for stability, reliability, and accuracy, from physical science to conservative investment services. Mark Twain needed one of these to handle his affairs. Maybe we all do.

The fourth Keepers clan is the ISFJ clan, which I call the *Server* clan. Members of this clan make up 6 percent of the population; they are the people who like careers where they can minister to needy individuals day after day. They are apt to be devoted secretaries, nurses, or teachers, conservative about following set procedures and established styles. *Servers* are usually willing to work hard and live frugally, and they want others to do the same. Ironically, they sometimes marry wasteful spouses and spend their lives trying to save them from drugs or gambling. They rarely find time to do much creative writing, I'm sure, but they turn up as faithful or longsuffering characters in other people's stories.

The Tribe of Doers

The S-P tribe, like the S-J tribe, includes 38 percent of the population. That's one of the few things that these two tribes have in common. Doers may not provide their fair share of authors to the world, but they certainly provide more than their fair share of lively characters for biography, fiction, and drama. Doers fill our corridors of power, and they also fill our newspapers, movies, television programs, roller derbies, and prisons. If Doers had a capital, it might be Las Vegas. Adjectives that describe Doers include bold, impulsive, footloose, spontaneous, playful, competitive, optimistic, fun-loving, freewheeling, adventuresome, and daring.

It has been claimed that most television programming is aimed at Doers (38 percent of the public) because there are so many of them. Keepers (38 percent of the public) usually go along with what Doers want to watch. There are not enough Growers (12.5 percent of the public) and Knowers (12.5 percent of the public) in the audience to have much clout in television ratings. Knowers and Growers often write dramas about Doers for the Doers and Keepers to watch. (In about 700 B.C. Homer [a Grower] wrote about Odysseus [a Doer] trying to get home to Penelope [a Keeper]. Some things never change.)

Just as Growers need inner meaning, Knowers need mental power, and Keepers need community position, so Doers need freedom to follow their impulses. They can hardly bear to feel constrained. They see life as negotiating an obstacle course, and they like the challenge. They are action-oriented and survival-oriented. They often love to use tools and implements and machinery. They live in the here and now, and they have the gift of great physical endurance. They are apt to take trips on short notice. They are apt to become athletes, dancers, hunters, construction workers, or racers. They may excel in the police, the military, or exciting kinds of business and politics. At their best they are supreme individualists with a zest for life, and at their worst they are dangerous criminals. At heart they are Huckleberry Finn people.

Although Doers make up 38 percent of the population, they provide only 2 percent of education workers. They not only avoid teaching school, but they also avoid attending school. I have never yet had one Doer student in a creative writing class, and I found only two Doer students in all my other college English courses combined. (I tested my classes for a few years to see what they and I could learn about types.) There are always a few Doers in our schools and churches, but their ratio is slim.

The first Doers clan is the ESTP clan, which I call *Negotiators*. They are one of the most common types, making up 13 percent of the population. They have a wonderful supply of jokes and stories, but they are not apt to write them down. These delightful, charming, and fun-loving people have amazing powers of persuasion. This gives them a great talent for corporate troubleshooting or international diplomacy, as long as someone else follows up on the details. They feed on excitement and risk taking. Some of these *Negotiators* live their entire lives as successful confidence artists, hoodwinking people all the time. Shakespeare's Falstaff was one of these *Negotiators*, and so was Molière's Tartuffe. They add great color and vitality to drama or novels, but they and their nimble-witted powers of communication are beyond the creative imagination of many writers. Truth is indeed stranger than the fiction that most of us can manage to invent.

The second clan in the Doer tribe is the ESFP clan; I call its members *Entertainers*. Like *Negotiators*, the *Entertainers* make up a hefty 13 percent of the public and radiate wit and charm. They have a festive spirit. They need to be genuinely happy-go-lucky because they have little tolerance for the sad or difficult part of life. They are apt to leave if tragedy strikes their own families, but they sometimes thrive upon the drama of other people's tragedies. This makes them good in social services or crisis work, because they love to look on the bright side and have fun with people and cheer people up. Lady Brett in Hemingway's *The Sun Also Rises* seems much like an *Entertainer*. Sometimes these people actually become professional entertainers.

The third clan of the Doer tribe is the ISTP clan, the one that I call *Stuntmen*. They make up 6 percent of the population. These people tend to be loners and like to deal with concrete physical realities in exciting or even risky ways. They are apt to develop great skill in their specialties, which are often sports, entertainment, crafts, or building. A chosen activity absorbs them completely; and it is the activity itself that satisfies them far more than the results. Perhaps the fictitious old man in Hemingway's *The Old Man and the Sea* was based upon a *Stuntman*. In contrast to *Entertainers*, *Stuntmen* are not apt to take much interest in relationships with other people.

The fourth clan of the Doer tribe is the ISFP clan; I call them *Dancers* because they tend to dance away. Like the *Stuntmen*, *Dancers* make up 6 percent of the population and are extremely independent. No matter how good they are with words, they have little or no interest in writing for its own sake, and they are not great talkers. Instead of seeking out exciting physical risks and challenges, as the *Stuntmen* often do, the *Dancers* are apt to seek intense sense impressions in the arts or nature. All kinds of physical pursuits can appeal to *Dancers*, from music to wilderness camping, so long as there is enough sense of freedom.

In conclusion, here are the two temperament nationalities, four temperament tribes, and sixteen temperament clans in chart form:

N-People (25 percent of the public)		S-People (75 percent of the public)	
Growers (NF)	*Knowers* (NT)	*Keepers* (SJ)	*Doers* (SP)
Pastors (EJ)	Leaders (EJ)	Managers (ET)	Negotiators (ET)
Performers (EP)	Entrepreneurs (EP)	Sellers (EF)	Entertainers (EF)
Poets (IJ)	Executives (IJ)	Accountants (IT)	Stuntmen (IT)
Priests (IP)	Professors (IP)	Servers (IF)	Dancers (IF)

Five Styles of Thinking and Nine Kinds of People

In addition to the Myers-Briggs temperament types, there are two other extremely helpful aids now available for understanding human differences.

The book *Styles of Thinking* by Harrison and Bramson appeared in 1982.[6] It includes a long test and an explanation of five thinking styles, and it was written primarily to help business people. Readers find out which mental style they unconsciously prefer and usually use, and this can solve a multitude of mysteries.

Most popular in our society is the "Idealist" style of thinking, which is pleasantly warm rather than rigorously exact; I call it the *Hallmark style*. Second in popularity is the "Analyst" style, which is the most theoretical and habitually views the world as logical, orderly, and controllable; I call it the *IBM style*. Third in popularity is the "Realist" style, which asks "What are the facts?" and then tries to improve things; I call it the *Mr. Fixit style*. Fourth in popularity is the "Pragmatic" style, which is practical and adaptive, aimed at getting things done; I call it the *Roto-Rooter style*. Least common of all is the "Synthesist" style, which is witty and skeptical, creative and flexible; I call it the *Law School style*. I think Mark Twain and Woody Allen might be that type.

Becoming aware of one's thinking style and the fact that most other people don't think that way can explain all kinds of misunderstandings and make life less frustrating. It also helps us to see why we read and write so differently from each other, and it helps to cut down on miscommunication.

There is much yet to be learned about the Myers-Briggs temperament types and the five styles of thinking, but a third mode of seeing differences has already joined them. The book *The Enneagram* by Beesing, Nogosek, and O'Leary appeared in 1984.[7] (*Enneagram* is Greek for *nine*.) This material describes the nine spiritual kinds of people, and the special qualities and needs of each. It emphasizes one unexpected besetting sin that dogs each kind. There is no test to take to prove Enneagram kinds; people simply recognize themselves in the descriptions. It can be a powerful revelation.

I have given the nine kinds of people catchy names to make it easier to keep them straight: 1. Quality Controller, 2. People Pleaser, 3. Go-Getter, 4. Special Star, 5. Mental Miser, 6. Model Member, 7. Pleasure Promoter, 8. Vigorous Vigilante, and 9. Placid Pacer.

Someone has claimed that most writers are in the first group; I am skeptical about that, although most writers of satire would certainly have to be in group one. I had a chance to present the Enneagram quickly to six book-author friends at lunch one day. They paid close attention, and every one of them chuckled and said she was a *one*, a Quality Controller. I believe them. But among my friends I also know so far of two *twos*, a *three*, a *four*, two *fives*, and a *seven* who have written and published books.

The Enneagram may or may not tell who writes, but it will tell much about why and how people write. In my opinion, the Enneagram material is the most surprising, the most revealing, and the most spiritually significant of the various approaches to human differences. But it requires more space than the overview of the Myers-Briggs material and cannot be included in detail here. It is available elsewhere for those who are interested.[8]

A growing acquaintance with the Myers-Briggs temperament types, the five styles of thinking, and the nine spiritual kinds of people is a way to grow in self-understanding and in awareness of how life is for everyone. We might as well notice and enjoy the differences. The more understanding we have of our differences and similarities, the more clearly we can think and communicate.

SUGGESTED ACTIVITIES

1. Which of the temperament types are you? Choose an author or fictional character whose life and mind you know fairly well, and attempt to "type" that person. Are your favorite authors and fictional characters rather similar to you, or are you attracted to your opposites?

2. Which of your temperament traits motivate you to be a writer and help you to write? Which of your temperament traits sabotage either your writing or your tenacity about getting published? Be specific.

3. Invent an imaginary critique group that you would like to belong to, where all five members would meet regularly to read each other's writing and to offer help and encouragement to each other. What personality types might most obviously nurture your own writing gifts? Why? Those are people for you to look for!

4. Assemble the cast of characters for a drama, novel, or short story. Decide upon their locale, their physiques, their vocations, their names, their relationships, and their temperament types. Remember that all of the temperament types can be either male or female.

5. A student leaves home to go to college. The mother immediately brings out a gun and informs the father that she knows he has a lover. Then what? Write out this brief story as it plays in your mind. Think about the temperaments of the characters. Remember to let your

readers see and hear what is going on instead of interpreting and summarizing it for them.

NOTES

[1] The Myers-Briggs Type Indicator and all writing by Isabel Briggs Myers are published by Consulting Psychologist Press, 577 College Avenue, Palo Alto, CA 94306. Some of these materials are sold only to qualified professionals, as indicated in the catalog.

[2] In 1975 Isabel Myers had established the Center for Applications of Psychological Type, a nonprofit organization at 414 Southwest 7th Terrace, Gainesville, FL 32601. Phone: (904) 375–0160. To promote the constructive use of human differences, this center offers a variety of materials and services to the public.

[3] Marilyn Bates and David W. Keirsey, *Please Understand Me: An Essay on Temperament Types* (Corona del Mar, Calif.: Prometheus Press, 1978). The name of the publisher was later changed to Prometheus-Nemesis Book Company.

[4] Between the writing of this chapter and publication of this book, a new book appeared on the market: *Type Talk* by Otto Kroeger and Janet M. Thuesen (New York: Delacorte Press, 1988). It is highly entertaining, informative, and authoritative. It, too, sidesteps the copyrighted tests.

[5] To qualify for MENSA, a person must pass a test demonstrating extremely high intelligence. For those who don't qualify, there is purportedly an alternative organization called DENSA.

[6] Allen F. Harrison and Robert M. Bramson, *Styles of Thinking: Strategies for Asking Questions, Making Decisions, and Solving Problems* (Garden City, N.Y.: Anchor Press, 1982).

[7] Maria Beesing, O.P., Robert J. Nogosek, C.S.C., and Patrick H. O'Leary, S.J., *The Enneagram: A Journey of Self Discovery* (Denville, N.J.: Dimension Books, 1984).

[8] I have prepared a kit explaining the Enneagram with a one-hour taped lecture and a set of twenty colored folders. It is available by mail and may be published in the near future in book form.

Chapter 9

Authors in Action

With sixty staring me in the face, I have developed inflammation of the sentence structure and a definite hardening of the paragraphs.

— JAMES THURBER

We learned to talk from other talkers, and we learn to write from other writers. We never finish learning from other writers — by admiring their strengths, spotting their weaknesses, hearing their concerns, getting glimpses into their lives, and taking or rejecting their advice.

Most writers like to take stock once in a while about how they got where they are, and they like to share a few profound thoughts or practical tricks of the trade with others. They like to praise their favorite authors, also. For this chapter I sent seven questions to some writer friends and asked them to respond to any that appealed to them:

— How did you happen to become a writer?

— What do you wish you had learned sooner?

— What do you need or prefer to use physically to write?

— Can you recount any interesting anecdotes or ironies in your career?

— Is there anything you particularly love or hate about writing?

— What have you learned along the way that you can pass on?

— Which authors do you prize and why?

The Heart of the Matter

John Alexander is cofounder of The Other Side. *He is a columnist and has also produced an independent newsletter,* Taking Jesus Seriously. *His first book is* Your Money or Your Life *(1987).*

Becoming a writer was not my idea. I was an academic who thought any sentence under forty words and any word under four syllables was a misprint. But since I was active in civil rights in the sixties I kept being asked to write about racism. Not by *Reader's Digest*, but by *The Other Side*, a magazine then entirely devoted to race and, coincidentally, published by my father with help from his son.

I hadn't yet noticed the active voice and in most of my sentences the main verb was *is*, but I had something to say — which seems to me to be the heart of the matter. You can write only as deeply as you live and feel. You can go to journalism school and write for years, and if you don't care deeply about anything, your writing will be boring and irrelevant — like that of most Christian journalists.

Nonetheless, writing is a craft. You can no more write well without years of practice, without laboring over the feel of each sentence and the organization of each section, than you can become a concert pianist without years of playing scales. In the arts, whether it's dancing, jazz, painting, or writing, people want to express themselves without discipline, but that is self-indulgence, not self-expression. You have to have the sense that no sentence you ever wrote is quite right, that no chapter comes close to what you meant — and then you have to be driven to try and try till you get closer. Keep playing scales.

Good writing is as hard work as is ballet. While I fall short of telling aspiring writers to learn Latin so they can understand the structure of their language, I fall only a little short of it. To write well, you have to develop an instinctive grasp of grammar and syntax and words. So don't bother unless you love words. Unless you are fascinated by dictionaries and grammar books and by whether *impact* is a verb, writing will turn out to be more work than you'll want to do.

188

Your writing grows out of who you are. If you have some depth, your writing will have some depth. If you are sloppy and undisciplined, your writing will show it. If you love beauty and are offended by ugliness, your writing will become beautiful. If you need to impress people, you will use big words and write long sentences or fall into weird styles. If you have forgotten yourself (died to yourself, in Christian language), then you are free to serve something bigger than yourself and to write well.

Having used a computer for the last three years, I'm not sure I could go back to any other tool. Computers obviously make rewrites many times easier. You can go over and over what you've written without rendering it illegible and without having to spend hours retyping unchanged parts. But for me the initial writing is also easier, and I'm not sure why. Maybe page after page half scratched out plus a wastebasket full of crumpled pages discourages me, and those you can't see on a computer.

Some of my favorite writers are Tolkien, E. E. Cummings, Kurt Vonnegut, Graham Greene, C. S. Lewis, Madeleine L'Engle, Sartre, Ursula Le Guin, Kenneth Patchen, T. S. Eliot, Emily Dickinson, and Dostoevski. I have probably been too much influenced by Vonnegut and Cummings, both of whom have self-indulgent, weird styles. I like those people because all of them have something to say and most of them say it simply and beautifully. Those are the things I care about in writing. They are also people who *show* what they mean rather than stating it; they don't preach it, but make you feel it.

Starting All Over

Lloyd Alexander is a master storyteller who writes both fantasy and realism, both about how we learn to be genuine human beings. Among his many honors, The Black Cauldron (1965) was chosen to be a Newbery Medal Honor Book and The High King (1968) won the Newbery Medal. His books have been translated into ten foreign languages. He says he wrote for adults for seventeen years before he began writing for young people—"the most creative and liberating experience of my life."

What I have mainly learned, during these past forty-five years of writing, is that writing does not get easier. On the contrary, it gets more and more difficult. It should, and writers ought to be glad of that. It means that we are continually trying to do better, to stretch our own limits. Otherwise, why bother to write in the first place? If we sense our work becoming easier, we could be in bad trouble and would do well to take careful stock of our hopes, motives, and goals.

Some things I have gained from experience. Large and messy piles of paper do not frighten me — as long as something is written on them; blank pages, however, do scare me. I'm no longer afraid of constant revision and rewritings, of doing hard work one day and throwing it out the next. I'm not afraid of not writing the perfect book. No one ever has; not yet, anyway, and probably never will. I have to be satisfied that I've done my best at that particular moment in my life.

Apart from that, each new work feels as if I've never written anything else before. It's a valid sensation because, indeed, I have never written that book before. The book and I are equally inexperienced, unknown to each other; we are both beginners.

Writing, for me, is always starting all over again.

Trust Your Instincts

Isabel Anders is the author of Awaiting the Child: An Advent Journal (1987) *and has published many articles in* Eternity, The Christian Century, *and other religious publications.*

I had a father who played word-games with me early on, and shared his deepest ideas about God and the world with me. Ideas were the first things I remember liking, that liked me back. Books excited me. I have wanted to be a writer since high school — perhaps even before that.

For me, growing as a writer has been partly learning to trust my own experience, my own voice and its expression. It has meant continually being willing to risk more, to follow my intuition as to what to work on next and how to go about it. When I became the wife of an Episcopal priest, John Throop, and then a mother, I think my perspective as a writer became much clearer. For years I had ideas that were developing, but I was identified mainly as an editor — and who wants to read the ideas of an editor? My various roles came together in my first book, *Awaiting the Child*.

I work at a keyboard — an electronic typewriter. I take a rough, typewritten first draft, and then edit it with a pen. Some parts I retype immediately to get better legibility. There may be several more versions after that. I have yet to get a chance to learn to use our basic word processor, which my husband uses. (He is a writer of articles and books also.)

I value writing as a valid and rewarding form of work, but I dislike the fact that people generally don't consider it so (unless you're making a lot of money at it), and I feel almost apologetic sometimes about having such a "sideline." To me it is much more than that, but it is easy to sound as if you take yourself too seriously if you come on strong about being a writer.

My advice is to listen to other people, but make up your own mind. How do you feel after you have finished a draft and reread it? Trust your own instincts if you feel you are on the right track. And read widely. Some of my favorite authors are Madeleine L'Engle, Annie Dillard, Frederick Buechner, C. S. Lewis, Charles Williams, Herbert O'Driscoll, and Evelyn Underhill.

Learning the Trade

Dennis Baker uses his writing skills almost every day while working for a group that ministers to kids in jail. As a free-lance author he has published twenty-four books, the most notable being The Gentle Giant *with Rosey Grier and Debby Boone —* So Far *with Debby Boone.*

My first intimation that I had any writing talent came in a freshman composition class in college. We got an assignment to describe some object or other. I chose my ROTC garrison cap which was close at hand when I sat down to do the assignment. It was just a page. I whipped it out and went on to other things.

But, a week or so later, I found myself sitting in class, listening to the teaching assistant read my paper to the rest of the class as an example of how the assignment should have been performed. Happily, he allowed me to remain anonymous. I savored the moment, but gave it little more thought.

I received a degree in English literature, but without taking any elective courses devoted to writing. Then, having undergone a conversion to Christianity while in college, I went on to seminary. Three years later, I was an assistant pastor in a surburban church in the Philadelphia area. When filling out my dossier form for my denomination's ministerial department, I remember noting, in response to a query on that form, that I had no interest in writing.

At the end of almost five years in pastoral work I — to reduce a complex series of events to a few words — experienced the truth of the adage that the guidance of God is often a kick in the pants. I took a job as a shipping clerk in a Christian publishing house.

After nine months, the publisher decided I was not going back into the ministry and invited me to join his editorial department. There I learned the trade from a former Doubleday editor and found myself having the time of my life. This was the sort of work, I realized, that I was born to do. I have been an editor and then a writer ever since.

Ted Bernstein was the managing editor of *The New York Times* and wrote a book I cherish, entitled *The Careful Writer*. His sage advice has always stood me in good stead. I love to recount the story he tells of the plumber in New York who was using hydrochloric acid to clear clogged drains. It's under the heading called "Windyfoggery" in which he discusses the ways in which wind and fog can often be found together in shabby writing.

Wells Root is an old Hollywood screenwriter whose book *Writing the Script* I found especially memorable. In explaining the importance of conflict in any piece of writing, he asks us to imagine the curtain parting to reveal an empty couch. A man and woman come onstage, sit on the couch, and begin to hug and kiss. Soon the audience is asleep.

But, Root goes on, imagine the audience's response and interest in the same scene if, before the couple comes onstage, a lone actor comes onstage and plants a time bomb beneath the couch. Then the couple could come out, engage in the most boring discussion imaginable, and yet maintain the audience's undivided attention.

Tell the Truth

K. L. (Lloyd) Billingsley says he has been involved in a kind of literary decathlon—mostly for purposes of survival. His card says: author, journalist, and screenwriter. He has now published one novel, A Year for Life *(1986) and five nonfiction books including* The Generation that Knew Not Josef *(1985). His journalism has appeared in* Christianity Today, *the* Wall Street Journal, *and the* Spectator *(London).*

I suppose one writes for the same reason a baby cries: to be heard. Writing was something I found myself doing more or less naturally. I asked myself why I should do it for free, and when I got my first book contract, I launched out full time. I do not consider myself a "success," whatever that is. I am still an apprentice, with much to learn, and to unlearn. I believe my most notable achievement is to have thus far survived in this rather unstable trade, in a century which increasingly prefers style instead of substance, fraud and lies instead of truth, and the image above the word.

I consider that a state-of-the-art computer is standard and indispensable equipment for the writer who would be competitive. The typewriter, once a boon, is now an instrument of torture by comparison.

All writers need editors, and that is something any writer should learn early. I wish I had learned sooner the importance of having fresh eyes look at my work, of the necessity for good editorial collaboration.

I realize that not all editorial advice is good, however. Once I wrote in an article about sports "Television did for sports what the automobile and drive-in theater did for sexual immorality." The editor lined this out and wrote in "Television put sports on the map."

Reactions from friends can be less than helpful also. For example, my old car had 160,000 miles on it when I suddenly received a royalty payment. So I went and bought a new car, a cheapo, bottom-of-the-line, "econobox." When a friend saw it, she said to me, "How can you buy a car? You don't even have a job."

I like what Flaubert said about writing. "Never mind whether they are good or bad, it is grand to write, to cease to be *oneself*, and to move among the creatures that one is describing. Today, for instance, I have been man and woman at the same time, lover and mistress together, riding in the forest on an autumn afternoon under the yellowing leaves; and I have been the horses too, and the leaves and the wind, and the words they spoke and the red sun that made them blink their eyes that swam with love."

Besides that, and more, writing is inside work, with no heavy lifting.

I wish that I had learned sooner that there is no hierarchy of writing, that fiction is not more exalted or important than other forms. In fact, books should not be classified as fiction or nonfiction, but as "fact" or "nonfact."

On the level of craft, I have learned not to try to write fiction or drama without a compelling story. To do otherwise is like laying the carpet first and then building the house around it. An idea, a vignette, a character, a gag, a gimmick, use of special language — these just won't get it done. Story is everything.

I have had a showcase production of two one-act plays, but have stopped writing for the stage. Dramatic writing is the most difficult of all, and the chances for financial reward are slim. I'm a member of the Writer's Guild of America, the union of film, television, and radio writers. I've sold three teleplays and done other screen work. This craft pays the best, but is most troublesome for the writer, who, in the overall picture is not very important. It's a producer's and director's medium, and the writer basically comes up with the instruction manual. But I do plan more screen work. It's a challenge.

In nonfiction, the idea and purpose are more important. Writers should ask: What do I want to say? What story do I have to tell? They should not start to write until they have something. Then, they should look for the most suitable and economical way of putting it down. It is important to learn the craft, but I believe there are some things which can neither be learned nor taught.

The best advice for a writer? Tell the truth. As Hemingway put it (but did not always practice), "Write the truest sentence that you know."

The writer should follow the example of the preacher in Ecclesiastes who "searched to find just the right words, and what he wrote was upright and true."

Malcolm Muggeridge has been my spiritual and literary Sherpa guide. I consider that he is the best writer of the English language now alive, mostly because his experiences have been so varied and because his prose is so alive and luminous. "Words are as beautiful as love, and as easily betrayed," he writes. The same honesty and lucidity are true of all the great ones: C. S. Lewis, Samuel Johnson, Evelyn Waugh, Boris Pasternak, George Orwell, T. S. Eliot, and others.

I admire Solzhenitsyn for his courage and sheer willpower. He wrote those huge books in complete secrecy and through great suffering when, humanly speaking, there was no chance that they would ever be published. That's inspiration, that's dedication.

These were all writers with a purpose, who did not fear to tackle the idols and buffooneries of this most bloody and pretentious of centuries. To me, they all say with one voice, in the words of a famous poem:

> Take up our quarrel with the foe
> To you from falling hands we throw
> The torch, be yours to hold it high.

Writing Changes Lives

Marian Bray has published articles in many magazines including Boys Life, Ranger Rick, Horseman, Mother Earth News, *and* TQ. *Her first three books for young people are* Springtime for Khan *and* Summer by the Sea *(1988) and* Stepping Over Stones *(1988).*

My first writers' conference, and I should have been thrilled — but I was furious. A fairly well-known writer had read one of my stories and looked up at me as if I'd suddenly grown antlers. "I don't know what to tell you," he said, putting my manuscript back in the manila envelope. "I've never seen a story like this before, so I can't help you."

I took my story and slunk off before I did bad things to him with a butter knife.

Fortunately, the conference lasted a week, and on the last day I met an editor who liked fantasy. He bought my story.

Rule One: Don't believe everything everyone tells you.

I suppose there are thousands of rules about writing fiction, but most of them don't seem to apply. Publishing is a crazy business.

Somerset Maugham said to a friend's English class: "There are three rules for writing a novel. Unfortunately, no one knows what they are."

Early on in my writing career, I decided that I might not be particularly brilliant or talented, but I could be diligent and hard working. Every day — well, almost — I write. Even if it's only a single page. I always meet my deadlines. I reject the common and try to be unusual — or, as some of my editors like to say, off the wall. These attributes increase sales.

I know too many people who talk writing. They only fantasize themselves as writers. Don't fool yourself. Writing is hard, hard work.

Rule Two: Writing requires a lot of heart and a belief in your work.

People always ask me, "Where do you get your ideas?" Even other writers ask me that, which I find strange. Don't we all go to the same place? I admit it, I daydream. A lot. Joyce Carol Oates once stated in an interview that she spends an inordinate amount of time doing nothing. I bet that means she daydreams.

I receive odd rejection letters. Editors tell me that my stories are well-written, but that they have no spiritual content or that they are too honest. I puzzle over those remarks, not understanding, or perhaps not wanting to understand. Then I always return to writing stories that I think kids will enjoy and identify with — honest, not preachy — and find brave editors to publish them. If I've learned anything, it's to follow the story because it knows the way.

Rule Three: As Madeleine L'Engle says, listen to the story. It knows.

Writers and editors often muck up stories. One of my frustrations as a writer is dealing with editors. Some I would lay down my life for, but the rest make me crazy. I have sent most of my editors this quotation I love from science fiction author Robert Silverberg: "I still get stories turned down by editors occasionally, you know, and so does every other well-known science fiction writer I can think of — if God were a science fiction writer, *he'd* get rejected once in a while too, editors being what they are. . . ."

My problem is idealism. I keep hoping for an editor who will care passionately for my stories. And like a great coach drive me on to writing heights. Well, someday. Until then I try to control my tendencies toward violence. Maybe suddenly I'll realize that the editor I've wished for has been with me all along.

Writing is hard, but sometimes it pays high. Only yesterday my teenage brother told me that his friend reads all my stories and thinks I'm a good writer. That means more to me than a contract. Well, almost.

The Final Rule: Writing changes lives, especially your own.

Creative Yen

Marjorie Lee Chandler is a former speech and language therapist turned freelance writer and journalist. She has published articles in many periodicals including Kids, Virtue, St. Anthony Messenger, *and* Moody Monthly. *She and her husband enjoy traveling with writing assignments, but most of their writing time is at their home in the San Bernardino Mountains.*

I wish I had read more classics as a youngster. The master word-artists are the best role models. Through their works I see the possibilities of turning my own mental pictures into word pictures.

I became a writer because it fulfills my creative yen as nothing else can. I became a *published* writer because it is affirming to know your work has value. It was a risk to begin sending off my very own stories — words scribbled on a phone pad, or heart-felt thoughts in a private journal, or freewheeling fiction tucked in a yellow file folder — to editors who often returned manuscripts with a rejection slip! Marketing is never as exhilarating as writing. But, when I crossed over from a would-be writer to "published author" the world seemed a rosier hue. I realized that people would actually read, enjoy, and profit from my composition!

Word processing has undoubtedly taken much of the drudgery from writing and rewriting, but the most important element in writing is still discipline whatever the writer's desk-top accoutrements. Also, the basics — spelling, grammar, colorful description — are the indispensable tools of the trade which I feel I can never fully master. I have a tight tether line to a good dictionary, thesaurus, atlas, books of quotations, etc.

Of course, I now have a great "in-house editor" — my husband — whom I met at a summer writing school. We enjoy planning future writing projects together, fine-honing each other's leads, and reading rough paragraphs to see if thoughts "hang together."

I'm glad I went to two writing schools (and took a longer correspondence course) after deciding to make my hobby my profession. Writers write, editors edit, and publishers ultimately hold the key to a byline. A writing conference is an excellent way to understand what those amorphous publisher-types are really like. Usually I find them discerning, demanding, and decisive. It is nice to be on a "first name" basis with a few of these eccentric word gobblers.

I have gained valuable "on the job" training as a writer by volunteering to put together newsletters for two organizations: The YWCA in Dayton, Ohio, and more recently, The Door of Hope, Home for the Homeless in Pasadena, California. The board of directors of nonprofit projects are usually grateful for even a beginner's attempt to initiate or increase their printed materials. As editor, I named each of the organs, created my own format, assigned columns, chose photos and — after many nonpaid hours — felt good about the results. Both publications resembled giving birth — a lot of labor and a lot of love. After I started these fledgling four-to-six-page newsletters, they continued to thrive through other volunteer efforts or paid assistance.

It is possible to tie in with a publisher willing to print the newsletter as a mission or as a tax write-off. Because the *Doorway* newsletter aided a mission to homeless families, nearby Focus on the Family made their editorial staff available to me for layout of art boards and printing runs. I learned a great deal about writing — from the drawing board to the press — by working with this professional staff.

Similarly, I have volunteered to do several brochures for other nonprofit groups. Brochures demand tight writing which clearly and quickly conveys information. This is good practice, and the volunteer experience might be a precursor to brochure writing in public relations, usually a lucrative activity. Brochures provide writing credits that help a portfolio look professional.

I've learned that ghostwriting is also a rewarding "job for hire" — if chosen wisely. Often the most effective mode is a first person story. And many people have great stories, but need a craftsman to do the telling. I find it a challenge to "get under the skin" of the subject and see life and relationships from their vantage point.

I enjoy reading authors who use strong visual word-pictures to describe our incredible physical world. W. Phillip Keller writes about the amorphous sea, a shepherd's tender care for his sheep, and wilderness trails with vivid description that I can nearly see in three dimensions and vibrant color as I read. Likewise, I appreciate the style in which Anne Morrow Lindberg describes the beauty of nature. And, although I got a late start reading the classics, I now like to keep the dust off our Shakespeare anthology, C. S. Lewis's Narnia series, and children's treasures like Winnie-the-Pooh by A. A. Milne.

Something Excellent

Russell Chandler is an award-winning journalist with the Los Angeles Times, *where he has been a religion writer for fifteen years. (In 1988 he was named United States "Religion Writer of the Year.") He has now published his fifth book,* Understanding the New Age *(1988), and he also writes free-lance articles for Christian periodicals.*

I always liked writing, and by the time I got to junior high my teachers gave me good marks. I particularly liked poetry and fiction writing, two things I don't do now. I went to a career day for writers in high school and learned that unless you are a super-popular author, you could hardly support a family with the writing habit. At that stage I parked my desires to be a novelist, majored in business in college, graduated from Princeton Seminary, and found an outlet for creative instincts in sermons and other materials for the church. But I was never published then.

After I had been a pastor several years, I went to the Billy Graham School of Writing sponsored by *Decision* magazine. I felt I was testing the waters at that conference to see if I could be a writer. I sent an article to *Guideposts* magazine and they liked it and bought it (although they never published it). That encouraged me to become a full-time writer, and journalism was the way to get a foot in the door. I took one journalism course at Modesto Junior College. I wrote a little for the *Modesto Bee*, and in 1966 I joined the staff. From there I moved around, including a stint as news editor at *Christianity Today*, and ended up at the *Los Angeles Times* in 1974. I think I'm there because of my interest, some talent, and my feeling that God could use my talents there.

Maybe in the divine economy the fact that I started my writing career at the age of thirty-four instead of ten years earlier doesn't matter a whole lot. I never attended journalism school, and I wished I had learned more about government and how the courts operate; but my seminary background, years in the pastorate, and reporter's coverage of the courts near Sonora have all been valuable. The latter helped me to understand legal proceedings when I covered church-state cases in Los Angeles.

I wish I had learned shorthand and touch typing, but I can type pretty fast anyway. Of course typewriters are absolutely passè. Marjorie and I both have Tandy 100 laptop computers. I have extra memory chips in mine, and I write a lot of my stories on the move and zip them in to the *Times* mainframe computer. Increasingly, Christian periodicals are having modem capabilities so that we can file a story directly; it takes only minutes to file a fairly lengthy story directly with the publishing house. I also now have a Tandy 1400 laptop computer with desktop capacity, which I just used to write my book on the New Age. I use the Word Perfect system.

Reporters can write in buses, planes, on park benches, in restaurants, and even phone booths when necessary — hang the noise. But to write a book I like an aesthetic setting, and we wrote most of this new one in the mountains with the tall pines to look at. But basically, you're looking at a screen. I wrote that 97,000-word book from January 11 to April 1, 1988. It has thirty-three chapters, glossary, and endnotes. A few weeks later, I still had a stiff neck and sore shoulders to work off gradually.

I find a comfortable posture chair and correct lighting most essential, and taking breaks to move around and shift the eyes to a distant horizon. I like the plug-in warmers that can keep a cup of tea or coffee hot right beside the computer. We have a portable printer that we take with us, and a daisy wheel at home.

In spite of all our modern comforts and conveniences, we still can't escape distractions that make it hard to write. I agree with Mark Twain that the best thing about writing is having written. I love the sound, cadence, and appeal of something that has the right ring to it. As a journalist, when I amass enough material so that I know I can advance knowledge on a given subject, and thus contribute something to my readers, it is a wonderful feeling. I also like to point out things of significance, so my readers can make an informed choice when they decide for themselves what to believe.

My advice to aspiring writers is to hone to its sharpest the instinct for curiosity, ask the hard questions, don't take things for granted, don't swallow people's assumptions and hypotheses, and don't fear intuition — the things that have to be perceived through the intuitive right hemisphere of the brain rather than the rational left hemisphere. Keep probing, make patience your specialty, and always be eager to ask one more question or check one more source. That makes the difference between something good and something excellent. Often some new insight will come after the interview is over, in casual conversation with your subject. Pick up on nonverbal clues and cues, and tune in to feelings that flesh out your story. Don't just tell readers about something, but take them there to experience the people and scenes for themselves.

When I had an interview with Oral Roberts once, he wanted to interview me first. He wanted to know if I had accepted Jesus as my Savior before he would answer questions. I am glad to be known as a Christian, but I didn't want to have to be screened that way. I wanted to be respected as a professional and granted the interview whether I was born again or not.

When asked about my favorite literature, I am apt to answer Ernest Hemingway, Frederick Buechner, and *Psalms* and *Proverbs*.

No Substitute for Living

Arthur C. Clarke is almost certainly the world's best-selling science fiction writer. He has published over seventy books of various kinds, including Childhood's End *(1953) and* 2061: Odyssey Three *(1987). This message is one that he has often sent to hopeful writers who contact him for help or advice, and he offers it here to encourage writers to write—but not to him.*

Read at least one book a day, and write as much as you can. Study the memoirs of authors who interest you (e.g. Somerset Maughham's *A Writer's Notebooks*). Correspondence courses, writers' schools, etc., are useful — but all the authors I know were self-taught. There is no substitute for living; as Hemingway wisely remarked, writing is not a full-time occupation.

So many publishers and authors have asked me to comment on books, or to write a preface, that I am forced to turn down all such requests, no matter how good the cause. I've always felt embarrassed by this as (a) it's an author's professional duty to help promising newcomers (and even more so, indigent oldcomers), (b) I did a fair amount of blurb-scrounging in my early days (e.g. from C. S. Lewis and Lord Dunsany), and (c) the editors/writers involved are usually good friends — as a result of which I've occasionally relented and knocked off a sentence or two for quotation.

I still get several requests every week — so now I simply have to be adamant.

UNDER NO CIRCUMSTANCES will I comment on MSS or story ideas.

If I responded to all the appeals I get for literary, financial, and educational assistance I would have no time (or money) for anything else. It is often difficult to ignore genuine and deserving cases, but I salve my conscience with the thought that I now directly support about 50 people.

Admiration Vs. Communication

Gracia Fay Ellwood has often contributed to The Reformed Journal *and other publications, and has served as editor of* Mythlore. *Her best-known book is* Good News from Tolkien's Middle Earth *(1970), and she is now at work on* The Faces of Faith, *a religion textbook for Prentice-Hall.*

I wanted to be an author since I was in grade school because I wanted to relate to people; my classmates nearly all treated me like the Invisible (and Inaudible) person. In my private fantasies my books were read far and wide and everyone wanted to hear what I had to say. I wrote my first book at about age twelve, and I'm afraid it still exists somewhere . . . luckily there's not much danger I'll meet the sort of world fame that might cause it to come to light. After a few years I sorted out the deep human need for communication from the lust for admiration, which might be compared, in Augustine's phrase, to "scratching the itching sore."

I prefer to write with pen and notebook rather than with my typewriter. Actually, I prefer to type with a secretary, but the secretary is waiting in the wings along with world fame.

I feel the best way for a style not to call attention to itself is to alternate short sentences with longer ones.

Aspiring writers should pretend they are salaried. They would do well to keep a schedule, put the phone on automatic, pool small children with a neighbor, lock the door, and let nothing short of a life-or-death crisis distract them. If they can't manage this at home they should go to the local library, or perhaps make an arrangement to be monitored by a friend.

In Your Bones

Eli Haugen, of Norway, does her creative writing in Norwegian but communicates here in English, her second language. Her first book Kjaere deg . . . (My Dear . . .) *was published by Lunde Forlag of Oslo in 1987, and the first printing sold out in three months.*

Being a writer is something that's in your bones — it was in mine. But I think I needed to grow up properly before I had something relevant and important to say. Becoming a published writer seemed to me to be too high a hope, so I slipped into it by writing things for our church newsletter. As I got positive feedback, I wrote more. The stack of pieces grew, until I realized I had enough for a book.

My manuscript was refused by two publishers. Then another publisher asked me to write some devotional material for children. They liked what I did for them and asked in an offhand way if I'd ever thought about writing a book for adults.

"Well — , I have a manuscript that's been refused twice. I can send it to you if you'd like to have a look at it. . . ."

For them it was love at first sight, and they accepted it! They published it as a beautiful little hardback with the cover, illustrations, and calligraphed section headlines by my brother, Anders Faerevaag, a professional illustrator.

Do I love or hate writing? My answer to that is simple: Both! Getting "into the flow" is horrible, and I do anything to avoid actually getting started. Once I'm "in," it's wonderful! It fascinates me that on the screen — on a limp piece of paper — I can create anything, absolutely *anything*.

I use a computer, which I needed because I am weakened by multiple sclerosis. After I got used to that, it's like going back to the stone age to try to use a typewriter.

I attended a writer's seminar in Amsterdam at Eastertime in 1988. The teachers were from the United States — John and Elisabeth Sherrill, experienced writers and wonderfully warm and gentle people. The best part of the course was that I finally got *words* for all my writing instincts. Now I know a lot more about the *how-to's* and *don't's*, and I'm sure I'll benefit greatly.

My own advice to aspiring writers is "Don't start writing unless you have to. It's too painful. But if you do, learn a few basics, then trust your instincts and don't pretend to be someone or something you are not."

My overall favorite writer is C. S. Lewis. His use of words and images is perfect, and he constantly makes me see, feel, hear, and *experience* the splendor and glory of God. On the other hand, I like P. G. Wodehouse for the sheer brilliance of his wordplay. And I like mystery writer Arthur Upfield (the Napoleon Bonaparte stories) for writing in a way that makes me taste and feel something I have never known — this time Australia.

Diamonds in the Dust

Virginia Hearn has edited about 250 books (usually behind the scenes) for more than a dozen publishers. She has led journal-keeping workshops for six years at New College, Berkeley, where from time to time she and Walter Hearn team-teach a course, "Communicating the Faith in Writing." In 1988 she "retired" after thirty years as a magazine/newsletter editor for various organizations (InterVarsity Christian Fellowship, Christian Medical Society, Berkeley Christian Coalition, Evangelical Women's Caucus) in order to read, write, and see what happens. Her own books are What They Did Right: Reflections on Parents by Their Children *(1974) and* Our Struggle To Serve: The Stories of 15 Evangelical Women *(1979).*

I became aware that I was a writer when as a ninth-grader I was appointed editor of the junior high newspaper, although the teacher in charge of it hadn't really known me. When I look at my eighth-grade compositions — whatever their imaginative inadequacies, they were letter-perfect, word-perfect, and at least somewhat creative — I realize that the teachers had talked among themselves about who could write. My work on that paper was primarily rewriting the stuff the other kids turned in.

That same year I started studying Latin under an outstanding teacher who took a personal interest in me. Since then I have gone on to learn Spanish, German, French, and Greek. I consider foreign languages basic to my competence in English. But I wish that I had deliberately and confidently tried to develop my writing talent in high school and college.

As a young adult I trained under Joseph Bayly, who edited InterVarsity Christian Fellowship's *HIS* magazine. He was a superb editor and encouraged me to follow in his footsteps. Later, I became a free-lance book editor, working for various publishing houses. When I saw the books that had been accepted for publication, and then were given to me to polish up before typesetting, I quickly realized, "I can do better than this."

I wish I had begun keeping a personal journal as a ten-year-old, and then on through my teens and early twenties, rather than the bare-bones chronology of events that I did keep. I had no vision for recording my inner rather than outer life. I am now working on a book about journal-keeping.

I still use paper and pencil, though now I'm glad to have a computer for rewriting, making format changes, and typing later drafts. Gradually I am composing more on the computer — though I suspect that my style, if handwritten first, is somewhat different, and perhaps better.

I have learned that even when I think something I've written is pedestrian or prosaic, I later on realize (as Flannery O'Connor said) that there are "diamonds in the dust."

In spite of all the writing I've done, I still always wonder if I'm up to the next project I face. I almost always feel great resistance to sitting down and getting started. It helps to tell myself that I'll do a rough draft, just to get something down. Then, all I have to do is polish that up — and I've done it. I pass that advice on to aspiring writers.

I also advise writers to work with a good editor, who can see flaws, problems, and mistakes in their work that they're oblivious to. Pray for such a person and then recognize her or him as a friend, someone who is really on your side, not an opponent. My husband and I edit each other's work, and my own first reaction to any change he makes is usually one of annoyance. But, almost always, I soon get over that and am able to see what strength my resident editor's emendations have brought to my writing.

I admire Flannery O'Connor for the quality of her letter writing, and the fact that she got so many of them written. Rosemary Radford Ruether for her research and productivity. Barbara Pym, for her novels. I readily identify with her lead characters, though they're in a British setting and live lives very different from my own; she pictures a world that seems authentic from a middle-aged woman's point of view. Another English novelist, Fay Weldon, has said that she began to write because as she was growing up she never read anything that fit the world as she experienced it.

Science and Sonnets

Walter Hearn is editor, founding editor, or contributing editor for assorted publications including Search: Scientists Who Serve God. *He is an active contributing editor for* Radix *magazine, where he used to be Poetry Rejection Editor. He is coauthor of the 1986 booklet* Teaching Science in a Climate of Controversy *and is now writing a book for parents about science in the public schools. He has edited many books, including Charles Hummel's* The Galileo Connection *(1986). He has published about a hundred articles and reviews, and has contributed chapters to seven books, from Mixter's* Evolution and Christian Thought Today *(1959) to Sider's* Living More Simply *(1980). Moreover, he has published over a dozen poems, and one of his sonnets won a prize in* Poet and Critic.

I was a university biochemistry professor when I married a professional editor. In fact, I met Ginny though a poem and later an article I submitted to InterVarsity's *HIS* magazine, of which she was then associate editor. We wanted to work as closely together as possible and after a few years of marriage we decided to share a single career. It seemed easier to turn me into an editor than to turn her into a biochemist, so I "dropped out" (as they said back in the late sixties and early seventies) and we eventually became a free-lance writing/editing team called Editorial Excellence.

I remember how Ginny and I moved into book editing. A friend of ours was told by his professor that he had to drastically condense his wordy dissertation, but he couldn't bear to part with any of his precious material. Ginny easily did the surgery and sewed up the wounds of both manuscript and candidate. When the acquisitions editor of Tyndale House asked me about a possible book, I told him I didn't think Tyndale was interested in my manuscript but might be interested in my wife, an experienced editor and "book doctor." Within three weeks Ginny received a manuscript Ken Taylor had promised to publish but which was reviewed by Tyndale's in-house editors as rather hopeless. She turned it into a book later recognized by one Christian magazine as the best book in a particular category in its year of publication. That was the way our joint book-editing career began, some two hundred books ago.

From early childhood I've loved to read. According to family lore I woke up one morning reciting an original poem, a big hit with my mother, who wrote it down. In elementary school I was on staff, maybe editor, of the school paper. My father's hobby was printing, so I grew up setting type and using a Kelsey handpress. As a Boy Scout in Houston, Texas, I was for a short time the editor, publisher, typesetter, and pressman of the *Troop Eleven Bugle*. I read voraciously, but rather narrowly, sticking largely to nonfiction "how-to" books.

I wish I had gained a more explicit understanding of the power of narration. Within the Christian community I recognized the importance of sharing ourselves with each other. But I wish I had given more thought to the overall human significance of one person narrating a story to another person. I would have read more fiction and might have tried writing some myself. More important, I would have seen everything I've written — even technical papers — as a personal story worth telling to other persons.

I also wish I had thought of myself earlier as a writer. I might have prepared myself better, kept a journal, and seized more of the opportunities to be published that I let go by. If I had thought of myself as a professional writer, even a part-time one, from the beginning, I would have kept better track of all the things I've written — and copies of everything published. I lacked a literary background, but my facility for language was fostered by four years of high school Latin. In college, besides the German required of chemistry majors, I took two years of French. In grad school I added a year of Russian and have since picked up a little Spanish and Greek. On my way up the academic ladder I contributed scientific papers to "the literature" (not to be confused with literature).

In about 1955, when I was teaching at Baylor Medical School, *HIS* published my slangy paraphrase of the epistle of James written to get a point across to a student I was counseling. I suppose that article, later reprinted in England, made me a published writer over thirty years ago.

I wrote verse for the fun of it as a pleasing change from the stiffness of technical writing. When I joined the faculty at Iowa State my parodies were a hit with home ec majors who had a frown-and-bear it attitude toward my required course. I turned *Annie Get Your Gun* into a smashing biomusical, with lines like:

> The girl that I marry will have to be
>   Loaded with glucose and ATP;
> The girl I call my own
>   Will have adrenocorticotropic hormone. . . .

I borrowed music from Georges Bizet for a metabolic opera entitled *Carbon*, which took place in the gonad of a brave Spanish bull and ended with a big reduction scene. A graduate student sang all the parts, including the glycolytic cycle to Carmen's "Habanera" and electron transport to the "Toreador Song." The opera had a short run (my eight o'clock class) but was acclaimed a critical success.

Editing newsletters is an unlikely route to literary fame and fortune but a lot of my writing has been in that genre. In the early sixties I began a newsletter for my department that was read all over the Iowa State campus for its occasional humor. I cranked out that newsletter weekly for over ten years. In 1969 I took over the editorship of the national

Newsletter of the American Scientific Affiliation, an eight-page bimonthly I'm still editing after nineteen years. That's a lot of copy, probably more than the million-word apprenticeship required of "real" writers.

I still write poetry, some of it quite serious, with a pencil equipped with a good eraser, but until about four years ago I wrote everything else on a standard typewriter bought as a rebuilt model when I was a teenager. My affection for that typewriter was such that I once gave "Ol' Underwood" coauthor status on an article we wrote about treating people as machines and vice versa. Now I use WordStar on a Kaypro computer whose CP/M operating system makes it as much of a dinosaur as Ol' Underwood — who looks on in sad amazement from a corner of my study.

I generally write in the study where my word processor is located, with the doors closed to keep the cats from entering and committing any acts of desecration on the papers piled around. I think I might be more productive if I filed away some of those piles, but a deadline seems always at hand to keep me from "getting organized." I dream of writing without having to face deadlines, but in fact I wonder if I would do much writing without them.

I hate the agonizing when a piece of writing hasn't yet come together, especially since people often say, "I wish writing came as easy for me as it does for you." Almost everything I write goes through about five drafts, sometimes after dozens of false starts on the opening paragraph. My wife edits just about everything I write. I don't know whether I love it or hate it when I finally let her see my fourth draft and she says, "It's coming."

I love finishing something after agonizing over it. And I love being a cocreator with God of something important. I love being able to lay my work before the Lord, sometimes waking up in the morning with exactly the right idea to break through the barrier I was up against the night before. Although such ideas never come "on demand," they *do* come after prayer, sometimes when I'm soaking in the bathtub (which has given baptism new meaning to me).

Writing and editing are different gifts. All writers need some of the editorial gift, exercised either by themselves or by someone else, preferably by both. Even the most experienced, most gifted writer finds it difficult to see things through the eyes of a reader, partly because the writer knows too much. For example, writers already know the importance of what they are writing, or they wouldn't be writing it. Readers have to be shown why it's important. Editors are go-betweens who read a manuscript with the naive reader's interest in mind.

Aspiring writers, especially those whose work has been rejected, sometimes regard editors as being against them, or as being ignorant for not seeing things the same way the writer sees them. I have encountered only one or two ignorant editors, but many arrogant writers who seek primarily to satisfy themselves. It is important to satisfy oneself, of course, but a writer who wants to be published must do more than that. A writer who wants to be published must learn to communicate, which requires one to see things from the perspective of the communicatee.

I have always admired the wisdom, humor, and storytelling ability of C. S. Lewis. I enjoy the popular writings of many literate scientists, such as Stephen Jay Gould, Loren Eiseley, and David Attenborough, when they show no disdain for the Christian faith. Luci Shaw is my favorite poet. As a young man I felt indebted to the committee that produced the Revised Standard Version of the Bible; today I also feel that way about Kenneth Taylor for producing *The Living Bible*.

Wrestling with the Angel

Melvin Maddocks was a semiweekly columnist for the Christian Science Monitor *for the past twenty years. He has written for several other periodicals including the* Smithsonian, *the* Atlantic, Sewanee Review, Sports Illustrated, *and, most often,* Time.

I really wanted to be a minister. I spent a few happy months at Harvard Divinity School, but I didn't have the "vocation" by the standards of those days. (Vocation: having slightly fewer doubts than your congregation.) Still, it started me *really* writing to clarify my thinking — to find out what I *did* believe, on the old expectation: How do I know what I think until I read what I write? The theory hasn't worked out — so far.

I wish I had learned earlier the things I *can't* write. I've wasted some time trying to write the sorts of things I like to read, but am not good at myself.

I especially like Gogol; Chekhov; Reinhold Niebuhr. *Dead Souls* and short stores like *Anna on the Neck* just seemed to go from terribly sad to heartbreakingly funny when I first read them. I know there are better theologians than Niebuhr in the history of Christianity. But *The Nature and the Destiny of Man* gave me such comfort and taught me so much when I was young.

I find writing pretty frustrating. The words slide off the meaning. The project wanders *so far* from the crystal-clear idea that possesses the mind with wonderful simplicity — in the beginning.

I think writing is like Jacob wrestling with the angel: all you can do is hang on until his name is pronounced, until the word is surrendered.

All I need is pen, paper, and a little privacy — but not too much. I've written with babies crawling over me. With pleasure.

The Making of Worlds

Bruce McAllister is a science fiction and fantasy author with stories in Omni *and anthologies. His first novel,* Humanity Prime, *was published in 1971, and his second,* Dream Baby—*based on the Nebula Award–finalist short story of the same name—is currently being prepared for publication by Tor Books. Since 1974 he has been directing writing programs at the University of Redlands in California as well as sometimes writing poetry, editing literary quarterlies, and doing advertising, public relations, and technical writing.*

Sometimes writing teachers aren't writers. But sometimes even writers who teach forget how they learned.

I was raised in the sciences by an oceanographer/engineering father and social science mother, so science fiction shouldn't be surprising. I was raised by an artist grandmother, too, and pursued art for the first fourteen years of my life — but started reading a lot of science fiction and fantasy at about fourteen (the usual time SF and fantasy readers start reading and writing it, it seems) and suddenly one day was writing it. It got to the point where I was reading a paperback a day, dreaming full-length epic cinemascope SF and fantasy dreams at night, and *writing.* When you immerse yourself in a fantasy world like that, creating your own fantasies on the page is easy.

First opus — at fifteen — was a history of the world in novel form . . . aliens visit and give rise to legends of gods 10,000 years ago . . . all the way through the end of human time. That done, more modest enterprises — short stories. All fantasy and science fiction. I loved it. I lived it and breathed it. I've come back to it at age forty-one after a ten-year hiatus in the academic and "literary fiction" community. SF and fantasy are where my heart and soul are, obviously. You can't escape your writer's destiny, they say.

Why do I keep writing? I remake myself — and the world — through writing. If I don't write for long stretches of time, I get unhappy and make others around me — three children and an outrageously supportive wife by the name of Caroline — unhappy. When writers say, "I'm not sane when I'm not writing," they mean it. That doesn't mean writing itself is easy or tranquil; the anxiety of it is remarkable. Stravinsky's "I sat down and looked at the infinitude of possibilities that lay before me" explains writer anxiety very neatly.

I started out long hand as a writer, fighting the typewriter. Then I became a typist and fought the computer. Now my typing muscles are shot and I can't use anything but a computer. I need a couple of hours of concentrated time. I'm easily distracted. I have an eight-by-eight office in the garage with a space heater and an air-conditioner. Writer's paradise. I never try to write in a beautiful place; it's impossible. Writers who go to Europe or Jamaica to write are crazy. You go to those places to *live*, then you come home to a hovel to write. Ask any writer.

What I hate about writing is the anxiety — and of course the long hours, even months if it's a novel, of shaping and polishing what was born of inspiration. Inspiration is the first joy — the seeing of a world and characters. The drudgery is the making of the words on the page evoke as precisely as possible the inspired vision and feelings in the head. At the end, when the work is done, there's a sense of completion — almost overpowering with a novel — which is the second real joy . . . and enough of a carrot if you've once felt it in a novel. On a first novel, you may not know it's coming, so you despair.

Editors are a Zen lesson. Just when you're *sure* one editor will like a story and another one will hate it, the former hates it and the latter loves it.

Self-doubt is also common for writers . . . and probably comes from knowing that you can't make it perfect. Fortunately, good fiction doesn't have to be "perfect" to be good . . . to move people . . . to be artful. But when we get glimmers of the degree to which we've failed to reach perfection, we always feel despair. Writing in that sense doesn't get easier because we keep striving for more, and we keep failing.

Writers must learn that all language fails, but that we're human and successful and dignified for trying — for using language and for reading it. Faulkner understood this. Every writer who is trying for more than simple entertainment knows this. In fact, good entertainment has craft rules that are just as sophisticated as "art's," and trying to entertain never achieves craft perfection either.

A horror novel may scare to three decibels . . . but if you've written it, you know you could have scared to eight decibels . . . if you'd only been a better writer. The next novel you'll get it to five, the next seven, and maybe some day you'll get it to near-perfection — to eight. In the meantime, people like your work, publish it, read it, anthologize it, nominate you for your awards — and that's the consolation prize against knowing that you *could* have done even better . . . and didn't. One is a personal knowledge; one is a public happiness.

I'm attracted to science fiction especially because it's interdisciplinary; it allows me to explore and build the future or alternative worlds using a great variety of fields. "Literary" fiction, while satisfying because it's about the human condition and the human psyche, is less satisfying: in science fiction — the best of it — you can get at the human condition, the psyche, "what it means to be human," but also at the entire globe, all of time. Imagination is more at work in *good* science fiction — it isn't just star wars; it's the bravest, most courageous fiction we have, in many ways.

Publication at an early age in the field of science fiction and fantasy isn't unusual. In my case I wrote a publishable story at sixteen because I lucked into what I could do well at that age — naive first-person narrator in an alien world mixed with a semi-invented language based on Latin (which I had just studied for two years in Italy). Also, I was most creative — almost obsessed — in Italy, dreaming every night, writing during the day — age fifteen and sixteen. Later I found out that we lived in the same village where Mary Shelley, after an evening of ghost stories, had her Frankenstein dream.

Stories come from a wide variety of sources — I'm never able to predict where and how good and why. A late-night image that makes no sense haunts and becomes a story. A 20,000 word novella in eight drafts fails with every fantasy and SF editor on the face of the earth . . . gives rise to the best story I've ever written in a single draft — 4000 words, different point of view, different plot — two years later. A single draft story works one time, a twenty-draft story is needed the next time.

What I love about writing is the *shaping* — the making of worlds. By shaping, I shape myself, come to understandings of the world and others. The subconscious is all about shape — dreams are shaping. Writing allows me to get in touch with my subconscious and to make and re-make my inner and outer worlds. If that sounds self-centered (in all senses of the word), hey, it is.

Self-expression — a passion for it — is the first prerequisite. After that (and intertwined with it) are reading, writing and rewriting. Weekend writers never get anywhere. Writers who never read never get anywhere. Writers who never rewrite never get anywhere. Writers who never embrace their favorite works in a humble apprenticeship never get anywhere. Ask them.

I wish I had learned earlier to *reread* favorite works, to copy out long hand or on a typewriter favorite works, to write my own versions of remembered portions of favorite works (and compare them to the better, original versions) — because this kind of embracing, out of love, of favorite literary models would have taught me much sooner all the craft techniques (style and structure) which I wish I'd learned earlier. For some reason writing teachers don't ask their students to reread and reread and reread favorite works, keep notebooks full of ideas and sections from their favorite works, memorize favorite works. This is how writers learn — by embracing works they love and by thereby becoming the craft used in their favorite works.

Some of my own favorite authors are Ursula Le Guin, Greg Benford, Nancy Kress, Connie Willis, Karen Joy Fowler, Greg Bear, Arthur C. Clarke — and many others in the science fiction and fantasy field. In the "literary" field Par Lagerkvist, Dashiel Hammett, Brian Moore, Thomas Mann, and many others. You need to find the writers who speak to you . . . and whose craft you can learn from. Trying to imitate their style won't work, but they may influence your structure, rhythm, tone. That's the level of influence you want. Embrace favorite authors (after reading ten times as many authors to find your favorite authors) and let them influence you in many subtle, passion-ridden ways.

My Right Hand

*Paul McCusker is a playwright, scriptwriter, lyricist, and copywriter. In addition to coauthoring the popular radio program "*Adventures in Odyssey,*"he has published many short plays and coauthored with Chuck Bolte the 1987 book* Youth Ministry Drama and Comedy: Better than Bathrobes but Not Quite Broadway.

I wrote when I was a child because I enjoyed it. My first "play" was based on a television series, rehearsed by my friends during recess, and performed for the fifth grade class on Valentine's Day with little acclaim. In college I consciously decided to be a writer by profession.

Writing has become such an integrated part of me that I can't love or hate it any more than I can love or hate my right hand. Yes, it could be improved: more agile, more dexterous. It could be stronger. It could be more attractive. And I would certainly suffer great loss if I didn't have it. But I have a difficult time looking at my right hand to determine whether I love or hate it. It is there. It is part of me.

My left hand is a different matter. It is the one I actually write with and it cramps easily. Back when I wrote everything first by hand, I thought through my words more carefully before writing anything down. (Avoiding pain gave me a better first draft.) I would then edit while typing up what I had written by hand. Now, I do whatever is most appealing at the time. For handwriting I prefer a fountain pen. For word processing, I alternate between Word Perfect and Microsoft Word.

When I was a teenager I learned increased respect for the power of the printed word. I needed county police assistance with a broken down car late at night. They refused. Indignant, I wrote a scathing — and somewhat exaggerated — letter to our county newspaper about the incident. I was going through a pseudonym phase at the time and didn't use my real name — then it was Mark Freed.

A few weeks later I was at a family gathering and my uncle, who is a county policeman, began talking about a letter in the newspaper that had been passed around the station. He expressed the police opinion in no uncertain terms. I cringed. I asked a few specific questions and, sure enough, it was my letter. I kept my mouth shut.

The next day I went to the library and found it — not placed as a small "letter to the editor," but located in a column all its own as a guest editorial. The headline: "Car 54 — Where Were You?" by Mark Freed.

My Heart stopped.

Out of curiosity, I looked in the same section in following issues to see if there might be responses. There was one. Another guest editorial written by the county police's public relations man.The headline: "Mark Freed — Where Are You?" The editorial went on to chronicle how the police had been looking for Mark Freed to discuss his complaints. They couldn't find him. This particular Mark Freed didn't exist in their files, and the newspaper had conveniently misplaced his address (thanks, guys). I wondered what they would do if they found Mark/me. I imagined receiving weekly traffic tickets the rest of my life.

I quickly retired Mark Freed from his career as editorial writer, and I try hard to be responsible in everything I write.

The authors I prize most are C. S. Lewis, Mark Twain, George Kaufman, Stephen King, Robert Bolt, Neil Simon, and Douglas Adams. A strange assembly, yes? I prize them for their unique perspectives on the world, how they communicate those perspectives, and their influence on my life and writing. I especially value this advice from C. S. Lewis: "In literature and art no one who bothers about originality will ever be original, whereas if you try simply to tell the truth you will, nine times out of ten, become original without ever having noticed it."

My advice to you — the up and coming writer — is: tell the truth.

I Was Hooked

Carole Gift Page has published her pieces in ninety Christian publications. Her twenty-three books include Misty: Our Momentary Child, *a personal story of the child she lost (1987);* Beyond the Windswept Sea, *a mystery-romance novel coauthored with Doris Elaine Fell (1987); and* Hallie's Secret, *a teen novel of incest and sexual abuse (1987).*

During my childhood I wanted to be an artist. I dreamed of someday traveling to California (from my tiny Michigan hometown) and becoming an illustrator for Walt Disney. But in junior high, several things happened. I read books like *Heidi* and *Treasure Island* and *David Copperfield* that fired my imagination and made me want to try my own hand at writing. At the same time I discovered so many new feelings I wanted to communicate that couldn't be conveyed easily through art. I was terribly shy — a true introvert — and therefore found it nearly impossible to share my feelings with my peers — until I discovered writing!

I experimented with short stories and poetry, pouring all my painful, jumbled, junior high emotions into them. The sense of catharsis was extraordinary. Even better, when I dared to show my fledgling manuscripts to friends and acquaintances, they liked them, considered them entertaining! I was hooked.

However, it wasn't until my last semester of college, as I was about to graduate with a B.S. in art education, with teaching fields in English and Spanish, that my vision to become a professional writer crystalized. I dared to show some of my stories and articles to one of the writing instructors on campus. "You will become a good writer, if not a great one!" His excitement was contagious. He advised me against settling for a safe, mundane teaching career in my little hometown; instead, he recommended that I strike out on my own, take a bread-and-butter job that wouldn't drain my creative juices, and spend all my free time writing.

I retreated to the prayer room in my college dormitory and spent hours searching for God's will for me. I caught a vision of what God was calling me to do: to make Christ known through stories and poems, through imagery and the beauty and mystery of words; to make known the Word through words! In that tiny prayer room, I accepted the challenge and claimed the marvelous, improbable mantle of Christian author (before I even knew what a Christian story might be!).

I, who had spent my whole life being safe, sane, and studiously circumspect, threw caution to the wind. I set out for Southern California with sixty dollars in my pocket, no job, no place to live, and no connections — except a college girlfriend who convinced me we would thrive in this lush, balmy land of opportunity.

We pooled our money for the first month's rent on a "luxury" apartment, went without lights and ate peanut butter for two weeks. I, who had avoided business courses like the plague (except for tenth-grade typing) landed a position as a clerk-typist and two weeks later was made private secretary to the sales manager of the company. As planned, I wrote in my spare time — when I wasn't dating.

Five years later, following marriage and two children, I seriously pursued the dream of all sincere, struggling writers: getting published. My first sale was to a Sunday school take-home paper, but it was enough to convince me that if I could do it once, I could do it again . . . and again

. . . and again. Several years later, I had free-lancing down to a science: If I could keep 150 manuscripts in the mail at all times, I could count on an average of three sales a week. But the paperwork took two hours a day.

Later, I discovered books — *writing* them, that is; and then I encountered the wonderful world of computers and word processing, and was able to go from one book a year to three — something I never could have accomplished with only my left-handed scrawl and trusty Adler.

I still enjoy drawing. I enjoy teaching. But I could live without them. Not so with writing. I must write. I will always write, because I can't *not* write. My advice about becoming a writer is, If you don't have to write, don't. But if you must — if you find it's part of the very warp and woof of your being, and without it a piece of you is missing — then tackle it with all your heart and mind and soul, and do it to the glory of God, because, the way I see it, there are precious few higher callings. Writing, at its best, embodies the roles of the minister and missionary, the prophet, the priest and the king — it is communication at its grandest, its impact immeasurable, and — wonder of wonders — it can be accomplished from the sanctuary of your own comfortable armchair.

Acceptance and Rejection

Richard V. Pierard is a professor of history at Indiana State University. He is the author or coauthor of seven books, the latest being Civil Religion and the Presidency *(1988). He has contributed twenty chapters to collected works and symposia, published about forty articles, and has lost count of his book reviews and entries in encyclopedic works.*

Writing is a very important part of being a historian. I got my start in high school where I worked on the staffs of the newspaper and annual. This on-the-job training provided the foundation for what I would be doing as a college and graduate student and then in my professional career.

What I soon found out was that there is a world of difference between putting one's words down on paper and seeing them appear in print. The rejection letter is a crushing blow for every aspiring writer, whether it be the impersonal printed slip of paper, form letter with the stock paragraph telling you that your piece does not fit our needs, or the outright insulting letter such as the one I received from a certain publisher telling me that they had an obligation to see that stuff like mine was not published.

Since every writer feels he or she has something to say and they want people to hear it, it is hard to separate a sense of rejection of oneself personally from simply a rejection of one's work. Since I have done a reasonable amount of editorial work through the years and served as a manuscript referee for several scholarly journals, I have seen the situation from both sides of the fence. Evaluating someone else's written output is indeed a hard task.

Perhaps the most difficult hurdle facing the aspiring writer is getting the attention of an editor who will take a chance on your work and then gaining some sort of public acceptance. There are so many people out trying to get their material published, and we who have never made the best-seller list often comment to one another how poor the literary and/or intellectual content of some of the big name personalities is. Publishing is an economic matter and firms and magazines accept the stuff they believe will sell. I painfully learned this twenty years ago with my first book-length venture.

In 1966, three of us who had been in graduate school together, were committed evangelicals, and were young assistant professors — Robert Linder, Robert Clouse, and I — got to talking about a situation that deeply distressed us. We saw our faith community in the grip of an uncritical acceptance of political, social, and economic conservatism which was enervating the gospel. The Vietnam War was raging and our evangelical leadership seemed to be one hundred percent behind it. The civil rights movement was making its greatest gains and our brethren for the most part stood on the sidelines carping at it. We were still getting massive doses of Cold War anticommunism and laissez faire capitalism from our spiritual mentors.

We decided that enough was enough — we had to do something. We recruited a number of like-minded younger people and put together a volume of essays on current issues modestly tilted *Protest and Politics: Christianity and Contemporary Affairs*. We were utter unknowns but we did score one coup; the newly elected U.S. Senator from Oregon, Mark O. Hatfield, agreed to write a chapter for our book.

After a year of intense effort, we were able to put the volume together, but then we hit a brick wall. Publisher after publisher turned us down and the material was rapidly getting cold. Finally, we located an obscure firm in South Carolina which agreed to publish it if we would provide a subsidy. It was painful to come up with the money on teachers' salaries, but we believed in our cause and knew the "kairotic moment" (a word not in the new *Random House Dictionary of the English Language*, second edition) was rapidly slipping past.

The book did not sell well because we had to market it ourselves, but it did attract a lot of attention in the right places and started all three of us moving as evangelical social critics. One thing in particular spurred us on: the late James Daane of Fuller Theological Seminary declared in a review that he did not know these young men but we were going to be hearing a lot from them in the future. In fact, I was at a party two years later where the editor of one of the firms that turned down the manuscript apologized to me and said they had made a mistake.

The problem of being a Christian writer who tries to swim against the current in social and political matters is a difficult one. I recall another book on contemporary issues which we published a few years later. It was doing rather well, but then the firm that released it was taken over by someone else who regarded the book's "liberalism" as an embarrassment and yanked it out of print. I deal with topics that most people do not want to think about except at the level of moralistic platitudes and the reinforcement of preconceived views. Thus, unless one has a keen sense of timing and can get a book out on an issue or issues at just the right moment, he or she will find it difficult to keep ahead of the competition, let alone get much attention.

From the standpoint of craftsmanship, I find that there is no substitute for careful planning of what you are going to say and the process of writing and rewriting. It is unusual that the first words I put down on paper or on the word processor screen will be the final ones that go to an editor.

Another thing I have learned is the value of trying out ideas in lectures and speeches. The experience of articulating my views and receiving audience feedback helps me in the long run to express myself.

Moreover, I find it helpful to have a pad of paper with me when I am driving or flying somewhere, as often an idea will jump into my head and then leave me as quickly as it came if I do not jot it down at once. The same is true when I wake up in the middle of the night, and, would you believe it, even in a church service. More than once I annotated a church bulletin with ideas that popped up when I was listening or my mind was wandering.

Also, my training as a historian with its emphasis on scrupulous accuracy and requirement for generalizations to be backed up with facts contributed immensely to making my written work more precise in quality. Still, the bottom line is that writing is work, but it is indeed rewarding, maybe not in monetary return but certainly in personal satisfaction.

Love Language

Rosalind Rinker is a writer of devotional books which lead the reader into a love relationship with Jesus Christ through prayer—which is the love language.

She has published fifteen books; the most popular of all has been Prayer: Conversing with God *(1959).*

I have liked to write ever since I can remember. My first letters from China were printed in our hometown newspaper. I also wrote articles for the *Oriental Missionary Standard.*

But I did not start to write professionally until I was fifty years old. Then I met Eugenia Price, who sent me to her publisher. They rolled out the Red Carpet of Welcome and I signed my first contract without them having seen a single sentence which I had written. That was in 1959.

When I have a contract and a title and sit down at the machine, the material just seems to pour out of me. It's fun and I love it. I prefer to have a quiet room. An electric typewriter. And a desk that has been cleared up. I only wish that I had learned sooner about getting better contracts.

When I help other writers with their manuscripts, I often find that they need to move good strong parts up to the beginning. There are three main things that I like to pass on to aspiring writers:

> First, write about something you know about.
> Second, keep it simple.
> Third, keep your readers in mind as you write.

My favorite writers now are Carlos Carretto, Edward Farrell, and George Maloney. These are all Catholic Jesuit priests. Their writing speaks to my heart. Next would be C. S. Lewis. His writing speaks to my mind and makes wonderful sense. I also like Catherine Marshall. She writes what she has experienced.

It Is Never Too Late

Jack Rowe is a novelist whose Brandywine *(1984),* Dominion *(1986), and* Fortune's Legacy *(1988) form a trilogy dealing with du Pont operations from 1800 to 1902. To say that these are historical novels would be stretching the genre a bit, because the historical events included are ancillary rather than pivotal. His first novel,* Inyo-Sierra Passage *(1980) is contemporary suspense with a mystical flavor, and his fifth is a mystery novel in process.*

It began with Shredded Wheat, crayons, and a stapler in the Brandywine freight office of the Reading Railroad. When I was in the second or third grade, Shredded Wheat biscuits came layered in fat squarish boxes with cardboard separators. I used the cardboard for all kinds of stuff, and when I saw the stapler, which was a new thing in the thirties, I realized immediately how easily I could bind those National Biscuit Co. (now Nabisco) boards into book covers. I could be a bookbinder, a publisher, a writer — more than that, by gosh, I could be an author. I did it. Authored my first book, *The Little Toot Tug*, lavishly illustrated in gleaming waxy color and slavishly plagiarizing *The Little Engine that Could*. At least I think it did, I think it did. But let's check the pub date; maybe it was the other way around. I am not a crook. I think I'm not, I hope I'm not.

Because the press run was disappointing, I decided to emulate my monastic Celt forebears and rest on the labors of only one illuminated manuscript until I was old enough to think I had something else to say.

When I was an undergraduate years later a teacher accused me of having plagiarized in a research paper. At the bottom of the last page he had written "B. Who wrote it?" When I protested, he snapped, "I know you didn't write that; I'd like to see your references."

After rounding up all my sources and dumping them on his desk, I requested a conference. This was a nervy thing, a confrontation really, because he was a Navy commander and I was a midshipman. The next time we met he admitted that my sources had been credited, but he challenged the opening, a page-long description of aircraft carrier landing operations I had composed.

"This is the part I won't swallow," he said. "You couldn't have written this."

I was angry because I had originated every word, but I was carefully respectful when I asked him why he thought I had not.

"Because it's too good." he answered with a chilly naval aviator stare, scribbled something on the manuscript, and handed it over.

Outside the office when I read his correction, revised down to a C, I was more upset about his conviction than the lowered grade. But after a while a greater truth dawned. He thought my writing had been good enough to publish! Somehow the commander's put-down was a greater endorsement than praise from any writing teacher.

I finally felt ready to follow up on *Little Toot Tug*. That was when I was nearly fifty, and Laura was so tired of hearing about writing a book someday that she told me to either shut up or start pounding the keys.

I wrote the first two novels on a wheezing Adler, composing on the keyboard with occasional handwritten preliminary copy. Now I use a computer (also a relative wheezer as CPUs go) and love it. This one is five years old but after two-and-one-half novels, I never cease to be amazed at the flexibility it offers. Maybe I should mention here that I lost parts of my hands in an overseas altercation years ago, and the editing ease of electronic writing is therefore more deeply appreciated. (Thank God I did not waste my formative years learning either the violin or the touch method of typing.)

I think my biggest disappointment as a published author is the limpwristed illustrations on book jackets wrapped around something I've written. I suppose that's because of my high Shredded Wheat standards.

It is never too late to start, but waiting too long for the "right time" is obviously counterproductive. I don't mean just numbers of books written; with over fifty thousand new titles published every year the reading public is not exactly starving for lack of volume. More important was my loss of the experience itself. Is there another artful craft more demanding of constancy and attention?

I wish I had learned sooner that the "barbaric yawp" Whitman sings of should be shouted out as soon as it is felt, rather than stifled by false modesty or fears of rejection and ridicule. Readers are a gentle lot for the most part, content to let us draw them into our intimacies. I should have embraced them sooner, risked the nakedness of my immaturity, and reaped the years of writing experience. Ultimately, writing must be learned by writing.

My favorite author is Thornton Wilder because in *Our Town* he touches us all with such a gentle hand, and because that play may be the one American literary piece without a single nonessential word.

The Wonderful Things in Books

Luci Shaw's public identity is tied to poetry. Of her four collections, Listen to the Green *(1971) is the best known, but she says that* Postcard from the Shore *(1985) is her favorite.* A Widening Light: Poems of the Incarnation *is her favorite of the three poetry anthologies she edited. Her first prose book is* God in the Dark *(1989).*

I didn't become a writer by conscious decision. As a child of five, putting pencil marks on paper that grew into words, I thought everyone wrote poetry. I kept at it even after I found that everyone did not. I had a British education, which meant that awful educational device, objective questioning, was no part of my experience. All assignments, quizzes, exams demanded essay answers, a rigorous rule, but one that forced me to think through an idea logically from beginning to end, and articulate it clearly and grammatically.

I became a writer because I was a reader and I wanted to write the wonderful kinds of things I found in books. I have never taken a "creative writing course," but I was an English Lit major in college, studying (and continuing to study) the great writers in our language. I also learned French, Latin, and Greek which gave me the origins of words and made word study a fascinating game. When I began to write mature poetry, the complex derivations of words played, and still play, an important part in the way a poem develops, pegged as it is to words and their associations.

When asked what I dislike about writing, I say I hate the guilt. During a current writing project, I almost invariably suffer from blockage — a sort of constipation of the will. That project is what I want most to get done, and what I want least to do. The more I want to do it, the harder it is to get to it. (Ah, there's the first line of a song!) Sometimes this is good, because as I wait to start writing, in a kind of serendipitous game, things start flipping into my mind. I see ideas in print, or a poem, or hear on the evening news, or in a discussion with a friend, the very detail that will make the writing *work*.

I think the guilt is left over from my conditioning as a child that I should only feel good about myself if I achieved the high goals set for me by myself and others. Of course, it is this inner pressure which forces me on, which grows so strong and makes me so miserable that eventually, once it gets started, the flow of words is like an open safety valve or a gusher of oil. I am productive because of guilt. I think most writers are.

What I love about writing is that once you get it right you feel like God on the seventh day, as Dorothy Sayers says, or a newly delivered mother with the baby she has only imagined for nine months and now holds, real, warm, sticky, furry, bony, in her arms, looking and looking at it as if she cannot ever stop. (She'll get over the euphoria. And the production of a good poem only produces a temporary high. And then you have to start over.)

I also love the randomness, the unplannedness of ideas for writing, the way they come at you like a headwind and all you can do is bend to them.

Once I heard a sermon about the fig tree which Jesus cursed because it bore no figs. I thought, as the Scripture was read — "How unreasonable of Jesus to expect figs out of season." From that thought came the poem "The Foolishness of God" which starts with the line "Perform impossibilities or perish. . . ." Months later I read for the first time Dorothy Sayers' *The Mind of the Maker*. In the context of the same parable she wrote, "Perform impossibilities or perish." How do I explain such a coincidence? I don't.

I have thought of myself, always, as an intuitive, imaginative thinker and writer, partly because I write from feeling and have learned structure as I had to, by simply *doing* it. Yet I've always sensed a lack in that part of me and wanted to be more of a mystic, a contemplative. Because I am a doer, very active, getting a charge out of conquering a risk or challenge, I've felt as if I have a flat tire in the right brain. Lately I am recognizing my intense need for logic, for rational thinking, for cause and effect.

Perhaps what I really want to be is whole brain — harnessing emotion and imagination with logic and plan on the one hand, injecting dogma with life through imagery and metaphor on the other. I hope someday to get myself sorted out and doing the thing I was originally planned for!

Here's a practical tip. Once you have a piece of writing done, test it by reading it aloud. This is good for prose, but even better for poetry. Latent weaknesses, flaws in rhythm and structure come into the open when you read the thing aloud. Also hidden benefits, new levels of meaning, unplanned correspondences show their lovely little heads.

What writers do I prize? In prose, I love Frederick Buechner's *Godric* and *Brendan* because of the rich, Anglo-Saxon or Celtic feel of the writing, very earthy, ugly even, but full of a kind of decaying humus that is the matrix of life. I prize Harold Fickett for his hard-edged, spare style, his casually tossed clues that are really very carefully planned, his aggressiveness and lack of sentimentality. I love Annie Dillard because for all her wonderful wealth of detail she has great control. And she's unexpected. Now there's a prize — writing that's full of unanticipated twists that turn you inside out.

In poetry, I respect Liesel Mueller, and Denise Levertov, and Maxine Kumin, and Elizabeth Bishop because when I read them I say "I wish I'd written that," and Howard Nemerov and Albert Godbarth because they are so witty and ironic and Hebraic. Galway Kinnell and Dylan Thomas cry out to the Celt in me; I love the singing line. And of course, the metaphysical poets, Donne and Crashaw and Herbert and Hopkins, because they join earth with heaven in a fusion as passionate as sex.

Keep the Child Alive

Robert Siegel is a poet who also writes fantasy. His books of poetry include The Beasts and the Elders *and* In a Pig's Eye. *His fantasies include award-winning* Alpha Centauri *(1980)*, Whalesong *(1981)*, *and* Kingdom of Wundle *(1982)*. *The first two fantasies have been translated into German.*

At the age of five I composed some new lyrics to "Oh, What a Beautiful Morning" (from the show *Oklahoma*) for my sister's birthday. I remember the surprise and delight of discovering that my version rhymed. It was that and later experiences of pleasure and surprise that led me to commit myself to poetry. At some point I said to myself, "*This* is what I most love doing."

And I think at that time I had some sort of realization like G. M. Hopkins' "*What I do is me: for that I came.*" Now that I look back, there seems to be a series of such moments. I recall another when I rounded a bend in the Morton Arboretum and saw a single red branch hanging down among green. Something was peeled away at that point and I saw (if that's the right word) a beauty in the world past describing. C. S. Lewis's phrase from *Perelandra* "an eatable, drinkable, breathable gold" comes to mind here.

As a senior in college, I permitted myself one of C. S. Lewis's Narnia books each month — to draw the pleasure out. (I had not read them before.) I think that I later turned to writing fantasy in an attempt to have that kind of intense pleasure again; those who love fantasy will know what I mean.

Though writing poetry remains my first love, the writing of fantasy fiction provides its own distinct rewards. One of these is to enter into a world where more is happening than one can possibly record.

I still type on my thiry-five-year-old Royal Quiet de Luxe portable with elite type. In recent years italic-nib pens have reconciled me to my handwriting, but I still use this typewriter that I bought new with summer earnings at the age of thirteen. (I have taught myself to touch-type after a girlfriend of my sister's laughed at my childish scrawl.) By now this old typewriter knows where to go on its own, and I just follow along — at least during its best moments.

I hate the distractions that take me from writing — that some part of my mind lunges after. I find that quiet and simplicity are helpful to writing and that these need to be sought out and protected.

I wish that I had learned when young that persistence is much more important than all that vague, fruitless questioning — "Do I have talent?" If one didn't have talent, one probably wouldn't want to write. Talent is fairly common (there lies a mystery).

Beyond a certain point in your development, do not take the criticism of others at face value. Use it, rather, as a guide to your own critical perceptions; your own deepest responses will help you to separate the wheat from the chaff in evaluating what others have said.

In this matter of looking at your own work it is vital to keep the child alive. Too many young writers allow the editor or critic in them to stifle the child.

I have loved with a special fervor Spenser, Milton, Blake, Wordsworth, Coleridge, Keats, and Shelley, Tennyson, Browning, Hopkins, and too many twentieth-century writers to name.

Called To Be a Writer

Kevin Springer is editor of Equipping the Saints *magazine and coauthor with John Wimber of three books which are also published in England and in seven foreign languages. The first of these is* Power Evangelism *(1986) and the latest is* Power Encounters among Christians in the Western World *(1988).*

I never set out to become a writer. In fact, throughout my teen years I aspired to be a physician. The science push that came in reaction to the Russian launching of Sputnik in the early sixties only solidified my commitment to medicine. Fortunately, my high school required that all academic students take four years of English and composition, reasoning that no matter what field one entered, one needed to write.

At the University of Southern California I majored in biology and minored in history. Between my sophomore and junior years I had a dramatic spiritual experience that changed the direction of my life. Much to my consternation, God called me to the ministry — though the exact nature of my calling seemed unclear at the time. I didn't like giving up medicine, but I obeyed. I never applied to medical school.

In my junior year I enrolled in a creative writing course that was a disaster for me. The first assignment was to write a short story. The professor, who had only recently arrived from England, used my story as an example of why American writers are inferior to English writers. I had taken a great risk in writing a short romance story, and I felt like an utter fool after he had finished criticizing it. His opinion of my writing, a curse of sorts, was a barrier that I had to overcome years later when I started writing in earnest.

I wish I had learned sooner, in my early twenties, that I was called to be a writer. I would have taken writing courses, especially in fiction writing, at nearby universities. There are still many technical aspects of writing that I know very little about.

When people ask me what I did to become an author, I say, "I picked up the phone. People kept offering me writing jobs."

By the time I was thirty I had graduated from seminary and was serving as a pastor in Michigan. At this time the group of churches of which I was a part invited me to become founding editor of a small magazine, *Commonlife*. (I had written papers and articles over the years, and they recognized a talent in me that I didn't recognize.) I accepted the job, and immediately fell in love with editing and writing. At the time I told my wife, Suzanne, "This is what I have been created for. I'm called to be a writer and editor." (Suzanne now edits also.)

After founding *Commonlife*, I received a phone call from *Pastoral Renewal* journal; I served as associate editor there for over three years. Next I was called to begin my association with John Wimber and Vineyard Ministries International. Looking back, I can see that my entire life and training has been preparation for what I am doing today.

I love the creativity involved in writing. I hate the deadlines.

I need a computer in order to write, because for me the art of writing is rewriting. I rewrite most book chapters twenty times, a task made much easier by the computer. After purchasing a computer I estimated that my production increased twenty percent, which translates into an extra workday each week. I also need an extensive personal library (currently over 3000 volumes) and access to a good theological library like the one at nearby Fuller Seminary. I also need my own office, a place to spread my papers and in which I have uninterrupted blocks of time.

Whenever someone asks me for advice about learning how to write, I always say, "If you want to learn how to write well, work under someone who writes well." Usually this means taking a low-paying job as an assistant editor under a seasoned veteran who is willing to teach you how to write. Don't take *any* entry level job; make sure that the person for whom you work is a writer that you admire and who will train you.

Before you take the job, insist on writer's training as part of your job description. Then, when you get the job, aspire to write *just as the good writer writes*. Don't worry about "your style" or "uniqueness." Style comes from personality, a natural by-product of good writing. Learn to write well technically, and your style will percolate through unconsciously. If you are too conscious about "your style," it is probably forced — a most unpleasant characteristic found too often among young writers.

If there is any "key" to all of this, I would say it is *obedience*. I have always been like one of the sons in the parable found in Matthew 21:28–31. When told by his father to work in the vineyard, he said, "I will not" — but later changed his mind and went. When God says, "Go!" I complain but then move out — even when I feel unqualified for the task.

I have never *striven* to be a writer; my primary goal in life is to serve Jesus Christ in whatever capacity he has called me to. My identity is not found in being a writer; it is found in being a servant of Christ. This means, should he call me back to pastor a church or to any other ministry, I will reluctantly obey.

Behind the Story

Hugh Steven is a historical biographer who has published over twenty books and several hundred articles. The central theme of his books has been to depict the truth of God's personal involvement in people's lives. His books are Manuel, Manuel, the Continuing Story; Good Broth To Warm Our Bones; A Thousand Trails; They Dared To Be Different; Never Touch a Tiger; *and* Behind the Story.

Somerset Maugham, in his book *The Summing Up*, said, "We do not write because we want to; we write because we must." It has been like this for me. From my earliest memory, I was captive to story and the power of words to transport me into wonderful new worlds. My first-grade teacher (a British woman) introduced me to the charms of *Winnie the Pooh* by reading aloud every afternoon. My mother read me Old Testament stories, and later, when I could read on my own, I discovered all those wonderful outdoor adventure stories by Jack London and the courageous and intelligent dog stories by Albert Payson Terhune.

These and other adventure stories fired my imagination and created an indefinable itch to travel and explore. I also believe spending long, solitary summers, with my dog as my sole companion, exploring tidal flats, estuaries, and backwaters of the Pacific Northwest was a link in my becoming a writer.

I had a friend — a kindly custodian at my elementary school. He wore baggy coveralls, plastered his hair with thick hair jell, and had wire-rim glasses. When I told him one day that I thought the waves at the beach looked like pages turning over in a book, he didn't laugh as my peers had done. Rather, he agreed. Unknowingly, he became an important link in my becoming a writer. And he taught me an important principle about creativity. Namely, we need at least one person to support us and offer encouragement.

With that kernel of encouragement, I allowed some of my "character flaws" — a natural curiosity, inquisitiveness and desire to explore, even my restlessness and sense of free spiritedness — to become tools. And here is a principle for all writers to celebrate. Writers should preserve and develop the childlike qualities of question-asking, open-mindedness, playfulness, curiosity, explorativeness, rather than suppress and crush them.

This leads me to my own dictum: Creativeness is part of our heritage, God's gift to all mankind. Yet social pressures, fear of rejection, conformity to rules and sterotypes, plus elevation of reason or judicial thinking over intuition, frequently inhibit our innate creativity.

I first began as a photographer who wanted to capture the mood and atmosphere of places I visited as part of my ministry with Wycliffe Bible Translators. Gradually, this interest led me to examine, in more detail, the dramas and forces, natural and internal, that give shape and meaning to people's lives. And out of that tangle of emotions and facts, I began to write.

At first I wasn't sure if I should or could be a writer. It meant a leap of faith, a cutting loose from all my comfortable assumptions. (I have since learned that to be safe and secure is to be uncreative.) This hesitancy was terribly mixed up with my own lack of self-confidence and fear of failure. I was part of a culture where the highest value is success, and I was about to enter a world that invited failure, or worse, ridicule.

My list of prized authors must include C. S. Lewis, J. B. Phillips, and Paul Tournier. These were men who, through their books, became my spiritual mentors. They were gateways to new worlds of theological understanding and taught me to live out my personal faith in Christ. In a real sense, they helped liberate me from what could have been a terrible life of legalism and conformity. To them and others like them I owe a great debt.

But I also owe a special debt to Alan Moorhead, a World War II correspondent, whose descriptive writing style held me captive from the moment I bought a sixty-cent paperback copy of *The Blue Nile*. I was immediately challenged by his ability to take sterile historical facts and infuse them with color, warmth, and high drama, yet without stooping to banalities or purple prose. When I finished the book, I told myself I wanted to be able to write about places and people with the same attention to detail, description, emotion, and drama as he had done.

A Book a Decade

Sheldon Vanauken is a former professor of history and English literature who catapulted to fame when he published A Severe Mercy *(1977) — the story of his extraordinary marriage, his conversion to Christianity with the help of C. S. Lewis, and the subsequent death of his young wife Davy. Since then he has published three more books; the latest one,* The Glittering Illusion *(1988) was really written first of all. What follows is in part drawn from* Under the Mercy *with the author's permission.*

As I said in *Under the Mercy*, one begins to ask questions as soon as one can speak. Indeed, my first utterance, If I am to believe Mother, was not a single word but a coherent question: "Where's Daddy?" I must have wanted to know. The young, at least, always want answers. And I was young — nine months.

The *only* reason for asking is to get an answer. The *only* reason for seeking is to find . . . The *only* reason for an open mind is to fill it with truth.

I knew very early that I *could* write. In fourth or fifth grade some story I wrote in school won a state competition I didn't know it was in. I was graduated with honours in prep school because of some essay I submitted. I attribute my ability to write to reading a vast number of books at an early age, especially English authors: Scott and Stevenson — Dad gave me *Treasure Island* at ten — The Wind in the Willows, etc.

Unconsciously I absorbed the rhythms of good prose, the use of words. Also the metrical rhythms of good poetry in the Great Tradition.

Anyway, reading is the key to writing. My advice to aspiring writers is that they read from the age of three or four or five . . . thousands of books. C. S. Lewis and Charles Williams both influenced my style, but there were countless earlier influences, including T. H. White, *The Once and Future King*, and other books of his.

I believe the first line of poetry I composed was while having a forbidden cigarette under the dining hall steps in boarding school, looking out through a crack at the brilliant winter stars: "The stars that wheel in deathless unconcern." (Later I incorporated that in one of the Oxford sonnets in *A Severe Mercy:* "Our Lady of the Night.")

What I need is quiet above all. I described my tiny cottage near Lynchburg College in the first chapter of *Under the Mercy:* It is old, said to have been a one-room schoolhouse just after the War of Secession. At all events, it is but a single storey and only twenty feet by twenty, plus a bathroom wing and the stoop. Now there is a main room that is twenty feet by twelve, almost a golden-mean rectangle, the interior wall lined with books to the ceiling except for the fireplace in the centre of it — the coal fire that is my only heat . . . The main room — drawing-room, library, dining-room, bedroom in one — is comfortable and, somehow because of its proportions and the glowing coals on the hearth, conducive to quiet talk. Its furniture and the Persian rugs were from Glenmerle — Glenmerle, my boyhood home — very old even then, including the narrow four-poster that was in my room there; and the windows have dark-blue curtains that are drawn at night. Above the mantelpiece are some of Davy's paintings — country scenes — and below them, glowing in the light, is the figurehead from the schooner *Grey Goose*.

People these days speak knowledgeably about the delights of word processors and laugh at my antique Royal portable that I bought in Glenmerle days, but I murmur: "It writes books." There is on the bed a low wooden desk with a slanting top that holds the portable, four headless nails going up into its four paws; and there very comfortably, the desk standing on its own legs on either side of me, I type with two or three fingers. Or, with the desk removed, read over what I've written. As I type the light comes in over my shoulder, and if I raise my eyes I see the wall of books and the fire. Thus it was that *A Severe Mercy* was written.

I love writing, seeing a book or essay take shape. Even more a joy, beyond expression, is a poem when it comes. I don't toss books off lightly. The writing itself may not take long because of the intensity and long hours, but the build-up of it does. At the end I hate the proofreading.

In replying to thousands of letters from readers, I resorted to post-office postal cards, on which I had room a-plenty for a serious and thoughtful paragraph. But, limited for space, I never wasted a word; constantly in mind was the need to say what I wished to say in the fewest words: it tended to make my style leaner, to the point.

Something to Say

Carolyn Vash is the author of two textbooks: The Burnt-out Administrator *(1979) and* The Psychology of Disability *(1981). She edits and illustrates* Rehab Brief, *a national newsletter for rehabilitation professionals. It is incidental to her writing that she has been a quadriplegic since a teenage bout with polio; with only partial use of her left hand, she writes, draws, and types 35 words per minute.*

It seemed destined that my sister and I would become artists/writers . . . she became the former, I the latter . . . she intentionally; I adventitiously. People who read my research reports and memoranda said, "You're such a good writer . . . you should WRITE!" I recognized that my memos did have a certain flair . . . and that my research reports were more readable than most, but could only answer, "But I have nothing to SAY."

In 1977 I "retired" from eight-to-five public-sector employment and went home to live like the control group for awhile . . . play at being a housewife, learn to cook at the age of forty-four, stuff like that . . . AND . . . I finally had something I wanted to say! Two books-worth, actually.

I was prepared to get 1000 rejection slips before my first acceptance and a friend leaked the first three chapters of my first book to his publisher, who called wanting to publish it. I felt cheated, momentarily.

After my books were complete, I slipped back into virtually full-time employment, doing consulting and research and profession-related writing and administering — serving as vice president of a Virginia-based research and consulting firm from my Altadena, California home. The book-writing well went dry. It seems obvious now that I was a tad overextended and why not . . . but for several years of dry-well, I wondered why I was having writer's block. Unquestionably more important than being overextended, I really didn't have any more to say . . . yet.

I used to be picky about using a specific type of pencil versus a specific type of pen . . . hard lead, soft lead, mechanical, colored, felt tip, ballpoint, fountain, etc. One of these possibilities would be strong . . . it had to be just that . . . and I never knew ahead of time which it might be . . . only when it was time to pick up my _____ and get started would I know that the muse wanted to write with a _____ this time. Now that I use a computer, I use a computer. Once in a while I need to scribble first, but it no longer matters with what.

Three books are now fighting to get out . . . each wanting to get ahead of the other two. At other times, it's after-you-Alphonse from all three. These are matters of the moment, however; in the main, I have now gestated or incubated or whatever it is you are doing inwardly when you're not writing, for over seven years and it's production time again! And with an interesting new wrinkle. My sister has moved away from making pictures to do sculpture . . . leaving a gap in the picture-making department of the family. I am filling it. I have started illustrating the technical publication I edit, and am illustrating all three of the books currently percolating. It seems I'm the same way about pictures as about writing . . . I can only do them when I have something I wish to convey. I've seldom been motivated to paint over the years . . . just a few times . . . when there was something I wanted to express that was not amenable to being *said*.

I wish I'd already learned how to market my books to the general public. Two of the three in progress are for folks in general, not the specialized professional audiences I've written for in the past.

Two of my favorite authors are Max Schulman and Ezra Pound. Pound once said, "Men do not understand books until they have had a certain amount of life, or at any rate no man understands a deep book, until he has seen and lived at least part of its contents."

Maybe I don't belong in this book. I CAN not write. In fact, I can only write when I have something I want to say.

The Pure Potency of Words

Walter Wangerin is an ordained Lutheran minister with over a dozen books to his credit, but he is best known for his award-winning fantasy The Book of the Dun Cow *(1978), followed by a sequel,* The Book of Sorrows *(1985). His poetry appears in* A Miniature Cathedral and Other Poems *(1987), and his short stories appear in* Miz Lil and the Chronicles of Grace *(1988).*

I write by old-fashioned typewriter. Approximately six hours a day: nine to three (since I'm responsible for the kids, the cooking, much of the cleaning in our house, and writing stops when children arrive home). I have (and need) a good spacious room in which to write, where all my library is available.

How did I happen to become a writer. . . .

If by "writer" you mean "one who writes" as opposed to "one who makes a profession of writing," it was more a matter of character than choice. Write: I've been writing material since elementary school, when it was the most natural step in the world to graduate from reading books to writing them — as my brother simply assumed that one moves from watching hockey to playing it. (We lived in Edmonton, Canada.)

But if there was a moment when I became acutely conscious that I was, in fact, writing, it was in the eighth grade. Two events. One, I wrote a short story which was, in effect, a lie. It was a fiction which did not acknowledge its fictive quality. People read it and believed what I wrote. Sitting, then, in a history class (the teacher writing our notes furiously on the blackboard because he was angry with student impertinence, as he said, and demanded that we take down word for word what he was scribbling) I was suddenly overwhelmed with the power of the thing I had done, overwhelmed with the pure potency of words: I had affected the souls of the people around me. I had persuaded them of a thing that wasn't, as though it was. I literally tingled while I sat in my desk and contemplated such a subtle dominance. For the most part I was a retiring child; but this means of control over others seemed eminently in my hands. I didn't, at that moment, recognize the evil of my discovery and its thrill.

Second event: I consciously chose to write a novel. And wrote it. (Though I recall that it grew to no more than about forty typewritten pages in length — I'd learned to type in third grade, a happy skill to gain so early.) The novel was science fiction and played with the notion of the relativity of time; two twins, one who travels the stars and stays young, one who remains earth-bound growing old. Not a particularly novel idea, but I supposed that my handling of it would make the difference. As I wrote it, I read it to my mother — through the bathroom door, since she was, each time I approached her with pages, seized with a sudden urge that required privacy.

In high school I consciously said (even before I ever had) "I'll write poetry." And in order to prepare myself I bought, as a matter of fact, *Leaves of Grass* because I recognized Whitman's name. I read it through, baffled. But I was, in those days, reading with great hunger the Russian authors, Tolstoy, Dostoevsky, Turgenev — and others, too (I remember Butler's *The Way of All Flesh* — and especially Wolfe's *Look Homeward, Angel*, which had profound effect). These books I discovered on my own, beginning with sophomore high school (because my brother had a copy of *Crime and Punishment*, and the insight into the spirit took my breath away — so I read constantly these books that so contented me with an acceptable vision of the world, not unlike my own).

I was not particularly social in high school. It was an all-boys prep school, a painful experience, in which I needed to wall myself round with a certain spiritual protection. Two things accomplished that keeping:

both my reading (which I did even in class and wherever people gathered; the book always seemed to justify my presence there and keep people away from me) and my writing. I wrote a very long story, meant to exorcise (though symbolically, since the story did not refer directly to the prep school) the horrors I was myself suffering. (That language is not exaggeration.) What the story did, psychologically, was to reinterpret an experience over which I had no perceptible control. The reinterpretation (and the secret execration which I heaped on my classmates, though they didn't know this) *was* my control. It worked. It worked, also, to raise a certain reputation for me at the school because my skill with words became recognized and applauded: I could do what they could not do. (Incidentally: Harper has now published a book of my short stories, one of which deals specifically with this time in my life, and that school.)

And the consequence of that writing's working? Well, fiction proved itself a means, for me, for meeting the world, an absolutely necessary companion — or if not a companion (a being of its own) then a necessary function of my spirit for my spirit's health and preservation. No, I did not fully know this then; and yet, yes: I did know it. From junior high on I wrote stories regularly in the night, copying no one in particular (and never truly thinking that this would lead to professional writing, which seemed a dream too celestial even to comtemplate: the prep school aimed toward the Lutheran ministry).

In my senior high school year a creative writing teacher named James Barber returned a sheaf of stories to us one day with a comment that shot blood immediately to my ears. He was a slouching, cigarette smoking, scar-faced, tenor-voiced, crew-cutted, carbuncle-butted, self-assured icon of a man (for all of which he had — but he didn't know it — our deepest, most boyish respect). When he'd plopped my story on my desk and turned away from me, while he slouched toward the front of the room, he fairly whined it: "Wangerin can write the eyes out of a turkey at fifty paces." That's the quote, word for word. One tucks such jewels deep in the pouch of one's memory, there to cherish it forever. If any single thing made me think of being an overt, evident, and public writer, it was that off-handed compliment.

Straightway I began also to write poetry. In college I focused most on the poetry. The first poet whose style I tried to match (should I be embarrassed?) was Frost — well, and E. A. Robinson. I was exceedingly formal. I attempted every kind of sonnet I knew (which, to me, merely meant a changing of the rhyme scheme and of versification: three quatrains and a couplet; an octet and a sestet; or a terza rima form). Again, I did this essentially on my own since the college was tiny and no one taught writing. The finest thing I got directly for my writing was a course (from Dr. Warren Rubel) in the seventeenth-century poets. Second best (but not as effective for me, since not yet compatible to my way of thinking) was a course in contemporary poetry.

I must say quickly that though I've published a book of poetry since those days, I do not consider myself a poet. I may yet be. I do sometimes write poetry. But I do not trust the continuance of my material enough to say that that is what I am or have become. I did, however, again discover the heady, threatful, astonishing power of plain words again — when I wrote a love poem (simply because love poems seemed a natural place to begin, whether one loved or not) which poem did indeed communicate love where I hadn't anticipated it; took my breath away when love was declared back to me; and then the declaration (but not the poem) caused me to love in return.

In graduate school (all my classmates having progressed to the seminary — I myself having veered out of the system to Miami of Ohio on a National Defense Fellowship; I myself — though I didn't truly know it yet — having lost any Christian faith), in graduate school, I say, I set myself the task of writing a poem a day. Which task I fulfilled — to my great anguish, since poem after poem seemed to me wooden, unworthy, incomplete, sophomoric, piping or puling, bombastic to no point whatsoever. But I shifted attitude, finally, and kept to the task by admitting to myself that this was an apprenticeship and I was permitted persistent failure. So I moved up another level of self-consciousness about writing: that is, I began, with full awareness, to learn the *sounds* of words by the writing of poetry (though the skill would specifically show itself in my prose thereafter), and more than sound (assonance, alliteration, rhythm) I learned (with a heady joy, I say) the *ambiguity* of words. That, for me, was like the creaking open of a treasure chest: how *much* one might say by implication and not just straightforwardly.

Yes, indeed: I read William Empson then, and I learned of the New Criticism (Brook and Warren) again, pretty much on my own. I was constantly being castigated by professors for a style in my papers which "called attention to itself," but I couldn't — nor wouldn't — cease it, because that was three-quarters my pleasure in writing papers at all, style. Sentences in all their variety. The use even of sixteenth-and seventeenth-century Brobdingnagian rhythms, a twisting, sinuous baroque quality to the sound. I plain liked that.

But still (even though I wasn't totally convinced that I'd end a teacher in college — though that was the track I was in) I did not consider that I could be a "writer." (Sometimes I wonder whether it would have moved me the more intentionally and clearly to the profession if I'd had some community around me involved in this long effort. Essentially, all this happened in isolation and under a faint embarrassment, since I didn't think that what I did was publicly presentable. It seemed, rather, a sort of quirk, a wrinkle in my personality.

If there's anything I'd say most to others intending (how perceptive such are!) to write in their future, it is that the apprenticeship is absolutely essential. I'll have not praise nor time for those who suppose that writing comes by some divine gift, some madness, some overflow of feeling (whether faithful, or romantic, or stuff recollected in tranquility, or junk that alcohol or drugs produce). I'm especially grim on Christians who enter the field blithely unprepared and literarily innocent of any hard work — as though the substance of their message forgives the failure of its form. FAITH HAD BETTER BE DRESSED AS BEST AND AS SKILLFULLY AS THIS WORLD DRESSES ITS LIES! For the world writes fine, fine; but again and again the Christian writes a nasal whine, a contemptible, mealy prose, and therefore deserves the judgment of the world. If there's any justification for the long history I've recounted here, it's to say to any aspiring writer: that, dear friend, is the necessary length of your own history before you commit to public print — *especially* if what you choose to write about is also holy.

The Writer's Hat

Ron Wilson agrees to contribute to this chapter from widely varying writers because he is a widely varying writer. He varies from fast to slow, left-brained to right-brained, hot to cold, and serious to semihumorous. Although he has books, an editing career, magazine articles, and a column to his credit (he wears many different hats), he prefers to be identified simply as "a writer." As an editor, he likes to quote T. S. Eliot: "I suppose some editors are failed writers, but so are most writers."

I wish I had learned sooner that you become a writer only by writing. It's like the old joke, "How do you get to Carnegie Hall? Practice! Practice! Practice!" I wish I had done more writing and developed my skills earlier in life.

After frittering away my high school years, I barely squeaked into college. I had some idea of "going into the ministry," whatever that meant. But I found that while I was a terrible communicator on my feet, I could do a half-decent job of writing. I also got involved in the student newspaper and became the editor. And found that I enjoyed writing and editing almost as much as eating.

From this awareness I concluded that my ministry was to be behind a typewriter and not a pulpit.

Actually, I learned to write with a pen and a pad of paper, and for years, I couldn't do any real creative writing on a machine. When I got into word processing five years ago, I forced myself to use it for the first draft. Now I do almost all my writing on the machine in my study.

On the other hand, I find the process of traveling conducive to creativity, and I still do a lot of writing while waiting for airplanes or in restaurants in faraway places.

I believe that many writers have a love-hate relationship with writing. Writing is hard work. Yet it brings a kind of satisfaction that few other activities bring. Writing is also something I simply can't turn on and off at will. At times when I need to write, I have to force myself to grind it out. At other times I can't stop the flow.

I like Ernest Hemingway for his clean, tight, no-nonsense powerful prose. John Steinbeck — not the world's greatest writer — perhaps for his subject matter more than anything else. Annie Dillard for her incredible imagination and ability to express it in unusual ways. Also, she combines humor, a reverence for life, and an appealing modesty in her writing. I find the results fascinating.

When asked for advice for aspiring writers, here is what I offer.

Victor Borge, the celebrated pianist with a sense of humor, often makes a great show of getting ready to play. He adjusts the bench, dusts it off, flexes his fingers, wriggles his torso. And the audience laughs.

Some people approach writing the same way — as a grand performance. They put on a writing hat, clear their throat, adopt a serious, if not austere, countenance, and "write." Only it's not funny.

They invariably overwrite. They try too hard and the prose bogs down of its own weight. It also gets in the way of communicating the ideas.

I don't mean that writing is easy. Finding fresh metaphors, searching for the precise word, trimming the fat is hard work. I simply mean that it should appear easy. Good writing has rhythm. It flows smoothly. It doesn't call attention to itself.

When Moses Malone stuffs a ball in a hoop or Boris Becker slams a backhand to the opposite court, we shake our heads and say it looks so easy. It isn't, of course. It takes dedication, practice, sacrifice, and concentration to achieve that effect. And that's true of writing.

The greatest compliment I ever received on my writing came from a friend who said that my letter sounds just as though I was talking to him across the table.

I know writers who put a picture of a friend on the desk or wall in front of them. That discourages pretentious writing, helps them relax, and adds an intimate quality to the prose.

Write to communicate, not to impress. Write the way you talk. Read your prose out loud. And remember the observation of Thomas Jefferson, a precursor of Strunk and White: "The most valuable of all talents is that of never using two words when one will do."

Here is another bit of advice I give myself.

Every morning when I turn on my computer, red lights flash on my printer and it begins a small dance. The print wheel goes *zitada*, *didida*, *dadada*, *eerrk*, vibrates to center stage, executes a practice pirouette, and tiptoes back. If it checks out, the lights turn green.

It occurred to me that all of us who aspire to influence those beyond the sound of our voice with print or broadcast media might profitably perform a similar examination. Whenever we pick up a pen or a microphone we need to check our motives.

For one thing, what we say will influence someone. We can count on that. When I went to journalism school, professors still talked about the power of the printed page. (Commercial television was only ten years old.) It was meant as much as a warning as a promise. Take responsibility for what you write.

Most important, I believe Christian communicators face some common temptations. In fact, it seems Satan dangles before us false promises quite similar to those he put to Jesus in the wilderness.

The first, of course, is the temptation to put money before the message. In college we were fond of asking, "Does philosophy bake bread?" We never answered the question to my satisfaction, but those of us who write for a living know what bakes bread. We can make a lot of money in publishing, broadcasting, films, etc. We can shape our work in a lot of little ways to make us or our message more marketable. And, as we set out to communicate a message, we can easily obscure it or dilute the gospel by trying to bake bread.

Christian communicators also face the temptation, as Jesus did, to test God and find a shortcut to success. If Jesus had jumped from the pinnacle of the temple, it would have been the ultimate publicity stunt. But that wasn't the way God wanted to usher in the Kingdom.

A clever communicator can arrange words, sounds, images, circumstances, etc., to get a carefully calculated response. If you and I package the pieces right, we can get an audience to give, get up and shout, or walk down the aisle. Relying on our own efforts and understanding, we can move the masses toward God — even if it's not just the way He'd do it.

Then, of course, to all of us comes the temptation to gain fame and power. Wouldn't you like to see your name on the marquee or your byline in sixty-point Cooper black or your picture on the cover of the *Music City News?* Edwin R. Newman once did a documentary he called "Land of Hype and Glory." That would describe more than a few publications or productions (or even conventions) that have carried the name "Christian." We have our own cultural variations of the temptation, but the lust for fame is as old as Lucifer.

This is why, to go back to my printer, I believe we need to check our circuits. Run a short self-test. Ask, "Why am I trying to communicate? Who am I trying to serve?"

I wouldn't press this analogy too far, but I understand that the printer doesn't do anything on its own. It waits for directions from the computer. I, for one, need to do that. I'm too eager to produce, either to meet a deadline or display my ingenuity. But first I need to listen, make sure my cable is connected, and wait for the green light to come on.

Earning a Living

Karen Ann Wojahn is a free-lance writer and editorial consultant who has written, ghosted, and edited over thirty books. She is best known for writing Growing Up with Roy and Dale *with Roy Rogers, Jr. She has also written articles for many Christian magazines, including* Moody Monthly, Christian Herald, *and* Charisma.

I'm constantly discovering writers who are new to me, although they are not new to writing. Today's favorites are sure to be joined — but not replaced — tomorrow. Frederick Buechner, Luci Shaw, and Madeleine L'Engle don't just write — they serve their readers a feast. Recently I discovered Maya Angelou, whose similes are as fresh as Sunday's breakfast. *Los Angeles Times* columnist Jack Smith writes with humor and candor. James Herriott has a gift for seeing and describing basic human nature with warmth.

Recently I revisited *Little Women*, a book I'd read perhaps as many as three dozen times in childhood. Reading again from the perspective of adulthood, I saw the profound influence of a nineteenth-century spinster on my morals, my values, my longings, and my dreams. Her name was Louisa May Alcott, and when I stood at her grave in Concord, Massachusetts just a few months ago, I thanked her again for her part in shaping my thoughts. She will, undoubtedly, be my favorite forever.

There are some things that I failed to learn from Louisa May Alcott or any other favorite writers, to my misfortune. Billy Wilder was probably right when he said, "Hindsight is always 20/20." Most of us could profit by watching the lives of others, but much of what we need to know in life doesn't come except through experience. There are many things I wish I had learned early in my writing apprenticeship, and I surely must have heard about them without really *hearing*.

The lesson I most want to share is that writing is a *business* as well as a craft. I've worked hard at developing my craft, but I haven't been as responsible about making wise decisions from a business standpoint. I don't believe that writers and artists are readily drawn to business and finance. We don't like to haggle over contracts or make demands, and some of us take a kind of romantic and/or spiritual (translate: foolish) pride in being "struggling artists" who are "writing for the Lord."

Because I've written and edited exclusively for the Christian market, I've bought into the "ministry" mentality. I've believed that people would deal honestly and fairly with me because they said they were Christian. In many cases, that has been true. But in some cases, it has not. I've also allowed myself to feel guilty about wanting to earn a living with my gifts and talents. (It rarely dawns on me that my pastors, doctors, dentist, teachers — all Christians — earn their livings with *their* gifts!) Consequently, I've frequently allowed myself to be underpaid, overextended, and sometimes manipulated into giving away my work as if it had no earthly value.

In only one case has anyone profited *substantially* from my work, a best-selling hardcover book (more than 300,000 copies sold), for which I was paid $700 in a flat fee, with no mention of my name anywhere. Someone else's name is on the book. (It's important to emphasize that the publisher did not trick me in that agreement. I knew what the agreement was when I did the work. I was too eager to help. I cheated myself, and I have no one to blame but me.) This amazing best-seller is the exception, not the rule. Most Christian publishers work on a narrow margin of profit; most are not wealthy. Nonetheless, editors and publishers and retailers receive regular paychecks, while writers are supposed to work "unto the Lord" and wait for "greater" reward in heaven. My grocer, dentist, doctor, and mortgage holder do not seem open to waiting to be paid until I get to heaven! I am obligated to myself, to my family, and to my creditors to be responsible from a business standpoint. I was slow to realize that it is right for me to expect to be paid promptly and adequately.

So my counsel to publishable writers is this:

1. Set reasonable fees for your work — fees that will cover expenses (including social security, taxes, mileage, supplies, electricity, and other overhead) as well as pay for your time *and* your skills and expertise.

2. Don't undermine your fellow writers or prostitute your profession by giving away your work to publishers for the sake of appearing in print. If you must give away your work, give it to struggling nonprofit ministries. For example, I edit, free, a quarterly newsletter for a local ministry. Recently, I developed, for free, a training manual for a national ministry that has earned my respect. The manual will not be sold for

profit. The money I earn writing and editing enables me to "tithe" my talents in this special way from time to time, and documentation of my "in-kind" service may eventually enable these ministries to receive grants.

3. Never work on the basis of an unwritten agreement. Get everything in writing, no matter how much you trust the person who made promises. If that is hard for you to insist upon, imagine that there is going to be a takeover at the company and that only written agreements will be honored. (As a matter of fact, written agreements are not always honored, but it is better to have one anyway.)

4. Recognize that because publishers are in *business*, they will create contracts and agreements that are in *their* best financial interest, not in the interest of the writer. Accept the fact that this is just common sense; there's no conspiracy, and it is foolish to become paranoid about the intentions of the publisher. It is equally foolish — and irresponsible — to be naive.

5. Don't expect to become rich or famous in the Christian writing field, any more than you expect to win a lottery.

In conclusion, there is some truth in these old words:

> The land of literature is a fairy land
> to those who view it from a distance,
> but, like all other landscapes,
> the charm fades on a nearer approach,
> and the thorns and briars become visible.
> — Washington Irving, *Tales of a Traveler*, 1824

Another Tolstoy

Charles Wrong, son of an Oxford professor, is himself an Oxford graduate who ended up teaching history in a Florida university and has now retired to Canada. As a student, he wrote essays for C. S. Lewis—who once said to him, "Sir, you are an adventurer!" He is a mystery buff.

I am one of the larger army of people who are firmly convinced they could be another Tolstoy, or anyway another Herman Wouk, if they could have found the time (by which they mean, taken the trouble). I didn't become a writer; I wish I had, but I was too lazy.

The time C. S. Lewis gave me lunch at Magdalen was when I was scraping around rather frantically for any source of income, and wanted to write an article about him. Although from his own point of view the publication of such an article would have been unwelcome, he was typically courteous and helpful. I can't remember what we had for lunch, except that we drank cider. (Cider in England is always alcoholic, but I have never met cider that packed such wallop as this.) The article never got written, and, to my lasting regret, I have lost the notes I took for it. I do remember his expressing great dislike for T. H. White's Sword in the Stone books about the young Arthur.

Earlier, when Lewis was my tutor, I saw him only once a week for a single term, I think; he was my tutor for political science, of which I did only enough to meet the bare basic requirement. It was neither his preferred subject nor mine. I wasn't even greatly interested in Lewis in those days, to my lasting regret now. (Since then, of course, I have read almost everything he ever wrote, and possess copies of nearly all his books.)

Work for a tutor consisted of writing a weekly essay, on a subject he would set, and reading it aloud to him — a practice Lewis regarded as immensely valuable as teaching people to "write for the ear." I agree with him. You would turn up at the appointed time, knock at the door of his rooms (we always used the plural word), and be invited in. He would sit in silence, listening to you, until you had finished, and then, if he was Lewis, tear your essay to shreds. Personally, I consider it to have been of the greatest value. I always knew nothing I wrote for Lewis could afford to have any loose ends or fallacies. He would be onto them at once. In his opinion (and mine) it was his job to expose bad writing or shoddy thinking for what it was; that was what the student came to college for.

I can remember almost nothing of what Lewis said in his tutorials. Once, after I had produced a string of rather adolescent wisecracks, he said, "Well, some of them came off and some of them didn't." (He was too kind; I'd hate, now, to remember any of them.) Once, when I mentioned Chesterton, he exclaimed impulsively, "What a good writer he was!"

I ran into Lewis on the station platform at Oxford some years after the war. It may have been then that he apologized for the unconvincing dialogue of the eldila in *Perelandra*. "I don't think I'm very good at Archangelese." And he told me of a friend who had told him that he couldn't read the description of the floating islands in that book, because it made him feel seasick. Lewis said he took this as a great compliment.

Of course Lewis's academic writing was superb. It's disheartening to see what a flood of unwanted books and articles the academic world produces, and how badly written many of them are. Even when they *aren't* badly written they're seldom useful. The universities have got themselves into a ridiculous bind; they know this perfectly well, but seem unable to do anything about it. A graduate school needs to keep churning out Ph.D.'s, to keep up its reputation. But there's no market for more than a small fraction of those Ph.D.'s, so at every slave market — like the meeting of the American Historical Association just after every Christmas — a horde of hungry job-seekers descend like locusts, a hundred applicants for every advertised post. The competition is so keen that, until they get tenure, they have to overproduce frantically; and as a rule they have to go on overproducing even after being tenured, in order to get promoted. Producing means writing, and being published.

And of course ninety percent of the stuff that's poured out is completely otiose (a word I like to use, without being quite sure what it means). In theory, it's a contribution to human knowledge. In practice, most often, it says nothing anyone needs or wants to know, and the chances are it's already been said by somebody else. It wasn't written to promote knowledge; it was written to secure tenure or promotion. The European Common Market has mountains of butter and lakes of wine nobody can use, and can't stop the farmers and wine-producers turning out more and more, because that's how they make a living. The academic world, for the same reason, has mountains of unnecessary verbiage. Lewis talked about this in "Interim Report," which was recently published in the book *Present Concerns*.

Another, different problem for writers that I've noticed is the widespread tendency to try and scrounge professional work out of professional people by freeloading on them. But at least the doctor or lawyer can refuse to give free advice. An author whose work is lifted has no recourse but legal action. It's only certain classes of professionals who are victimized this way.

Nobody takes a taxi, and then informs the driver that he can't expect to be paid because the ride was undertaken in order to convey soup to deserving paupers. (I'd like to see somebody try it.) But they do it to historians all right. I was asked to contribute to an encyclopedia of the French Revolution; the remuneration to each contributor being one book (out of a list of six) which he was told he was forbidden to sell. At least they gave the contributor the option of telling them to drop dead; which I took. I told them, in effect, that if their encyclopedia was a professional job, they would pay their contributors professional rates; if it wasn't a professional job, I didn't want anything to do with it.

But publishers don't seem to have any sense anyway. Some are just mildly goofy, while others are crazy as bedbugs. P. G. Wodehouse speaks somewhere of the "brisk delirium" in which all business in a publishing house seems to be conducted, and I'm sure he's right.

I think of my unpublished mystery with fond affection, but have an uneasy feeling at the back of my mind that it's really an unpublishable turkey. My father's own effort in the same direction certainly was. However, when I was about ten I read my father's introduction to his anthology *Crime and Detection* (nowadays the only thing he's remembered for), and then dug out of his bookshelves all the mystery works he'd mentioned: Hornung's *Raffles*, Barry Pain's *Constantine Dix*, and so on. It may have been this that started me off as a mystery buff.

I have found (though I have yet to make practical use of the discovery) that with writing, as with many other things, you have to work yourself up to a proper pace. Once you have done this, it becomes both easy and enjoyable — which does not, of course, necessarily mean you're doing it well. Your easy writing's "curst hard reading," as Sheridan said.

What I've learned about writing is that the thing is to *do* it; do a lot of it; do it all the time. (Not that I do.) You remember Sinclair Lewis being invited to give a talk to would-be writers at college. "How many of you want to become writers?" asked Lewis. A forest of hands shot up. "Then for God's sake why aren't you *writing?*" snarled Lewis, and turned on his heel and walked out. He is not my favorite author, by any means, but he was quite right.

C. S. Lewis is a favorite of mine, of course; because he's right about so many things most other authors are wrong about or ignore; and because of his superb descriptive talent. Edwin O'Connor, Margaret Kennedy, Kate O'Brien: novelists with a Christian orientation. Michael Gilber, Rex Stout, Dorothy L. Sayers, Elizabeth Daly: the best of the mystery writers (and Sayers of course so much more). Tolkien, at least in the Trilogy. Tolstoy, Jane Austen, O. Henry, P. G. Wodehouse, at his best. Garrett Mattingly, the historian who united incomparable style with meticulous scholarship; and in that field F. W. Maitland and Veronica Wedgwood; also Fernand Braudel.

Another author I prize is Anthony Boucher, who told a writer friend that writing is the only profession from which no one ever retires. You find retired soldiers, retired civil servants, retired engine drivers, even retired politicians. But as long as any writer *can* write, he *does* write; it doesn't matter whether he's published or not.

I have a hotshot Smith Corona that corrects your spelling mistakes for you, but I have yet to master the secret of how to use it; in fact, I don't even know how to take the wretched thing out of its case. What I use is an Olympia Portable. As long as it doesn't jump too many spaces, I'm quite satisfied with it. I agree with Andy Rooney: what I want is not a thinking machine that corrects my spelling mistakes for me, but a machine that will simply put my words down on paper. Damn and blast all these miraculous inventions that supply us, at vastly inflated prices, with technological breakthroughs we don't need and don't want, and in the process make it impossible to get honest, humble typewriters serviced any more.

How should I be identified as a writer? As an Awful Warning: the man who knew what should be done but was too lazy to do it. All I have published is a handful of essays. I have written a number of papers for my own edification or amusement (e.g., "The Impossible Lecture," the lecture I would have liked to give my Canadian history students if I'd had the nerve). I plan to write a lot more of these now that I'm retired. You can classify me as a man who writes, when he writes at all, for the most appreciative audience in the world: himself.

SUGGESTED ACTIVITIES

1. Which of the thirty writers in this chapter interested you the most and why? Which would you most like to interview? Pretend that you have been asked to participate in writing the chapter. Write your own present factual answers to all seven questions, imagine what your answers might be ten years from now, and add your factual or imaginative response to the other thirty.
2. If you are in a writing class or writing group, try interviewing another member and being interviewed in return. Present your finished products to the rest of the group. This gives you some experience in conducting and writing an interview, lets you feel what it is like to be an interviewee, and is also a means of getting better acquainted. Then the interviews can be compared and critiqued by the entire group.
3. Here is a playful way for some writers to come up with a story plan. One member of a group is excluded while the group supposedly makes up a fictional plot. In reality, all that the group does while the victim is away is to get the following scheme in mind. The victim is to ask questions about the story that can be answered by yes or no. When a question ends with a consonant, the group answers yes. When a question ends with a vowel, the group answers no. The victim then inadvertently invents a story line while trying to get yes answers and tie them together. This exercise is not apt to create any great plots, but it can serve as an icebreaker and stir up some story ideas.
4. Authors and editors are real people, and some of them probably live in your neighborhood. Meeting them at workshops, writing classes, and critique groups provides a wealth of insight into the craft and business of writing. Check with colleges, libraries, and local publications for leads; make a list of writers and publishers in your area; and consider forming a writers' group if there is none available to you. (Many experienced writers and editors are willing to come to speak to such groups even if they are too busy to join.)

Chapter 10

C. S. Lewis's Free Advice to Hopeful Writers

Your manuscript is both good and original; but the part that is good is not original, and the part that is original is not good.

— SAMUEL JOHNSON[1]

C. S. Lewis was so fond of crusty old Samuel Johnson's writing that he thought of him as a member of his family and said he looked forward to meeting him in heaven.[2] He never tired of reading Johnson.

I think every writer should have a beloved author to admire and feel close to that way, a chosen mentor. My own favorite author was C. S. Lewis himself, and I didn't have to wait to meet him in heaven. Thanks to what felt like a miracle at the time, I managed to meet him in Oxford.

I was an English major at the University of Redlands in California when I first sampled a book by C. S. Lewis one summer and was caught for life. When I was invited to do an honors project in the field of English, I chose Lewis for my subject and plunged in. I read everything by and about him that was available in the Los Angeles Public Library and wrote a thesis showing that all of Lewis's major beliefs were present in his brand-new series of Narnian fantasies for children.

I worked part-time in the cafeteria for seventy-five cents an hour in those days and had no hopes of getting to England. Then in the spring of my senior year I happened to see an announcement about scholarships for a summer course at the University of London, and I applied. As soon as I got word that I had won a scholarship, I wrote to C. S. Lewis for the first time — telling him that I had been studying his work for a year and a half and asking if I could hear him lecture or meet him while I was in England.

Lewis said that I should write again when I got to England and that I could come to meet him in Oxford. My dream was coming true. I graduated from college; crossed the United States by train; and crossed the Atlantic — economy class on an old ocean liner, seasick all the way. I got to England on July 7 and wrote to C. S. Lewis immediately.

On July 20, 1956, I finished my London classes for the week and caught an afternoon train to Oxford. Lewis was meeting me in the lobby of the Royal Oxford Hotel for four o'clock tea, and I had a panic attack as I approached the place. If I had been given free choice of all the famous people who ever lived, Lewis was the one I would have chosen to meet. I was a penniless California student who looked only sixteen and felt like an ignoramus, getting a personal visit with my favorite author. My awe for Lewis's mind was so great that when I finally sat on the hotel sofa by him, I had to fight for a minute not to faint and fall on the floor.

He was so entertaining that we chatted and laughed without pause for well over an hour. I have never met anyone more enjoyable before or since. I knew at the time that this little afternoon tea was bound to be a high point of my entire life, and that has proved true. But it is what Lewis's books have been giving me ever since that has enriched me far more, and they are available to everyone. I don't think I could possibly have chosen a better mentor to help me to grow in understanding of what I want to understand about life.

- I didn't try to strike up a regular correspondence with Lewis after our meeting, because I didn't want to take up too much of his precious time; and that was a proper decision. But in 1957 I mailed him my thesis, and he read it all and replied that I was right in the center of the target. Then he pointed out one weak sentence where I could have been misread, and he included the following bit of free advice: "Most readers will misunderstand if you give them the slightest chance. (It's like driving cattle; if there's an open gateway anywhere on the road, they'll go into it!")

Later I discovered that for a span of fifty years C. S. Lewis gave away pointers like that to both friends and strangers. He did this in personal letters; and, fortunately, many of them have survived.[3] I have dug out much of this writing advice, and I have grouped it into six generally chronological sets: letters to Arthur Greeves (Practice, Practice, Practice), letters to other early friends (The Best Words in the Best Order), letters to children (Seeing One's Mistakes), letters to an American lady (As One Rhymester to Another), letters to a variety of adult correspondents (Simplify! Simplify!), and letters to Sister Penelope (Raised in Print).

Practice, Practice, Practice

All of C. S. Lewis's earliest advice about writing went to Ireland to his earliest friend, Arthur Greeves.[4] It seems that Lewis followed his own eager advice to Greeves far more than Greeves did. But we can be deeply grateful to Greeves for saving the letters all his life. He finally sent them on to C. S. Lewis's brother Warren, and Warren Lewis contributed them to the Wade Center in Wheaton, Illinois. Lewis's momentous decision against literary ambition is spelled out in one place only: in a pair of 1930 letters to Greeves. But that was a turnaround in his maturity.

Just before his sixteenth birthday Lewis wrote from England that all he needed for his art was paper and pen, in contrast to Greeves' unfortunate need for a piano or a box of paints and drawing paper. Soon Lewis was urging Greeves to join him and become a writer.

In 1915 Lewis teased Greeves for his "gems of orthography" like "simpathise" and "phisically," admitting that his own spelling was almost as bad. A few days later Lewis criticized Greeves again and hit upon his lifelong theme: the first point for a letter writer to master is to make himself intelligible to his reader. For the next fifty years Lewis would constantly urge himself and others on toward the goal of clarity. That became his hallmark.

When he was seventeen, Lewis was temporarily on guard against feelings. (He had lost his mother to cancer and had to put up with an emotionally stormy father.) He cockily told Greeves that feelings should be saved for literature and art, where they are delightful, and kept out of real life, where they are a nuisance. Several months later he decided that his own letters were becoming mawkish. He told Greeves that they should publish their letters someday in a book to be called *Lamentations*.

(About sixty-five years later, his letters to Greeves really were published, under the title *They Stand Together.)*

At this point Lewis began seriously urging Greeves to try to make his mark in literature. "I cannot urge you too strongly to go on and write something, anything, but at any rate WRITE." He usually followed his advice to Greeves more than Greeves did. He advised Greeves not to try humor because it is a dangerous form of writing and there is enough humor in print already. (Ironically, Greeves comes across as rather melancholy; it was Lewis who developed a flair for wit.) Lewis obviously wanted an audience and companionship. He promised to tell Greeves the absolute truth about his writing and begged Greeves to do the same for him.

"Whenever you are fed up with life, start writing: ink is the great cure for all human ills, as I have found out long ago." Lewis was still seventeen when he wrote that. He was convinced that it didn't matter what they wrote at that age, just so they wrote continually, as well as they could. What Greeves needed, Lewis claimed, was practice, practice, practice. Lewis felt that every time he wrote a page of prose or verse, with real effort, he was making good progress as an author — even if he burned the page as soon as he finished it. On the other hand, he felt one can't write one's best if one never submits one's writing to a reader.

Lewis told Greeves that the beginning of his first story was superb and that only laziness could keep him from producing something good. Now that they were both writing and knew how much work there is in a short piece that can be read in a few minutes, they could both begin to realize the labor that went into writing a great and lengthy work.

On a practical note, Lewis advised Greeves to stop referring to the character in his story as "our young friend" or "our hero."

Greeves complained that he sometimes found the same word coming into his prose repeatedly; Lewis answered that this is the common experience of all writers. Greeves complained that he sometimes had to sit and think before he could go on writing; Lewis answered that good work is never done in a hurry. When one does write a good passage quickly, it always needs further work later, Lewis believed.

Lewis mentioned that he planned his writing in his head while he was walking; his imagination worked only when he was exercising.

Lewis hoped that Greeves would continue his story, but he admitted that authors rarely complete their first projects. By this time Lewis had begun and abandoned several. Further, he thought that Greeves gravely underestimated how much time it took Lewis to write.

At this point Greeves accused Lewis of flattering him about his story, and Lewis reminded him that he hardly let a sentence go past without picking holes in it. But Lewis's efforts were wasted; Greeves gave up on the story and decided to try a novel instead. At the same time, Lewis gave up on the epic poem he had been trying to write in antiquated English. He told Greeves that they had both gained valuable experience while their projects lasted, but Lewis didn't want much more of this kind of quitting.

"The Bible (which you don't read) has very hard things to say of people who put their hand to the plough and turn back," Lewis warned Greeves. (Greeves was proud of being a Christian, and Lewis was proud of not being a Christian.) Lewis thought it would be better to complete one small work than to begin and abandon twenty more ambitious projects.

Lewis felt an almost urgent need to be able to say that he had written a book and finished it, no matter how it turned out. Perhaps that was because of the First World War, which he and Greeves ignored in their letters. It was raging on, and Lewis would soon be pulled into it. (Greeves suffered from the idea that he had delicate health and never went to war or held a job.) When Lewis was eighteen, he was recruited. He intended to gather his poems and send them to a publisher before he was sent to France, he said, because if he died in France, his friends who knew nothing about poetry would be in awe of his book and believe that he had been a young genius. Behind his jaunty tone was the fact that literary immortality was the only kind that Lewis had any hopes for then.

Just before Lewis sailed for France he wrote to Greeves that thought can be expressed in a number of ways, and style is the art of expressing a thought in the most beautiful or rhythmical way. An example of poor style is "When the constellations which appear at early morning joined musical exercises and the angelic spirits loudly testified to their satisfaction." The same thought is expressed in good style in the King James Bible: "When the morning stars sang together and all the sons of God shouted for joy." With that point made, Lewis went off to the front lines.

Soon after Lewis returned to England to recover from war wounds, he was pointing out to Greeves how easy it is for readers to misunderstand a writer's words. Greeves had said that he was driven to town; he meant that someone took him in the car, but at first Lewis thought he was driven by circumstances.

At that point Lewis hired a typist to prepare his poems and began submitting the manuscript to publishers, starting with his first choice. Macmillan turned him down with a polite rejection letter; but Heinemann, his second choice, accepted his book. He was overjoyed. Later he wrote to Greeves that he was disappointed every week over the delay of his book. When it was published in 1919, he wrote to Greeves that he was *not* famous yet, but that perhaps he had slunk into a "modicum of notoriety." He was still urging Greeves to write and get published.

A decade passed. Lewis completed his lengthy education, became an Oxford professor of literature, and kept on writing.

In August, 1930, Arthur Greeves complained that he might be doomed to failure as a writer; and Lewis wrote an extraordinary letter in response. At this point Lewis had published two books of poetry that were almost completely ignored by the public, and Greeves had not come close to publishing anything. Both men were in their thirties.

First, Lewis declared that facing the possibility of being a literary failure, like facing the possibility of surgery, can drive a person crazy if he vacillates between hope and fear. It is better to resign oneself to the worst and deal with it.

The side of Lewis that longed for success as a writer, he admitted, was not the side that was worth much. (The desire to be a writer is another matter, because no one could stop Lewis and Greeves from writing.) Greeves no doubt believed that it would be bliss to have a book published, whether anyone bought it or not. But such an idea is an absolute delusion. If Greeves had a book that did not sell, he would soon be as disappointed as he was when he had no book. Lewis knew that from experience.

From the age of sixteen onwards Lewis had staked his whole contentment upon one single ambition: literary success. He had pursued that goal without wavering. And he had failed. He was an expert on suffering the pangs of disappointment as a writer; that was his special subject, his real profession. (He realized how absurd it is in such a world as this to dignify his disappointment with the word *suffering*.)

At this point in his life, Lewis believed in God and was on his way to becoming a Christian. He told Greeves that unless God has abandoned us, He will burn away our literary ambition someday. We need to endure the pain and be healed of our wish to outdo other people. When one gives up one's ambitions, one can for the first time have a restful state of mind and say with true sincerity, "Thy Kingdom come." In God's kingdom there will be no competition, and a person must stop caring about status to enter there.

How difficult it would be to reach this stage after succeeding as an author, Lewis exclaimed. Perhaps God had been kind to Greeves and Lewis by saving them from making literary success the center of their lives. Literary ambitions can be a dangerous idol.

Lewis shuddered to think what he would have given at one time to be a successful writer. One has to die to personal ambition. Greeves had written to Lewis for literary encouragement, and Lewis apologized for telling Greeves the moral truth instead. He said he had to.

Greeves thanked Lewis for his honesty, and Lewis took up the theme again. He said that since he had given up hope of publication and fame, his poetry had actually improved. The second book of poetry was not much noticed by the public, but he had got good out of writing it. Perhaps the true use of a book lies in its effects upon the author. Publication and sales are not the real test of the value of a book.

Some people are bound to write, just as a tree is bound to bear leaves, Lewis said; it is their way of growing. But for others, the desire to write is a form of vanity. When hope of literary success is gone, the former writers continue to write and the latter writers stop. Lewis believed that those who continue to work devotedly at their writing without success are not wasting their efforts; they or others, in this world or elsewhere, will eventually reap some kind of harvest from the work. That was Lewis's faith. And he included himself in that category. Perhaps unsuccessful writers like Greeves and himself, who used to think that the world was waiting for their words, were really ministering to something within themselves.

This very letter was an example of what he was talking about, Lewis exclaimed. He was writing to Greeves and trying to give something to Greeves; but by the time he finished, he had benefited himself so much that even if the letter became lost in the mail, it would not be wasted.

The Best Words in the Best Order

As a young man at Oxford, Lewis found friends other than Greeves who were interested in writing, but he usually talked with them instead of sending letters. The first of these friends was Leo Baker, who eventually turned out to be an actor with the Old Vic Company rather than a writer. Before long Lewis and Baker and a third friend were putting together a collection of poems that they tried to publish.

Lewis advised Baker that struggling after originality is like trying to pull oneself off the ground by pulling up one's own suspenders — as if shutting one's eyes to the work of earlier writers would make one more likely to create new things. Homer and Virgil wrote great lines not for their own works alone, but for the use of all poets who followed them. The notion that one should not honestly refer to other authors and give to other authors is a heresy.

When a second publisher turned down the poems of the three friends, Lewis gave up on that project. But he reflected about what poetry really is. Coleridge had said that poetry is "the best words in the best order," but Lewis pointed out to Baker that this applies to any piece of good writing. "The train will leave at 7:30" gives us the best words in the best order and we can't improve upon them. Lewis made up a few lines of Wordsworthian poetry about the hissing locomotive and the laboring coaches and the grim chronometer, all worse words in a worse order. The real test of a poem is "Could this be said as well in prose?" If the answer is yes, the poem is not valid.

In another letter Lewis told Baker what he disliked about the prologue of a poem by Owen Barfield. In theory, a poet should be able to include anything he wants to in a poem; but in reality, some things make a reader squirm or laugh at the poet. Lewis complimented Baker for his use of the old phrase "God the father almighty" in one of his poems; he used it so skillfully that it seemed to become his own.

Another early friend of Lewis's at Oxford was A. K. Hamilton Jenkin, later known for his books about Cornwall. When Lewis learned that Jenkin had married, he sent him congratulations for marrying an author's daughter, because such a woman would probably already be accustomed to living with genius. Then he went on to condemn women's letters, full of so-called news about people going here and there. Lewis claimed to hate writing letters unless he was in the middle of an argument about ideas. Soon Lewis was begging Jenkin to find an excuse to come to Oxford for a visit. When that did not work out, Lewis wrote to Jenkin that he was by his absence a gap in Lewis's bookshelf and in the manuscript of his mind, as well as a drawn tooth in his psychic jaw and a broken lace in his spiritual boots. For Lewis, letters never served long as a substitute for talking with friends.

In 1929 Lewis first wrote to his fellow instructor J. R. R. Tolkien with advice for improving some of his poems. Soon Tolkien was reading his fantasies to Lewis in person. "He was for long my only audience," Tolkien reflected later. "Only from him did I ever get the idea that my 'stuff' could be more than a private hobby." Lewis's unflagging enthusiasm finally pushed Tolkien into fame and fortune.

Sometime before 1939 Lewis drew to himself a circle of male friends including Tolkien who met weekly for literary discussion and response to each other's writing. At last Lewis had the writing companionship that he had been reaching out for all along, his personal critique group. By this time he had also started to receive letters from strangers who had read his books, and some of these were hopeful writers themselves. Lewis was especially helpful to American children.

Seeing One's Mistakes

In 1956 C. S. Lewis wrote to an American girl named Joan that if she became a writer she would be trying to describe the indescribable essence of life always. Then he jumped from sublime thoughts to her practical question about correct English; *amn't I, aren't I,* and *am I not.* Good English is whatever educated people speak in a given time and place, he told her. When he was a child, *amn't I* was good in Belfast and bad in London, and *aren't I* was just the opposite. Don't trust teachers, textbooks, or logic in these matters, he warned her. Then he gave her five rules for writing:

1. Be clear, and make sure that your sentence can't be misunderstood.

2. Use plain, efficient words rather than long, vague ones. ("Keep promises" rather than "implement promises.")

3. Use concrete nouns rather than abstract nouns. ("More people died" rather than "mortality rose.")

4. Don't rely on adjectives like *terrible* and *wonderful* that tell the reader how to feel instead of making him feel that way. Such adjectives say to readers, "Please will you do my job for me."

5. Avoid word inflation; don't use *infinitely* when you mean *very.* Save words for when you need them.[5]

A couple of years later Lewis responded to some stories from Joan. "One can learn only by seeing one's mistakes." In her animal fantasy the talking animals were still in our real world, yet they had lost their real relationships; the small animals were in no danger from the owl. That works only in a more thoroughgoing fantasy world like Narnia. In Beatrix Potter stories, set in the real world, an owl is a threat to small animals. Reality and fantasy need to be mixed in one of the ways that work. Joan's spy story was better, but it was too condensed. And the police looked silly for failing to suspect the talented opera singer because he sang so well. Joan's poem had good content, Lewis said, but the verse "creaked" a bit.[6]

In 1959 he congratulated her about an Easter essay with sentences that were clear and taut and didn't sprawl. He said that she would be able to write a good prose, but that she exaggerated her point in her essay's ending. She had claimed that her reader had everything he needed in his soul. Lewis told her that he certainly did not. Never exaggerate, he said. Don't say more than you really mean.

She had sent him two poems, and he told her that one of them was really just prose, but not so good as her ordinary prose, typed like verse.

That was not good for her, he said. Ten years of writing strict, rhyming verse would be good for her before she ventured on into free verse.

In 1963 Lewis wrote to Joan that her poetry was developing. She would probably go too far with invented names for a while, but it would do no harm. It was like going through the measles. He mentioned to her that E. R. Eddison's invented name *silvamoonlake* had been spoiled for him recently by the advertising slogan "Drinkapintamilkaday" that everyone in England was tired of. Spelling counts as well as sound in creating a beautiful word. And of course the beauty of the object itself plays a role. The lovely sound of *velvet* was spoiled for Lewis because he hated the fabric itself.[7]

In 1957 Lewis congratulated another girl, named Jane, for the excellent fantasy story she had sent him, and told her that her next book could be at least twice as good. He pointed out six mistakes she could avoid in the future, explaining that she would get plenty of bad advice, and so he felt he should send her some good advice:

1. In a fantasy land of enchantment the story should be high, reckless, heroic, and romantic — not like earth's humdrum politics and conflicts.

2. Commonplace technological luxury breaks the spell in fairyland.

3. Don't use adjectives and adverbs like *exciting* that tell readers how to feel. Make them feel the emotion you want them to feel.

4. Write by ear, not by eye. Test the sound of every sentence to make sure it is nice to pronounce and has the right texture or speed to go with its meaning.

5. Don't bore your reader with descriptions of ordinary clothes. Such habits can be picked up from reading poor-quality magazines. Read great fantasy books in order to pick up good fantasy-writing habits.

6. Fantasy names should be beautiful and suggestive, not merely odd.[8]

In 1954 Lewis wrote to an American boy named Martin that his story was good and kept Lewis guessing to the end. But a word about how the policeman felt (was he afraid?) and a name for him would help to make him more real.[9] Five years later, Lewis was still writing to Martin. "Remember this if you ever become a critic [book reviewer]: say what the work is like, but if you start explaining *how it came* to be like that (in other words, inventing the history of the composition) you will nearly always be wrong."[10]

Martin, a scholarly boy, had the idea of trying to translate some solemn Latin poetry into English and had chosen a rollicking rhythm that he liked. Lewis told him that his chosen rhythm was not appropriate for his lofty theme and wrote the following ditty to show him why:

"A pound of that cheese and an ounce of the butter,"
Aeneas replied with his usual stutter.[11]

Later in 1959 an American schoolgirl appealed to Lewis for writing advice, and he sent her a list of eight rules for good writing:

1. Turn off the radio [and television].
2. Read good books and avoid most magazines.
3. Write with the ear, not the eye. Make every sentence sound good.
4. Write only about things that interest you. If you have no interests, you won't ever be a writer.
5. Be clear. Remember that readers can't know your mind. Don't forget to tell them exactly what they need to know to understand you.
6. Save odds and ends of writing attempts, because you may be able to use them later.
7. You need a well-trained sense of word rhythm, and the noise of a typewriter will interfere.
8. Know the meaning of every word you use.[12]

Two weeks before he died, Lewis wrote to a young woman named Kathy about some "maddening experience" that she had just suffered as an author. (Perhaps she had worked hard on some project and it hadn't turned out well and she threw it away.) He assured her that this is one of the occupational risks of authorship and that the same sort of thing had happened to him more than once. "There is nothing to be done about it!"[13]

As One Rhymester to Another

At the midpoint of the century C. S. Lewis heard from an American widow who corresponded with him until his death, telling him her troubles and occasionally sending him a poem she had written. He analyzed one of her poems metrically for her, pointing out that where she collapsed into a four beat rhythm it was not so good. He suggested that the ending, "God speed," was weak — especially because it seemed to be spoken by God, unaware that He was referring to Himself as humans do.[14]

When the woman sent Lewis a Christian poem by someone else, he found it very good Christianity but not good poetry. It was free verse (no rhyme and no metrical pattern). It had no rhythmic vitality, no reason why the lines should end where they did, and no melodious words. He admitted that he was old-fashioned; he thought that free verse succeeded in only a few exceptional poems.[15]

The American lady mentioned the "cult of the obstuse" to Lewis, and he asked her frankly if she meant "abstruse," "obtuse," or "obscure."[16]

"The pen has become to me what an oar is to a galley slave; then (God be praised) influenza and long half-comatose days in bed," he wrote to her in 1955. A few months later he responded to another of her poems and added "Between ourselves, as one rhymester to another, it's a great pity that *world*, such a good important word and often so emphatically demanding to come at the end of a line, has so few rhymes in English. *Furled, hurled, curled* — none of them very serviceable — and what else is there. Let's invent a verb *to churl* (behave churlishly)."[17]

In 1956 Lewis let off steam about book reviewers. "The review is of course a tissue of muddles and direct falsehoods — I don't say 'lies' because the people who write such things are not really capable of lying. I mean, to lie — to say what you know to be untrue. But to know this, and to have the very ideas of truth and falsehood in your head, presupposes a clarity of mind which they haven't got. To call them liars would be as undeserved a compliment as to say that a dog was bad at arithmetic."[18]

"People in real life are often so preposterous that one would not dare to put them in a novel."[19]

Simplify! Simplify!

C. S. Lewis sprinkled snippets of advice about writing throughout his correspondence that is yet unpublished. I have collected some samples.

On August 3, 1943, Lewis wrote to J. B. Phillips thanking him "a hundred times" for making Colossians more clear with his modern paraphrase. Lewis said it was like seeing a familiar picture after it had been cleaned. The only complaint Lewis had was about the phrase "Life from nothing began with Him." It was a bit ambiguous and could be misread to mean that Christ was created out of nothing.

On January 3, 1944, Lewis sent Phillips a list of suggestions for improving the manuscript of his next paraphrased epistle. First, Lewis advised Phillips to use fewer exclamation marks. Many of Paul's sentences call for them, but together in print they tend to give a childish or hysterical appearance to the letter. Similarly, "Never!" might be better expressed as "Not at all," or "By no means."

"Filial duty" is too hard, Lewis claimed; how about "duty to parents?" "Believe on Him" is not modern English; we use "in Him." "*Ipso facto*" would puzzle some readers, and Latin often annoys people.

"Your *members*" is archaic; would "organs" do? "A commonplace metaphor" could be replaced by "an illustration from ordinary life." "What *fruit*" would be more clear as "What was your harvest?" or "What sort of crop did you raise?" "Erstwhile" is too archaic. "Who have written this epistle" would be more clear as "to whom he's dictating this letter." Again and again Lewis pointed out what uneducated readers might misunderstand and suggested that even more clarity was needed. He was highly enthusiastic about the project.

On March 29, 1952, Lewis wrote to Miss H. D. Calkins of Los Angeles that he had read her book manuscript *India Looks* and found it as interesting as an adventure story. He would not write a preface for it because he was not qualified; for all he knew, the book could be a mass of errors (although he was sure it was not). Aside from that, Miss Calkins spoke well of Lewis in her book, and it would look like a mutual admiration society if he wrote the preface.

Lewis wrote out a list of thirteen suggestions for improving her book. Some of them were about getting quotations and facts exactly perfect and avoiding false impressions. He also advised her to write "enamored of," not "enamored with" and "Christocentric" rather than "Christ-centric"; and he told her not to write that *the reason* for something *was because* . . . One can correctly use either "*The reason* for his reluctance *was that* . . ." or "He was reluctant *because*. . . ." The latter is better because it is more concrete and less abstract, and this helps to avoid gobbledygook.

Lewis found two sentences in Calkins's book that conveyed no clear meaning at all to his mind. A knot of abstract nouns (such as *aspect* and *framework*), he warned, is usually a danger signal. Simplify! Simplify! But Lewis cited a sentence that he particularly liked and ended his letter by saying that that's the way to write.

On June 10, 1952, Lewis wrote to mystery writer Katharine Farrer that he greatly enjoyed her book *The Missing Link*, although he was an inexperienced reader of whodunits. Then he told her that her dialogue needed improvement. Lewis himself found dialogue frightfully tricky to write for two reasons. First, his own characters tended to talk too much; and second, because what works in real conversation often looks different in print. "Huntin'," without the *g* at the end, takes on unwanted significance in print that it does not have in real conversation. The word reminded Lewis of all the odious literature by authors who admire those people who say "huntin'" and all the more odious literature by authors who dislike people who say "huntin'." Then Lewis came up with the idea that authors would be wise to reread all their dialogue as it might be read by a dull, vulgar, or hostile reader. That would be a test. And he concluded with the idea that the hardest dialogue to write well is light dialogue such as banter between lovers or small talk at a party.

On February 3, 1954, Lewis wrote to Mrs. Farrer praising another book of hers and finding fault with the fact that a certain character giggled. Even if she would have giggled, he said, the word is too damaging. He was always reminding people, he said, that nothing gets into literature without becoming a word, and that sometimes the *things* are okay but their *words* are not. For example, no matter how deeply one feels about Czechoslovakia, it is impossible to use the word in a lyric poem. Then he scolded Mrs. Farrer for describing a moon, which we have all seen, by likening it to something that most of us have not seen — the white face of an idiot lost in the wood. This was disrespectful to the moon; if he were her spiritual director, he would make her learn Psalm 136 by heart. (He knew Mr. and Mrs. Farrer; Austin Farrer was a theological author.)

On August 14, 1954, Lewis wrote to a Mrs. Donnelly telling her that he thought she had a mistaken idea of a Christian writer's duty. We are all obligated to avoid writing anything that will increase in our readers lust, pride, or the ambition to outdo others; but we are only obligated to use the particular writing talent we have, not one we don't have. Not all Christian writers are called to write specifically Christian works, and it is a mistake to tack on bits of Christianity. A good story and a good meal are both innocent pleasures that don't need Scripture verses tucked in. The first job of a story is to be a good story; and if God wants the story to carry a Christian message, that will come in of its own accord. Lewis believed that some writing that is not obviously religious may do more good than some that is.

Lewis concluded his advice to Mrs. Donnelly by saying that first we must fulfill whatever duties life imposes on us, and then we are to do well whatever job our natural talent points to. Any honest work can be done to the glory of God, whether it is making stories, shoes, or rabbit hutches.

On February 2, 1955, Lewis wrote to Father Milward, who sent him thanks for his writing, that all teachers know that those who needed their help least are the ones who acknowledge it most fully. Then on Christmas day in 1959 Lewis wrote to Milward that he used to carry on deep discussions with friends in letters when he was young, and it was much like writing a book. But when he was actually a writer of books later, it finally became too hard to keep up discussions in letters. One shouldn't fill one's leisure with the same activity that is one's major work. Both Lewis's mind and his hand got tired.

On March 7, 1960, Lewis sent some preaching advice to Milward. The joints in the sermon or lecture cannot be made too clear (We have finished point A; now for B. . .). And if you want people to weep at the end, make them laugh at the beginning. Lewis added that he agreed with Milward that "the greater the author, the less he understands his own work."

One day after his first letter to Father Milward, on February 3, 1955, Lewis wrote to a Mrs. Johnson in Canada that many people don't seem to understand what fiction is. If a writer says what is untrue with the intention of making people believe it, that's lying. But if he says it with no such intention, that's fiction. Fiction is apt to express an author's deepest thoughts, speculations, dreads, and desires. Writing a story is only imagining out loud.

On September 2, 1956, Lewis wrote to I. O. Evans that he had done a frightful thing. He read the galleys of a story that Evans had sent him before properly reading the Evans letter that came also, and tore up the galleys. Then he saw that Evans wanted the galleys back. Lewis had never heard of an author keeping his galleys before. He had no ashes on hand because he heated his house with gas, he said, but he could order himself a little sackcloth. He signed his letter "Yours abjectly."

On April 19, 1958, Lewis wrote to Jane Douglass of New York that he did not find her dramatic adaptation of *The Lion, the Witch and the Wardrobe* very promising, but he assumed she would get other advice before deciding. He didn't want her to waste any more time than necessary on the project. Our lives are littered with false starts, he said; at least his was.

On March 29, 1962, Lewis wrote to his old friend Owen Barfield about his exciting new book and added, "Your language sometimes disgruntles me." He didn't like Barfield's word *polyvalence* and his phrase "He bases on. . . ." instead of "He starts from. . . ." Lewis preferred plain English.

Raised in Print

Sister Penelope, a Church of England nun, had come into C. S. Lewis's life in 1939 and became a friend of his. She lived in a convent at Wantage. When C. S. Lewis dedicated a book to Sister Penelope and her fellow nuns, he used the words "To Some Ladies at Wantage." The Portuguese translation accidentally changed it: "To Some Wanton Ladies." Lewis enjoyed that story.

Sister Penelope had first contacted Lewis with a letter of praise and a copy of her book *God Persists*. He said he didn't know how to respond to praise from his readers; he trusted that someday he could enjoy such compliments with the same innocence as if the compliments were for someone else. "Perfect humility will need no modesty." He was becoming a successful writer, and he saw pride as a continuing threat. He complimented Sister Penelope on her own book and told her that her phrase "God sat again for His portrait" (the New Testament) was daring and good.

He also told her that convincing good characters are uncommon in fiction because in order to imagine a man worse than himself an author only has to stop doing something (pushing back evil). To imagine one better than himself, an author has to do something new (come closer to goodness). He also told her that it is hard to invent something that isn't there already. He had learned to his surprise that some of his invented words in *Out of the Silent Planet* resemble real words in Arabic.

A couple of years later Lewis sent Sister Penelope a disreputable looking copy of his *Screwtape Letters* for safekeeping. The only other copy was with his publisher in London, and there was a danger that it might be destroyed in the London bombing. He did not say so to Penelope, but it is a matter of record that Lewis expected to be executed if the Germans took England. He no doubt thought that until publication his manuscript would be safer with her in her convent than with him in Oxford.

In 1942 Lewis answered Penelope that he used "all right" to mean that all items in a group are right, but *"alright"* to mean "perfectly right." It is an old Anglo-Saxon custom to double the *L* for the shorter sound in the middle of a word like *already*. (This distinction is not observed in the United States, where *"alright"* has usually been judged incorrect.) Penelope had also asked Lewis about people making up myths, and he told her that he thought they really come from good and bad spiritual sources. And what *is* the process we call "making up," he asked her. He agreed with her praise of a book by his friend Charles Williams, and he too wished that Williams would write more clearly.

In February 1943, Lewis found himself sharing Sister Penelope's frustration about book publication. His *Perelandra* was delayed at the bindery, and her book on Saint Athanasius had been sent back for rewriting. He advised her to try different publishers first. "Do fight." He likened their frustrations about their delayed books to the long waiting of God through the centuries to see His plan for mankind work out. When will the divine books he meant us to be actually lie on God's table in perfect form without faulty text or printer's errors? An author's desire for a perfect book is like God's desire for us, Lewis believed.

Human authorship is not real creation, of course. We only rearrange elements that God has provided. We can't imagine a new primary color, a third sex, a fourth dimension, or even a monster that does not consist of bits of previous animals stuck together. That is why we can't control exactly what our writing means to other people. And we can never know the entire meaning of our works. The meaning we never intended may be the best and truest one. Writing a book is like planting a garden or begetting a child; we are only one cause among many in the flow of events.

"But how dull all one's books are except the one you are waiting for at the moment!" Lewis observed. The author is like a shepherd, and the delayed book is like a lost sheep.

Later in 1943 Lewis read some radio dramas Sister Penelope wrote to teach the Bible to children. He suggested that she should not have characters say "Alas," which is not living language in our day, unless the entire play is in antiquated language. She should avoid trying to sneak descriptive matter into the dramatic dialogue. And she should try to keep her writing simple and concrete instead of abstract. Even if Ezra were the kind of man who would talk about the "agricultural aspect" of a ritual, that term seems a poor choice for children. "The parallel is as close as possible" also sounds too lecture-like for such a play. Victims of the Assyrian conquest would not have said that they were ground under the enemy's heel; they would have named specific terrors and cruelties. Lewis compared these weaknesses to surface stains that could be easily removed; he encouraged Penelope in her work and also urged her to have a rest.

Lewis was six chapters into his book *Miracles* at this point and told Penelope that he was surprised to find that writing about the supernatural turned out to include much praise of nature. "One never knows what one's in for when one starts thinking."

Lewis couldn't offer Sister Penelope much advice about publishers, although he had had many manuscripts rejected and accepted. He sent his books to one publisher after another, in the order of his choice, and he found it a great distraction to have to do so. He disapproved of her publisher's plan to alter her radio plays "not to disturb the children's minds." What staggered him about publishers, he said, was not their wickedness ("in fact they may not be wicked at all"), but their muddle-headedness.

Twelve years later, it turned out, Lewis would announce to Sister Penelope that he had put himself into the hands of a good literary agent and would never deal directly with publishers again. He advised her to do the same. When news got out that Lewis was in touch with an agent, one of his publishers went all the way from London to Cambridge and offered to raise the terms on all his previous books if he would promise not to hire an agent. Lewis took that as a sign that he should do so. An agent means increased royalties, but he also means relief from work and thought and frustration that is not good for an author. "Study to be quiet. . . !" he reminded her.

In May 1948, *Out of the Silent Planet* was temporarily out of print, and Lewis explained to Penelope that his pestering the publisher would do even less good than anyone else's pestering.

She had sent Lewis a story idea that intrigued him, but it lacked a good ending. He suggested several endings for her and exclaimed, "What fun it is writing other people's books!" He didn't know if she was capable of writing a good novel or not, but he encouraged her to try. In a couple of months she sent him the beginning of the novel, and he was so excited about it that he answered at once. He thought that the first two chapters might need to be rewritten later, after the story was finished. The readers should be kept guessing about the nature of the odd experience in the first chapter instead of finding out the truth almost before their curiosity was aroused. One character's wife should be left out unless she was going to play a real part in the story; there were already two good female characters, and this housewife seemed to add nothing. There was too much guidebook information in the first chapter. The priest tended to lecture when he would have done better to hint. And people don't say "my boy" or "my friend" to another person now.

Lewis's main point was that Penelope needed to go through her manuscript and remove adjectives of praise, replacing them with adjectives of description. It is no use telling the reader that things were lovely, exquisite, and superb, because the reader won't believe it. The writer must tell the reader about the color, texture, size, shape, or motion of the shadows instead of saying they are lovely.

"God speed!" Lewis concluded warmly after all his advice.

A month later Lewis congratulated Penelope on her progress and pointed out some more weaknesses that he compared to skin troubles, not heart disease. First, he claimed that the word *tense* had been overworked by cheap writers, and so "a voice tense with interest" didn't work well; and it didn't need to be said anyway. Second, "had nothing outward seen" in dialogue was unclear and didn't sound like ordinary spoken English. That was true of some other odd-sounding phrases in the dialogue also. "If so be that the difference in size. . ." should be replaced by "If it's really true that the difference in size." Lewis pointed out that a certain bad sentence managed to be as clumsy as real conversation and at the same time as stiff as a lecture.

"Does a grin really go through a telephone?" Lewis wondered.

When the adult male hero made remarks like "it was just topping" and "I just loved. . ." he sounded too much like a child. In real life he might say those words, but the impression would be modified by his mature face and voice. On the printed page one doesn't have those and must be more careful. Lewis revised some of those sentences to show how to make them seem like what a grown man would say.

It is useful for an author to imagine dialogue being read aloud or acted on the stage. Listen for anything that an actor would find difficult to say or that one would feel embarrassed at in front of a large audience. The fictional dialogue must always sound like real conversation but must always be clearer and more concise than in reality. "Literature is the art of *illusion*."

Six months later, at the beginning of 1949, Sister Penelope was considering a pen name, and Lewis suggested a couple. The first he mentioned was Pevensey. She did not use it, but a few months later Lewis used it himself — as the name of the four children who entered the land of Narnia.

He told Penelope that all he could suggest for possible publication of her novel was stocking up on postal supplies and fortitude, finding a magazine that might want to publish it as a serial, or putting it aside in order to rewrite it in a few years. Rewriting it would probably be impossible in the near future, but he suggested that the story would be better without its improbable coincidence. *Real* life isn't often probable, but stories have to seem probable.

Next Penelope titled her story *The Morning Gift* and hoped for a preface from Lewis himself. He said no, that he had written too many prefaces already. Later that year he read the entire manuscript and said that it was better than he had expected. His curiosity about the story kept him up past his usual bedtime. Once again he told her what he liked and how she could make the novel better.

One of the characters was not much more than a mouthpiece for doctrine. What he said was interesting, but he was not interesting. The ideas could just as well have come from a book that the main character was reading. Anything, even oddities, to bring this character to life would be a great gain. Perhaps she could draw him in part from a real person. Lewis told her not to be timid, to let her imagination and humor go to work. He also suggested that her new convert should perhaps not find church going entirely pleasant at first and that there should be a clear reason for the bride and groom's decision that they would never consummate their marriage. This sacrifice was artistically right in the story, but the reading public would dislike it; and it seemed to have no ethical or theological basis.

The style was now satisfactory, Lewis said, except for cliches. He advised Penelope to cut out stale phrases such as "all too little," "sands of time running out," and "three score and ten." But her image of Jesus leading an old man down to age like an old horse brought tears to Lewis's eyes. "I wish I had thought of it myself."

Early in 1950 Lewis expressed sorrow that Penelope had no luck finding a publisher for her novel, and he reminded her that many a book that succeeded later was first rejected by several publishers. He said he couldn't help her to revise it. He congratulated her on the status of her biblical plays, which had done him good. "They may be, in a way, your most important work."

At this point Sister Penelope asked Lewis what he would think about other people bringing out their own "Screwtape Letters," using his ideas. He told her that a literary idea ought to belong to anyone who could use it and that exclusive ownership of literary ideas is a kind of simony — the misuse of holy things for financial profit. However, he said, his publisher might not hold his view.

Finally in 1956 Penelope wrote to Lewis and asked for permission to sell the manuscript of *Screwtape Letters* that he had entrusted to her fifteen years earlier during the bombing of London. He replied that he hadn't the faintest notion that she had it, or that it existed. She was welcome to sell it if she could find a buyer and to use the money for any pious or charitable purpose she liked.

Then he asked her if it had ever occurred to her that the replacement of the scrawled old manuscript by the clear, printed book in mint condition was an excellent symbol of our bodily resurrection. "It is sown in inky scratches, it is raised in print."

In 1960 Reverend E. T. Dell wrote from Massachusetts and asked C. S. Lewis to consider writing a book about death. Lewis answered on March 5 that it was a tough proposition, but he would think about it. The idea that death is a hideous enemy is scriptural, he told Dell; and the idea that there is no death or that death doesn't matter is blah. He was starting to write the book already, he half-joked.

It never got written. His health was sinking fast.

In 1963 Lewis found himself slowly parting with the inky old manuscript of his mortal life. One of the last letters he wrote before his death was to Sister Penelope. He concluded their long correspondence with some final thoughts on life and death and closed with the message, "It *is* all rather fun — solemn fun — isn't it?"

Yours always, C. S. Lewis."

That could stand as his last word on creative writing as well. It is all rather fun, solemn fun.

SUGGESTED ACTIVITIES

1. "Dear Mr. Lewis. . ." Write a long letter to C. S. Lewis in response to specific things he has said in his letters to other hopeful writers. Argue with him, question him, agree with him, or tell him what it's like for writers like yourself in the United States today. Polish this letter so that it can possibly be used as an article in a writers' magazine.

2. Make a list of your favorite authors with a note telling why you like each one of them. Which one would you most like to resemble as a writer? (Don't worry; you will find your own voice, even if you emulate the author you admire.) Which would you most like to resemble in your values and thinking?

3. The most common human motivations, according to some people, are money, fame, and power. Write a personal statement for yourself, in light of Lewis's 1930 credo that he sent to Arthur Greeves, analyzing your present writing goals in the light of your real values. Be as honest and specific as possible.

4. There are published writers in most communities, and many writers make public appearances. Have you attended any of the many lectures given every year by famous and infamous authors? If so, have you asked them to autograph their books for you? Have you ever sent letters of thanks to writers of books or articles that you particularly appreciated? (You can send such letters in care of the publisher or magazine, and they usually get to the authors.) Many book authors give their addresses and much other information about themselves in *Contemporary Authors*. Browse in a few of these volumes in your library and see what you find out about some of the interesting people who can't not write.

NOTES

[1] Samuel Johnson (1709–1784) was a prominent London author and wit, the foremost conversationalist of his age. He was most celebrated for his monumental *Dictionary of the English Language* (1755).

[2] C. S. Lewis (1898–1963) was born in Belfast, Ireland, and was educated at the University of Oxford. He taught medieval and renaissance literature at Oxford and Cambridge and wrote many scholarly and popular books. He was converted to Christianity at the midpoint of his life and became an unusually successful exponent of the faith.

[3] Some of these letters are in print, and others are available to researchers in the Bodleian Library in Oxford and in the Marion E. Wade Center at Wheaton College in Illinois.

[4] C. S. Lewis, *They Stand Together: The Letters of C. S. Lewis to Arthur Greeves (1914–1963)*, edited by Walter Hooper (New York: Harcourt Brace Jovanovich, 1979).

[5] C. S. Lewis, *Collected Letters*, edited by W. H. Lewis (New York: Harcourt, Brace & World, 1966), 270–271.

[6] *C. S. Lewis: Letters to Children*, edited by Lyle W. Dorsett and Marjorie Lamp Mead (New York: Macmillan, 1985), 80–81.

[7] C. S. Lewis, *Letters to Children*, 109–110.

[8] *Collected Letters*, 278–280.

[9] *Letters to Children*, 40.

[10] *Letters to Children*, 85.

[11] *Letters to Children*, 86.

[12] *Collected Letters*, 291–292.

[13] *Letters to Children*, 113.

[14] *Letters to an American Lady*, edited by Clyde S. Kilby (Grand Rapids: Eerdmans, 1967), 18.

[15] *Letters to an American Lady*, 27.

[16] *Letters to an American Lady*, 29.

[17] *Letters to an American Lady*, 40.

[18] *Letters to an American Lady*, 49.

[19] *Letters to an American Lady*, 80.

Appendix: Pure Poppycock

It all started when I began the new year wrong. On January 1, 1983, I was unwillingly coerced into watching the evening news on CBS in Los Angeles. Fortunately, I had pen and paper handy, and here are three of the astonishing statements I heard.

1. "At the Rose Parade today there was only elbow room." (Only?)

2. "At Venice Beach on New Year's Day some people went into the water where only penguins fear to tread." (I always assumed that penguins were more cowardly than angels, but not in cold water.)

3. "You say, 'What will the weather be like in Los Angeles tomorrow?' It will improve! Of course, it was excellent today. But if it gets even better, we'll have too many people at the broadcasts of the parade and game." (The parade and game, broadcasts and all, would not occur again for a full year; in the meantime, I puzzle about what it means to have too many people at broadcasts.)

No wonder that our nation's melting pot is full of mental mush. Young people today grow up listening to television announcers who sound as if they cleared their sinuses with cocaine before going on the air.

Shortly after the new year began I ventured where not only penguins fear to tread — into the freshman composition classroom of my local college, to rejoin the fray on the side of clear thinking and good writing. I had been out of the fight for twenty years, like Rip Van Winkle. I opened the bright-covered, high-priced English textbooks expectantly and got the shock of my life.

"There are varying degrees of bilinguals," someone intoned cryptically in the model outline for a model research paper. I flipped a few pages to see how such a model research paper would conclude.

> If the oral phase of learning a language can be mastered before a child starts school, the other interrelated phases (reading and writing) should follow with relative ease.

If a child learns to talk before he enters school, he will probably learn to read and write in school?

I flipped a few more pages and found direct instruction about how to write such a research paper:

> To put it another way more bluntly, it is not enough to demonstrate that you have read; you must in turn have something to say about what you have read, and you must be able to say the "something" at least clearly, and hopefully even gracefully.

This is not satire; I checked.

Here is a suggested thesis for a research paper:

> The current fear of human's [*sic*] being displaced by machines, or what alarmists term the "automation hysteria," seems to be based on insubstantial reports.

To me that thesis seems to be based on insubstantial comprehension of both apostrophe use and alarmist rhetoric. I decided to skip the section on research papers.

The next section was on writing about literature. Students were warned:

> Passages from the work should be liberally quoted to support your paper's interpretation of it. Above all, never assume that any reading of a work, no matter how unsupported or farfetched, will do.

I don't even assume that any reading of that sentence will do. Ever.

"Write a 'third bear' story in the style of your favorite author," the book suggests to students. Ignorant about what "third bear" stories are, I checked the previous pages and learned that the editor was referring to "The Three Bears," which he seems to have confused with something else. (I know of an excellent book called *The Third Peacock*.)

The writer concluded this section with what he may have meant as a flourish:

> Saying that Hemingway's male characters suffer from machismo is a little like an anthropology student opining that humans are bipedal. Both remarks are undoubtedly true, but they are neither original nor insightful. You should, therefore, check out the prevailing critical opinion on a writer before attempting to rashly dogmatize on your own.

I have not yet checked out the prevailing critical opinion on this writer, but I bet I could rashly dogmatize on my own anyway.

As their inadvertent contribution to the ongoing problems that freshmen have with quotation marks gone to seed, the editors included this:

> In modern existentialist terms, you are what you do; so change what you do and you change what you are. After all, isn't "growing up" a matter of adopting views and roles consistent with our concept of being "a man" or "a woman" of the kind you would like to be?

My answer is no, it isn't. I wouldn't be "a man" or "a woman" for anything. Those cute quotation marks serve as a broad wink and a poke in the ribs.

I turned to more basic, traditional teaching:

> That prose literature has unity is easily seen by examining almost any book or magazine article.

Come again?

> Very often, when skilled students read a book, they underline certain passages. This is a good technique — if the proper sections are selected. The single sentence that should be underlined is the thesis or purpose statement of the book, its generative sentence.

Are students supposed to laugh or cry over the price they paid for this book that tells them they should underline just one sentence in every book? Perhaps what they should underline in this one is the price mark; it serves as a kind of purpose statement.

> In the beginning was the *logos*, says the Bible — the idea, the plan, caught in a flash as if in a single word. Find your *logos*, and you are ready to round out your essay and set it spinning.

Somehow this new exegesis of a key New Testament passage makes me into a blasphemous unbeliever right off. But how does one find one's *logos?* The author explains:

> The *about-ness* puts an argumentative edge on the subject. When you have something to say about cats, you have found your underlying idea.

The spinning of this particular essay about how to form and spin an essay makes me queasy. Some poor students still don't know how to hone their *logos* with *about-ness*.

Well, perhaps Harcourt Brace has been having a bad decade since it started publishing *Readings for Writers*. With some confidence I turned to the *Macmillan Handbook of English*, which is over forty years old and hence one of my peers. But it has been spruced up. It was all right until I got to page 7.

Precision and clarity are the primary requirements of effective writing, and weaknesses here are most vulnerable to attack from casual readers and instructors.

This means, I take it, do as we say, not as we do. It's these casual readers and instructors who are always out to get you.

The evidence is convincing that recognized expository writers use precise, uninflated Anglo-Saxon — not multisyllabic — words in their essays.

Humph.
All goes well again until page 10.

No doubt you have experienced the sense of dismay with which ideas tumble out of your head when someone mentions topics like abortion. . ."

Frankly, when ideas tumble out of my head they don't seem dismayed at all. They are glad to get loose. I am the one who is dismayed, and the thing that dismays me is a grossly misplaced modifier on the printed page of an English book.

Modern English, however, is an uninflected language, that is, the position of the word in the sentence determines meaning, function, and so forth.

I don't know what "and so forth" means here, but I do know that this is a run-on sentence, otherwise known as a comma splice.

We know *sail* is the verb in the following sentence because it comes after the subject and before the object: "They sailed to Sicily."

Nice try, but there is no object in "They sailed to Sicily." Maybe no one will notice.

It is of course quite possible for communication to function, as it were, on a single plane without degrees of structural emphasis.

How many degrees does structural emphasis usually have?
Maybe that's what I long for — for communication to function as it were.
Not that I'm an impractical idealist or a mossback intellectual snob. Sometimes I dream of angling my way onto teams that write new improved math textbooks for college students. I think I could write math textbooks with as little precision as some of our present English textbooks. The results might seem innovative or liberating to people who don't care about math. And a decline in the dependability and accuracy of math instruction might make our English instruction look better.

In the long run, though, I think the low quality of English textbooks is bound to come to the attention of high-quality publishers ready to fill our need. In ten years we will probably have excellent texts again. We'll import them from Japan.

Bibliography

CHAPTER ONE: *The Wonder of Creativity*

Koestler, Arthur, *The Act of Creation* (New York: Macmillan, 1964). This hefty volume about the nature of creativity is still unrivaled.

May, Rollo, *The Courage to Create* (New York: Bantam Books, 1976). This celebrated book explores creativity and how to use it.

Yukawa, Hideki, *Creativity and Intuition: A Physicist Looks at East and West* (New York: Harper & Row, 1973). These observations about creativity by a colleague of Einstein draw heavily upon the Japanese concept of intuition.

CHAPTER TWO: *To Communicate or Obfuscate*

Barzun, Jacques, *Simple and Direct: A Rhetoric for Writers* (New York: Harper & Row, 1975). This book illustrates the clarity and discipline that Barzun recommends.

Graves, Robert and Alan Hodge, *The Reader Over Your Shoulder* (New York: Random House, 1979). This little classic demonstrates the myriad ways that dignified writers can write imperfect prose.

Huff, Darrell, *How To Lie with Statistics* (New York: Norton, 1954). This playful and practical guide puts readers and writers on guard.

Mitchell, Richard, *Less Than Words Can Say* (Boston: Little Brown and Company, 1979). This jeremiad and its companion *The Leaning Tower of Babel* make fun of today's pompous jargon and sound a serious alarm.

Zinsser, William, *On Writing Well: An Informal Guide to Writing Nonfiction*, 3d edition (New York: Harper & Row, 1985). For all writers who need to brush up on their skills.

Zinsser, William, *Writing To Learn* (New York: Harper & Row, 1988). Zinsser shows how anyone who can think clearly should be able to write clearly about any subject at all. He writes with warmth, logic, and enthusiasm about writing with warmth, logic, and enthusiasm.

CHAPTER THREE: Pitfalls and Pratfalls

Bernstein, Theodore M., *Miss Thistlebottom's Hobgoblins: The Careful Writer's Guide to the Taboos, Bugbears and Outmoded Rules of English Usage* (New York: Simon and Schuster, 1984). The former editor of *The New York Times* shows that the rules of grammar you learned in school were often wrong.

Bernstein, Theodore M., *Watch Your Language* (New York: Atheneum, 1965). A distinguished journalist steers his readers away from common pitfalls and provides some fun in the process.

Hudson, Bob and Shelley Townsend, *A Christian Writer's Manual of Style* (Grand Rapids: Zondervan Publishing House, 1988). This book addresses problems unique to Christian writers, but also presents the basic rules of written language for all writers, editors, and proofreaders.

Pinckert, Robert C., *The Truth about English* (Englewood Cliffs, N.J.: Prentice-Hall, Inc., 1981). This lively all-purpose guide to proper English is innovative and practical.

Quinn, Jim, *American Tongue and Cheek* (New York: Pantheon, 1981). This provocative retort to the self-appointed protectors of English mixes a libertarian spirit with an outstanding grasp of facts about our language.

Strunk, William and E. B. White, *Elements of Style*, 3d edition (New York: Macmillan, 1979). This is the classic collection of writing advice from one of America's most delightful authors and his own favorite writing teacher.

Tibbets, Arn and Charlene, *What's Happening to American English?* (New York: Charles Scribners, 1978). This alarming report on the decline in writing ability since 1960 points out some power plays in academia and publishing that did us all harm.

CHAPTER FOUR: Eye, Ear, Nose, and Throat Specialists

Ciardi, John, *A Browser's Dictionary: A Compendium of Curious Expressions and Intriguing Facts* (New York: Harper & Row, 1980). For browsers interested in the origins and shifting history of many of the most interesting words and idioms in American-English use.

Dickson, Frank A. and Sandra Smith, *Handbook of Short Story Writing* (Cincinnati: Writer's Digest, 1970). The essays in this collection are light and practical.

Oxford English Dictionary (Oxford: Oxford University Press, 1971). Every writer should browse in this most complete dictionary of our language, seeing the kinds of information it offers us about our words. Librarians can explain how to read the word histories.

Tuchman, Barbara, *Practicing History, Selected Essays* (New York: Knopf, 1981). Tuchman teaches writing by example as well as advice.

CHAPTER FIVE: English, the Marvelous Mess

McCrum, Robert, William Cran, and Robert MacNeil, *The Story of English* (New York: Viking, 1986). This book was produced from a series of television programs that show the history, the flexibility, the drama, the pervasiveness, and the power of English.

CHAPTER SIX: A Foot in Your Mouth

Espy, Willard R., *The Game of Words* (New York: Bramhall House, 1972). In this and other books Espy shows what magic tricks are inherent in English.

Jarrell, Randall, *The Bat Poet* (New York: Macmillan, 1963). In this profound little tale one tastes the joy and loneliness of a person full of poetry.

Paterson, Katherine, *Gates of Excellence* (New York: Elsevier/Nelson, 1981). This collection of essays by a master author of fiction for children gives glimpses of what it is like for her to write children's books.

Perrine, Laurence, *Sound and Sense: An Introduction to Poetry* (New York: Harcourt, Brace and Company, 1956). For readers of writers, this beginners' overview of poetry cannot be matched.

CHAPTER SEVEN: A Foot in the Door

Aycock, Don M. and Leonard George Goss, *Writing Religiously* (Grand Rapids: Baker Book House, 1984). While this book is mainly geared toward explaining how to write for the religious market, much of what is said is certainly applicable to writing in general.

Block, Lawrence, *Telling Lies for Fun and Profit: A Manual for Fiction Authors* (New York: Arbor House, 1981). These peppy essays by a *Writer's Digest* columnist are both witty and wise.

Bonham-Carter, Victor, *Authors by Profession*, volumes 1 and 2 (Los Altos, Calif.: William Kaufmann Inc., 1978 and 1984). This set from England is full of little-known facts about the business end of writing.

Goss, Leonard George and Don M. Aycock, editors, *Inside Religious Publishing* (Grand Rapids: Zondervan Publishing House, 1989). This book will help writers with the actual thinking through of the writing, editing, marketing, advertising, and selling of their work.

Herr, Ethel, *An Introduction to Christian Writing* (Wheaton, Ill.: Tyndale House, 1983). For those asking the question, "Do I want to be a writer?"

Holmes, Marjorie, *Writing the Creative Article Today* (Boston: The Writer, Inc., 1986). This best-selling author gives easy-to-read, practical advice about breaking into print with articles that don't require research.

Meredith, Scott, *Writing to Sell*, 2d edition (New York: Harper & Row, 1974). A literary agent's advice to those interested in making their living in writing.

Whiteside, Thomas, *The Blockbuster Complex: Conglomorates, Show Business, and Book Publishing* (Middletown, Conn.: Wesleyan University Press, 1981). This book reveals radical changes in the realm of United States book publishing.

The Writer. This is the second most popular magazine for writers.

Writer's Digest. This is the most popular magazine for writers.

Writer's Market. This annual book lists current markets for free-lancers.

CHAPTER EIGHT: *Writer-Types (How To Type Yourself)*

Harrison, Allen F. and Robert M. Bramson, *Styles of Thinking: Strategies for Asking Questions, Making Decisions, and Solving Problems* (Garden City, N.Y.: Anchor Press, 1982). This book aimed primarily at business people explains the five basic styles of thinking and includes a test to show which style one prefers.

Kroeger, Otto and Janet M. Thuesen, *Type Talk* (New York: Delacorte Press, 1988). This is the best-written basic overview of the sixteen Myers-Briggs temperament types.

CHAPTER NINE: *Authors in Action*

Auchincloss, Louis, *A Writer's Capital* (Boston: Houghton Mifflin Company, 1974). The memoir of a well known author giving his origin and development as a writer.

Buechner, Frederick, *The Sacred Journey* (New York: Harper & Row, 1982) and *Now and Then* (New York: Harper & Row, 1983) together tell the story of how Buechner has became the writer and person he is today.

Farrar, Larsten D., *Successful Writers and How They Work* (New York: Hawthorne Books, 1959). Advice and tips from established writers from many fields.

Gardner, John, *On Becoming a Novelist* (New York: Harper & Row, 1983). This spirited advice from an outstanding writer and teacher of writing was published one year after he died in a motorcycle accident. His friend Raymond Carver, who wrote the foreword, died prematurely in 1988.

Hersey, John, *The Writer's Craft* (New York: Alfred A. Knopf, 1947). A distinguished writer and teacher offers insight into what it means to live by and for the craft of writing.

Van Gelder, Robert, *Writers and Writing* (New York: Charles Scribner's Sons, 1946). A compilation of interviews the author had with many of the best known writers of the first half of this century.

Welty, Eudora, *One Writer's Beginnings* (New York: Warner Books, 1983). This best-selling book of memories and insights from one of America's favorite fiction writers shows what words and stories mean to our hearts.

Wirt, Sherwood Eliot, *The Making of a Writer* (Minneapolis: Augsburg Publishing House, 1987). A practical book which discusses what it takes to be a successful writer who can communicate with readers and get along with editors.

CHAPTER TEN: *C. S. Lewis's Free Advice to Hopeful Writers*

Lewis, C. S., *An Experiment in Criticism* (Cambridge: Cambridge University Press, 1961). This scholarly little book written near the end of Lewis's life explores in an original way the real difference between "good" literature and "bad."

Index